UNDERSTANDING CURRICULUM AS RACIAL TEXT

SUNY Series, Feminist Theory in Education
Madeleine R. Grumet, Editor

UNDERSTANDING CURRICULUM AS RACIAL TEXT

Representations of Identity and Difference in Education

edited by

LOUIS A. CASTENELL, JR.

University of Cincinnati

and

WILLIAM F. PINAR

Louisiana State University

State University
of New York
Press

Acknowledgement for Permission to include the following is expressed:

Chapter 4: Whatley, Mariamne H. (1988). Photographic images of blacks in sexuality texts. *Curriculum Inquiry,* 18(2), 137–155.

Chapter 7: Gomez, Jewelle. (1986, March/April). Black women heroes: Here's reality, where's the fiction? *The Black Scholar,* 17, 8–13.

Chapter 8: Luttrell, Wendy. (1989, January). Working-class women's ways of knowing: Effects of gender, race, and class. *Sociology of Education,* 62, 33–46.

Chapter 9: Murphy, Lindsay, and Livingstone, Jonathan. (1985). Racism and the limits of radical feminism. *Race & Class,* 2b(4), 61–70.

Chapter 14: Gordon, Beverly M. (1985, Winter). Toward emancipation in citizenship education: The case of African-American cultural knowledge. *Theory and Research in Social Education,* 12(4), 1–23.

Published by
State University of New York Press, Albany

Production by Susan Geraghty
Marketing by Fran Keneston

Printed in the United States of America

For information, address State University of New York
Press, State University Plaza, Albany, N.Y., 12246

Library of Congress Cataloging in Publication Data
Understanding curriculum as racial text : representations of
  identity and difference in education / edited by Louis A. Castenell,
  Jr. and William F. Pinar.
      p.   cm. — (SUNY series, feminist theory in education
  Includes bibliographical references and index.
  ISBN 0-7914-1661-5 (alk paper). — ISBN 0-7914-1662-3 (pbk. : alk.
  paper)
      1. Education—United States—Curricula.   2. Discrimination in
  education—United States.   3. Intercultural education—United
  States.   4. Critical pedagogy—United States.   I. Castenell, Louis
  Anthony, 1947– . II. Pinar, William. III. Series.
  LB1570.U44   1993
  375'.00973—dc20   92-38899
                                                                    CIP

10   9   8   7   6   5   4   3   2   1

CONTENTS

PREFACE

This is a book about categories. Race is a category, and so is gender. They, along with categories like class, nation, neighborhood, and religion, order our worlds. This series, Feminist Theory in Education, is dedicated to examining these categories as they function in curriculum. We speculate about their relationship to the world they name; we investigate the social processes that have constructed them and identify their presence in curriculum where they recapitulate and renew the common order.

What is the relationship of the category of gender to what is real? Well, primary sex characteristics signal distinctions in reproductive function. Whether or not we use this anatomical equipment in sexual or reproductive activity, there it is. What we make of it (also known as gender), what we make *from* it, is not determined but made up in the course of human history.

So over here we have gonads, vaginas, and penises.

And over here we have EVERYTHING ELSE: maleness, femaleness, mothering, patriarchy, madonnas, machismo, equal pay for equal work, women's history month, football, heroes, romance, reading, testing, schooling.

The EVERYTHING ELSE list goes on and on. And as we compare the length of the list of what we are with the list of what we have made of what we are, we recognize how little of our lives we can ascribe to nature. This project in this series is a very optimistic enterprise, for as we discover what has been constructed through human history we simultaneously recover the possibility for change.

The category of race is even less substantiated—rooted in substance—than the category of gender. The formation and deformation of race is even more poignant because we can find no anatomical or functional referent for the centuries of bias, exploitation, and oppression that this category has supported in Western history. Nevertheless, we are the children of this history, constructed and confined by the categorical creativity that has spawned us.

Understanding Curriculum as Racial Text: Representations of Identity and Difference in Education joins other books in this series in exploring the categories that position us in relation to other people and in relation to history.

We may not escape these categories completely, but we can, as Peter Taubman reminds us in the final chapter of this book, scramble up their sides and dance together on the rims.

> We who cling to our various identities and freeze ourselves and others in them, we who become the critical theorists or poststructuralists, the feminists or postmodernists, the autobiographers or the Marxists, we who look at multicultural and antibias education from these identities, we might ask how we have used and been used by those identities and how we have distorted ourselves and distorted others with them. . . . [H]ow can we look at and through these identities so that we can begin to see ourselves in one another and one another in ourselves, so that we can hold unity and differentiation in a tension that holds us all together?

Louis Castenell and William Pinar have brought together a book of essays that catches us committing categories. The authors, writing from a broad variety of scholarly discourses, practice the phenomenological stance that takes whatever seems familiar as strange and requiring justification. They also duck under the category in question to consider what its existence means to use who spend our everyday lives under its shadow and shelter. By bringing these essays together, by bringing a consideration of curriculum as racial text to a series identified as feminist theory in education, these editors refuse the categorical etiquette that declares where and when who can speak about what with whom. And so in this book you will find arguments and perspectives that often demand a room of their own. Here, they join in open conversation, and together, as authors, editors, and readers, we celebrate freedom of assembly.

Madeleine R. Grumet

CHAPTER 1

Introduction

Louis A. Castenell, Jr.
William F. Pinar

In recent years public debate over a "common" or core curriculum has revealed an explicit racial aspect. The exchange at a 1989 Madison Center[1] conference is illustrative. The center's president, John Agresto, characterized the conference as a "response to the academy's current trivialization of liberal education and the continuing attacks on the canons of traditional collegiate instruction." "Under the cover of pluralism," criticizes Agresto, "is the dismissal of the past" (O'Brien, 1989). In opposition, Houston Baker, noted literary critic and professor of English at the University of Pennsylvania, charged that the continued curricular emphasis upon Western civilization constitutes "a willful ignorance and aggression toward Blacks" (O'Brien, 1989). Regarding the so-called Great Books curriculum of St. John's College (Maryland), Baker commented: "The Great Books won't save us . . . but rap may because it might finally allow us to recognize that the world is no longer white and one might even say no longer bookish." Jonathon Culler, professor of English at Cornell University, cited a 1988 study of that literature taught in high schools conducted by the Center for the Teaching and Learning of Literature at the State University of New York at Albany. Albany researchers found that twenty-seven books were required in more than 30 percent of the schools surveyed. Culler commented: "I find it scandalous that long after the

---

[1] A conservative research and education policy center founded by former education secretary William Bennett and *The Closing of the American Mind* author Allan Bloom.

civil rights movement, there are no books by Black authors in the top 27, and books by and about women are so poorly represented" (O'Brien, 1989). It is an understatement to observe that issues of race are paramount in contemporary curriculum debates in the public sphere.

To contribute to the understanding of the racial issues embedded in the public debates over the canon, we offer a collection of essays which complicate the curriculum controversy. To introduce these essays, we suggest that curriculum is racial text, that is, that debates over what we teach the young are also—in addition to being debates over what knowledge is of most worth—debates over who we perceive ourselves to be, and how we will represent that identity, including what remains as "left over," as "difference." To help us think about curriculum in this way, we rely on three interrelated concepts. These concepts organize our formulation of curriculum as racial text. They are race, text, and identity. In this introduction we will suggest that understanding curriculum as racial text implies understanding the American national identity, and vice versa. The essays in this collection exemplify in diverse ways these concepts through their articulations of representation and difference. The essays, representing scholarship in the humanities, social science, and education, point to the complexity of race and identity and, in particular, how racial representation—including the splitting off and projection of difference—portrays, suppresses, and reformulates racial identity. Curriculum is one highly significant form of representation, and arguments over the curriculum, we suggest, are also arguments over who we are as Americans, how we wish to represent ourselves to our children. Although we will speak of an American "self," of an American identity, clearly—as these essays assert—'self' and 'identity' are multivocal concepts. We ask readers not to mistake the implicit unity of a concept of 'American self' or 'American identity' for its constituent diversity.

The Concept of Text   Why employ the concept of 'text'? The concept of text implies both a specific piece of writing and, much more broadly, social reality itself. A term borrowed from poststructuralism, and more particularly from the work of Jacques Derrida, *text* implies that all reality is human reality, and as human reality, it is fundamentally discursive. In contrast to the phenomenological view (Pinar and Reynolds, 1992) that language is derived from a more fundamental and prior substratum of preconceptual experience, the poststructuralist view is that all experience has been deferred (hence the famous construct *différance*) from original experience, and in this "gap" occurs language and history. Reading, in Derrida's words, "cannot legitimately transgress the text toward something other than it, toward a reference (a reality that is metaphysical, historical, psychobiographical, etc.) or toward a signified outside the text whose content could take place, could have taken place outside language" (Derrida, 1976, p. 158). In one sense, race points to the "gap" between self and other. We aspire to read this text in such a way as to contribute to understanding curriculum as a discursive formation of identity and difference. What discursive formations are written in our unconscious, which selectively we represent in the curriculum, splitting off the excess as "difference"? Susan Edgerton's essay, relying on Ellison and Morrison, provides one answer to this question. Of course, what is "different" from majority culture is not reducible to the unconscious of the majority culture, and in this collection we read affirmative statements of African American history (Kincheloe, Gordon) and culture (Young, Gomez). As Toni Morrison asserts, "we are not, in fact, the 'other'" (1989, p. 9).

The Concept of Race   What is the meaning of race? It is hardly an unchanging, biological concept, as the Livingstone and Murphy essay underlines. Race is a complex, dynamic, and changing construct. Historically, those identified as "people of color" have changed according to political circumstance. For instance, before the Civil War southern Europeans, Jews, even the Irish were considered "nonwhite" (Omi and Winant, 1983). The racial category of "black" grew out of slavery. "Whites" collapsed the diversity of African—and native—peoples into monolithic, racialized categories. "By the end of the seventeenth century, Africans, whose specific identity was Ibo, Yoruba, Dahomeyan, etc., were rendered 'black' by an ideology of exploitation based on racial logic. Similarly, Native Americans were forged into 'Indians' or the 'red man' from Cherokee, Seminole, Sioux, etc. people" (Omi and Winant, 1983, p. 51). In nineteenth-century California, the arrival of large numbers of Chinese provoked a "crisis" of racial classification. In *People v. Hall* (1854), the Supreme Court of California ruled that the Chinese should be regarded as "Indian" and thereby ineligible for those political rights afforded whites (Omi and Winant, 1983). Race intersects with class and gender, as we observe in essays by Patricia Collins, Wendy Luttrell, and Lindsay Murphy and Jonathan Livingstone.

The Concept of Identity   Identity becomes a central concept in the effort to understand curriculum as racial text. *Identity* is not a static term either, reflective of a timeless, unchanging inner self. Rather, identity is a gendered, racialized, and historical construct. For involuntary immigrants such as African Americans, the notion of 'caste' is not inappropriate. Castelike minorities tend to construct a collective identity in opposition to the dominant group, arising from the experience of oppression (Ogbu and Mattute-Bianchi, 1986). Additionally, "the formation of a collective oppositional identity system is usually accompanied by an evolution of an oppositional cultural system or cultural frame of reference that contains mechanisms for maintaining and protecting the group's social identity" (Ogbu and Mattute-Bianchi, 1986, p. 94). Identity formation is constructed and expressed through representation, that is, the construction of "difference," and negotiated in the public sphere. As we shall see, what is at stake is the identity not only of minority groups but of the American nation as a whole.

For those readers who are curriculum scholars, we wish to acknowledge that curriculum is not only a racial text. It is also a political text, an aesthetic, a gender text (Pinar, Reynolds, Slattery, and Taubman, 1994), but it is, to a degree that European Americans have been unlikely to acknowledge, a racial text. We will lay out the broad outlines of this concept of curriculum as racial text, linking knowledge and identity, by focusing upon issues of representation and difference. Then we will introduce the essays which work with these issues, focusing upon African Americans.

IDENTITY

"We are what we know." We are, however, also what we do not know. If what we know about ourselves—our history, our culture, our national identity—is deformed by absences, denials, and incompleteness, then our identity—both as individuals and as Americans—is fractured. This fractured self is also a repressed self;

elements of itself are split off and denied. Such a self lacks access both to itself and to the world. Repressed, the self's capacity for intelligence, for informed action, even for simple functional competence, is impaired. Its sense of history, gender, and politics is incomplete and distorted. Denied individual biography and collective history, African Americans have been made appendages to European Americans (Bulhan, 1985).

In this collection of essays dealing in diverse ways with issues of race and representation, we seek to link current debates regarding the "canon" with questions of self, identity, and difference. Such an understanding enlarges the curricular debate from an exclusive preoccupation with equity or with multiculturalism to include debates regarding the relationship between knowledge and ourselves. We maintain that the "Eurocentric" character of the school curriculum functions not only to deny "role models" to non–European American students, but to deny self-understanding to "white" students as well (Castenell, Jr., 1991). We would argue that the American self is not exclusively or even primarily an European American self. Fundamentally, it is an African American self. We refer here not only to well-publicized demographic trends (minorities are predicted to constitute the majority by 2050); we refer to the American past and the present. To a still unacknowledged extent, the American nation was built by African Americans. African Americans' presence informs every element of American life. For European American students to understand who they are, they must understand that their existence is predicated upon, interrelated to, and constituted in fundamental ways by African Americans (Goldberg, 1990).

The American self—repressed and fragmented—"acts out" repression via imperialism in foreign policy and political, economic, and cultural repression domestically. The refusal—sometimes unconscious, sometimes not—to incorporate African American knowledge into the mainstream curriculum can be understood as a psychoanalytic as well as political process of repression and suppression. *Understanding curriculum as racial text suggests understanding education as a form of social psychoanalysis* (Kincheloe and Pinar, 1991). That is, what we as adults choose to tell our children in schools—the school curriculum—represents who we want them to think we are and who they might become. The stories we tell them are presumably only about the disciplines, disinterested bodies of knowledge unrelated to who we are as civic creatures. Particularly in the humanities and social sciences, this view has been largely discredited. Knowledge is rarely politically neutral or disinterested. School knowledge communicates—not always explicitly, of course—assumptions regarding many features of human life. Moreover, it communicates that which we choose to remember about our past and what we choose to believe about the present. Our interest here is how representations of race and difference communicate a sense of the American identity. We maintain that the American identity is constructed partly by denial, by maintaining fictions. The American identity, the American "self," is not exclusively or even primarily European. That delusion represents a fantasy, a flight from historical and cultural reality. As James Baldwin wrote, "White Americans . . . are dimly aware that the history they have fed themselves is mainly a lie, but they do not know how to release themselves from it" (Baldwin, quoted in Taubman, 1987).

The absence of African American knowledge in many American schools' curriculum is not simple oversight. It represents an academic instance of racism, or in Baker's apt phrase, "willful ignorance and aggression toward Blacks." Just as African Americans have been denied their civil rights in society generally, so they have been denied access to their history and culture in school. Not only African Americans have been denied, however. Institutional racism deforms white students as well. By refusing to understand curriculum as racial text, students misunderstand that they are also racialized, gendered, historical, political creatures. Such deformity occurs—for most "whites"—almost "unconsciously." Many European American students and their parents—and many curriculum specialists—would deny that the curriculum is a racial text. Such denial is done "innocently"; it represents an instance of repression in its psychoanalytic sense. Socially, psychological repression expresses itself as political repression (Schwartz and Disch, 1970; Kovel, 1971).

Repression impairs intelligence because it siphons off energy from, for instance, problem solving to maintain the repression. Further, repression implies that information is limited, as well as distorting that information which is available. The contemporary crisis of American education is complex in its nature and causes; it is not reducible to one factor or one set of factors, such as poorly prepared teachers, an out-of-date curriculum, malnourished students, developmentally and/or culturally inappropriate examinations, and other school practices. One overlooked factor is repression, the repression of African Americans in American society, the repression of women, the repression of other marginalized groups, and the repression of non-European knowledge. Such repression is evident in the schools in several ways, including funding inequities, tracking, teaching practices, and a curriculum that is Eurocentric and unrelated to the lived experience of students.

Freudian imagery of the self is provocative here. During the decade of the 1980s the businessman represented the American prototype. Lee Iaccoca, Donald Trump, Michael Milken: white, male, savvy, shrewd, calculating, devoted to the bottom line. If this prototype represented the American "ego"—realistic, adaptive, adjusting in self-profiting ways to "reality"—then African Americans represented the "id"—pleasure seeking, unpredictable, accomplished in athletics and the arts. European American culture projected African Americans as the "id," and in classical Freudian style, maintained relative repression of the "pleasure principle" so that—presumably—ego stability and hegemony could be maintained. Those elements of American life which could be said to represent the "superego"—fundamentalist religious groups—were permitted by the "business" ego to grow in size and influence. Those groups marginal to this version of the "ego"—African Americans, other marginalized ethnic groups, women, children, gays—were undermined via public policy and in political practice. In her essay, Susan Edgerton explores the dynamics of marginalization.

Christopher Lasch (1984) has argued that the conservative political prescription for schools and society during the 1980s can be characterized as "superego" in nature. Illustrative of this "superego" voice are slogans such as "more homework," "just say no," "work harder." Conservatives insisted that the problem with American society was simple laziness (not their own, of course), and in this simpleminded analysis African Americans were assigned a major blameworthy role. Liberals continue to call for rational deliberation, incorporating aspects of the unconscious (African Americans in the parallel) into the conscious ego (mainstream society), but in controlled and planned ways (as in the liberal conceptualization of an orderly, incremental civil rights movement). Our point is that the question of school curriculum is also a question about the self, the American self. *Understanding curriculum as racial text means understanding the United States as fundamentally a racialized place, as fundamentally an African American place, and the American identity as inextricably African American as well as European, Hispanic/Latino, American Indian, and Asian American.* Debates over the canon are also debates over the constitution of the American self. They involve as well the private self, as Taubman's studies of "canonical sins" and "separate lives"—which open and close the collection—indicate.

In this collection we focus upon African American issues, especially those of identity (including gender, race, and class) and representation (especially in curriculum). Our position is that historically European Americans and African Americans are two sides of the same cultural coin, two interrelated narratives in the American story, two interrelated elements of the American identity. Projected as "other" and repressed, African Americans' presence in the American, indeed, "Western" self has been understood, perhaps most precisely, by Frantz Fanon. Like James Baldwin and others, Fanon understood that 'white' is a fabrication made by the construction of the concept 'black.' Briefly, there can be no 'black' without 'white' and vice versa. One cannot understand the identity of one without appreciating how they are "codependent" upon each other. So it is that European Americans cannot hope to understand themselves unless they are knowledgeable and knowing of those they have constructed as "different," as "other." The sequestered suburban white student is uninformed unless he or she comes to understand how, culturally, he or she is also—in the historical, cultural, indeed, psychological sense—African American. Because 'white' does not exist apart from 'black', the two coexist, intermingle, and the repression of this knowledge deforms us all, especially those who are white and male. All Americans are racialized beings; knowledge of who we have been, who we are, and who we will become is a story or text we construct. In this sense curriculum—our construction and reconstruction of this knowledge for dissemination to the young—is a racial text. Cameron McCarthy reviews past efforts to represent the American multicultural reality in its school curriculum, recommending the formulation of a "collective identity politics oriented toward change."

Such African American cultural affirmation is indicated in the Gordon, Young, and Gomez essays as well.

During the past decade much has been made of the failure of public school students to learn even the most elementary and necessary facts regarding their history, geography, and culture. Cultural literacy is a noncontroversial requirement for any citizenry. What becomes controversial is the composition of such literacy. In the popular press voices express views of cultural literacy that are informed by, primarily, Eurocentric and patriarchal knowledge systems. Without question American students must know and understand the European antecedents of contemporary American culture. However, this knowledge ought not be used as a defense against "otherness" and "difference," a denial of what we might term our "cultural unconscious."

We believe that understanding curriculum as a racial text is especially urgent in the present time of neoconservatism during which racial attacks and racial antagonism have increased. In November 1990 in Louisiana, as is well known, David Duke's white supremacy candidacy for the U.S. Senate brought him 60 percent of the white vote; even in his November 1991 defeat in the Louisiana gubernatorial election, Duke captured 55 percent of the white vote. The increase in racial attacks, particularly on college and university campuses, is dramatic (McCarthy, 1990). We have been struck by the silence of curriculum specialists during the public debates of the decade. We worry that this silence results from both ignorance and avoidance. While making enormous strides during the recent reconceptualization of the field (1969–1980) toward understanding curriculum multidimensionally (Pinar, 1988), mainstream curricularists have yet to incorporate racial considerations in any significant way. Even multiculturalism—inadequate as that curriculum movement is viewed by scholars of race such as Cameron McCarthy—remains relatively marginalized and unincorporated in the scholarly effort to understand curriculum. Even those scholars who accept and study the profound ways in which the curriculum is a political text seem reluctant to assert and teach curriculum as a racial text. Instead, race tends to be subsumed under politics (McCarthy, 1988a, 1988b). It is past time for the curriculum field to acknowledge the significance and relative autonomy of the scholarly effort to understand curriculum as a racial text. We hope this collection will take its place alongside such seminal contributions as Cameron McCarthy's *Race and Curriculum* (1990) and Warren Crichlow and Cameron McCarthy collection *Race, Identity, and Representation in Education* (1993). No course on curriculum can ignore this vital sector of scholarship.

THE ESSAYS

Race and Representations of Identity

To understand curriculum as racial text suggests understanding ourselves as racialized beings whose stories are racial stories, even when denied. By exploring the denied past, we might push back the blacked-out, repressed areas of memory and in so doing be able to offer more of ourselves to our students, as we have more of ourselves to offer. We begin this labor of self-understanding in an exploration of identity and curriculum politics.

An Opening: Identity and Curriculum Politics   Opening with Peter Taubman's framing of the contemporary debate over the literary canon, the first four essays depict issues concerning representations of identity. Taubman's essays both open and close the collection. They do so not because we believe they represent the "first" and "last" word on this subject, but because they frame issues of race and difference in terms of life history, of identity, the organizing idea of the book. On the margins of the collection they provoke what Edgerton (see Chapter 3) regards as those issues of inter-referentiality and intertextuality which lace debates over multi-cultural representation.

Taubman accuses canonical conservatives of being guilty of idolatry, of fixing selected "classics" in an ahistorical realm in which "they are worshiped for their embodiment of the Western metaphysic." He characterizes canonical radicals as heretics, as they seek "to stretch the canon's boundaries to include noncanonical texts or to dissolve those boundaries altogether." Both radicals and conservatives, he alleges, might be guilty of a decontextualism: "Perhaps both discourses [radical and conservative] do violence to the quirky and unique ways books move through our lives, flatten out our private relationship to reading, and force us to read and hear a prior discourse in the words which meet our eyes and ears and the intentions which move our hand to pull down the volume from the shelf." He proceeds to locate his reading in his life history, asking, with Foucault, "How is it, given the mass of things that are spoken, given the set of discourses actually held, a certain number of these discourses are sacralized and given a particular function? Among all these narratives, what is it that sacralizes a certain number and makes them begin to function as 'literature'?" He regards the knowledge of marginalized groups as a kind of discursive unconscious, and this realm he suggests is "fueled by Desire in the Lacanian sense." From Freud and Lacan, Taubman continues, we have learned that "the unconscious is formed by the No! which separates mother and child and introduces the paternal or patriarchal realm of language. . . . I am suggesting that the formation of the canon introduced a No! into the individual's relationship to reading and thus opened the space for a canonical unconscious, one structured by the canon but not articulated by its discourse." He sketches pedagogical as well as curricular implications of his view of the canon, worrying that the welcomed demise of the traditional canon may result in a "new canon," which in turn will produce its own canonical unconscious. He worries also, as does Henry Louis Gates, Jr. (1990), that a radical interest in the margins, in the molecular, and in dispersion rather than unification (in those radical discourses associated with poststructuralism) risks undermining the political initiatives of marginalized groups. "The fetishizing of the molecular in particular is a denial of difference. Each unique molecule is finally the same, since no identity lasts long enough for difference to exist. I suspect such a fetishizing of the molecular and the temporal reflects the fear of any real relationship between reader and reading, reader and text."

This collection, in its diversity and nonlinear design, illustrates difference within identity. Just as Taubman's essays suggest that marginalized literature is not monolithic, not unified, and ought not to represent a new set of timeless, ahistorical, and sacralized texts (a new canon), so this collection asserts difference and nonsynchrony. Understanding the curriculum as racial text implies curriculum as social psychoanalysis, implies knowledge conscious and unconscious, functioning to maintain and disturb illusions of identity and power—indeed, reality. Understanding the curriculum as racial text may also illustrate a notion of knowledge as revelatory, in which identity becomes complex enough to support and express difference and contradiction. Such an understanding of curriculum might reflect a historically and culturally accurate, nonsynchronous American identity.

Race and Representation   Susan Edgerton understands that marginality is created by centrality (and vice versa), that marginality "lives within the very language/world that makes it necessary and that it must oppose." Marginality can suggest invisibility, as portrayed in Ellison's *Invisible Man*. As the novel indicates, it is possible to be invisible to others but not to oneself. By the end of the novel the Invisible Man notes that he is "invisible, not blind." Others so marginalized may internalize their social invisibility, may suppress their interior life, indeed, their humanity. Edgerton quotes from the Ellison novel: "Already he's learned to repress not only his emotions but his humanity. He's invisible, a walking personification of the Negative. . . The mechanical man!" Hidden not only to himself, the African American is hidden to "white" America. Again, Edgerton quotes from the Ellison novel: "You're hidden right out in the open. . . . They wouldn't see you because they don't expect you to know anything, since they believe they've taken care of that."

The second novel Edgerton consults—Morrison's *Beloved*—enables her to depict how the fantasies of European Americans become realized in the marginalized "other." Edgerton quotes from the Morrison novel:

> White people believed that whatever the manners, under every dark skin was a jungle. Swift unnavigable waters, swinging screaming baboons, sleeping snakes, red gums ready for their sweet white blood. In a way, he thought, they were right. The more colored people spent their strength trying to convince them how gentle they were, how clever and loving, how human, the more they used themselves up to persuade whites of something Negroes believed could not be questioned, the deeper and more tangled the jungle grew inside. But it wasn't the jungle blacks brought with them to this place from the other (livable) place. It was the jungle whitefolks planted in them. And it grew. It spread. In, through and after life, it spread, until it invaded the whites who had made it. Touched them every one. Changed and altered them. Made them bloody, silly, worse than even they wanted to be, so scared were they of the jungle they had made. The screaming baboon lived under their own white skin; the red gums were their own.

In this brilliant passage the inextricability—psychologically and culturally—of "whites" and "blacks" is vividly portrayed. This inextricability is not only an empirical historical fact; it is a psychological reality. European Americans are what they displace onto others, and their self-representation requires repression of the "other." The dynamics of racism are complex, much deeper than a catalog of attitudes which workshops might aspire to change. The very complexion of one's skin, the nature of one's blood, and one's view of the world are all experienced racially. These dynamics cannot be decreed away; perhaps, as Edgerton suggests, "love in the margins" might make them visible.

Photographs make the dynamics of racism visible as well. Such images become representations of identity, especially when reprinted in textbooks. Because photographs appear "objective," they can communicate a sense of truth that, say, a drawing might not. In her study of photographic illustrations of black people in college-level sexuality textbooks, Mariamne Whatley reports that although images of black people were intended to be positive, negative patterns or themes were discernible. She characterizes these negative themes as blacks as "exotic," blacks as "sexually dangerous," and blacks as asexual. The photographs she studied functioned to communicate a sense of "difference," of blacks as "other." A message of racial tolerance seemed merely tacked on.

The theme of blacks as "sexually dangerous" extends our earlier observation that in contemporary "white" American culture, African Americans are, in Freudian terms, the "id." One form of this projection of fantasy takes involves the long-standing and powerful myth of rape. White women and men have feared black men for centuries (Jordan, 1971). However, Whatley reports rape statistics indicating that at least 90 percent of sexual assaults involve same-race rapist and victim. How are we to understand the persistence and intensity of the rape myth? Psychoanalytically, fear is sometimes inverted desire, and in another place Pinar (1991) has speculated—after Eldridge Cleaver—that the pervasive fear that African American men will rape European American women might represent a denied and displaced (onto white women) homoerotic attraction of white men to black men. Aside from these possible sexual dynamics, the fear has, as we know, also functioned to justify white violence against black men.

Whatley discovers that these textbooks tended to ignore the

dangers of sexually transmitted diseases to African Americans; only the risk to European Americans was viewed as a problem. Whatley suggests that "the stereotype of the Black woman as 'depreciated sex object,' in this instance disease-ridden, serves to warn white men against inter-racial interrelationships." Regarding the depiction of AIDS, she reports that the disease's origin in Africa is overemphasized, underlining the stereotype of Africans and African Americans as carriers of disease, especially sexual disease. This aspect of race and representations of identity is studied in the next chapter.

In "Til Death Do Us Part: AIDS, Race, and Representation," Brenda Hatfield examines an example of racial representation in the electronic media, namely, in an educational film on the AIDS epidemic produced by and for an African American student audience. Hatfield learned that student viewers were "critically concerned" over what appeared to be their roles as carriers and victims of the disease. Student responses included the following: "It makes it look like only black people have it." "If whites see it, they might say 'Oh, only blacks have AIDS.'" "On TV always lots of things about black people. Like they are the only ones to get the virus, use drugs and stuff. Act like they are the only ones to have the problem." Statistics indicate otherwise, Hatfield reports: of the infected population, 57 percent white, 27 percent black, 15 percent Hispanic, 1 percent others.

There were positive aspects of the film. Students liked the presentations of "rap" in the film. One student wrote: "What I like about the film, I have never seen in a film like this before. They have new changes such as rap, and someone dressed represented AIDS." Unfortunately, the film featured only male rappers. Females were assigned to background positions in the dance routines, only indicating, Hatfield writes, "their subordinated gendered positions." Further, "African American females were stereotyped in roles of anguish, suffering, and singing the hymns. Ironically, the strongest character in the play among all of the roles was a female, but this powerful role figure was depicted as a supernatural white female. In this case, the message of white racial domination is clearly signified above black characterizations in the film."

Understanding Curriculum as Racial Text begins by locating the debates over the canon in issues of identity and representation. In these first four essays we have seen these issues as they are discernible in novels, textbook photographic images, and an educational film about AIDS. In each of these gender has surfaced as a theme, and the concluding five chapters of this section focus upon gender and women specifically. In different ways, each of these following essays illustrate dynamics of race, representation, and identity.

Gender, Race, and Class   The introductory chapter on gender works within the African American community, calling for "breaking the silence" on gender in African American studies. Patricia Hill Collins begins by acknowledging that the survival of African American studies departments on predominantly white campuses has required the elevation of the category of race over class and gender. The external threat to African American studies has thus functioned to undermine diversity and dialogue among black intellectuals. Collins asks, "Can African American studies accommodate the scholarly diversity essential for producing analyses of black life and culture responsive to race, class, and gender?" If the answer is to be an affirmative one, then the silence on gender must be broken. Gender must join class and race as a major analytical category of research in African American studies; indeed, these must be considered interlocking dimensions of the African American experience. After listing the contributions and directions feminist research in African American studies might take, Collins poses a "final question":

> how [might] black feminist thought [produce] unique analyses that do not confirm, complement, or challenge existing African American studies paradigms but instead produce something that is entirely new. Reconceptualizations of rape, violence, and the overarching structure of sexual politics; of power, political activism, and resistance; of the relationships between work and family; and of homophobia and its impact on the interlocking nature of race, class, and gender oppression are all neglected topics explored in black feminist thought.

The relationships among gender, race, and class raise crucial theoretical questions, not only within the sector of scholarship on race and curriculum, but across curriculum studies as well (Pinar, 1988). These are questions of identity, which get framed differently according to which dimension one emphasizes. In the remaining chapters in this section we observe four different representations of gendered and racialized identity.

Jewelle Gomez begins by noting that imaginary representations of idealized figures are essential to cultural life. Oddly enough, Gomez discovered, heroic black women characters are difficult to find in those genres she terms "fantasy fiction." Certainly, historical figures are not uncommon, as Gomez's survey of them reminds us. In fact, she writes:

> African history has provided the role models for an expansion of our concept of what heroism can be. But few of us have taken the cue. When this store of wealth has been exploited, it has generally been by white male writers who bleach the history of Dahomean Amazons and turn them into Wonder Woman and Queen Hera. It is clear that the history of African women has many epic figures for those interested in the fantasy genre. But why have so few black women writers been intrigued by either this genre or this history?

One answer might reside in European American representations of heroism, which typically are male. Typically, women are portrayed as deferential and dependent, mere appendages to male conquering heroes. Further, Gomez continues, those women who are independent are characterized as "bitches."

And, to take this analysis a step further, Gomez concurs with Barbara Christian's analysis:

> The stereotypic qualities associated with lesbian women: self-assertiveness, strength, independence, eroticism, a fighting spirit, are the very qualities associated with us (meaning black women in general). Qualities that we have often suffered for and been made to feel guilty about because they are supposedly 'manly' rather than 'feminine' qualities. . . These are the charges leveled at the 'bitch' but the same words are accolades for the male hero.

This sexism is reflected, Gomez asserts, in creative thinking and writing. Black women have suffered the inability to see themselves as the center of anything, even of their own lives. Black men sometimes resent black women's efforts at autonomy. Gomez lists examples of female heroism in science fiction, noting that these cited works replace images of black women as passive victims with representations of an identity constituted by "fighting spirit, strength, eroticism." In an argument that could be extended to include representation generally, Gomez insists that fictional representations affect everyday experience, including how we think about ourselves, upon which action is predicated. Gomez concludes:

> While critics have often neglected to scrutinize fantasy or science fiction or place it within the context of literary and social constructs, the genre—like any other popular art form—is very intimately related to the sensibilities of the broad-based populace. It can be a barometer of our secret fears and secret dreams: dreams of solidarity, strength or heroism. And we, as a people, should be acutely aware of just how powerful dreams can be.

From fictional representation we move to the present time to examine a different order of identity representation. Wendy Luttrell's "Working-Class Women's Ways of Knowing: Effects of Gender, Race, and Class" describes how black and white working-class women define and claim knowledge. Based on participant observation in adult education classrooms and in-depth interviews outside school, Luttrell finds that these women's experience challenge those feminist analyses which posit a single, universal mode of women's knowing.

Before describing differences among these women, Luttrell describes similarities. Both black and white working-class women tend to share similar conceptions of knowledge and a similar framework for evaluating their claims to knowledge. Both differentiate between that knowledge associated with school and textbook and that knowledge associated with living, with experience. Both groups tend to share ideas regarding their commonsensical abilities "to take care of others." That is, their ideas of knowing and knowledge are situated in community, family, and work relationships. They cannot, Luttrell asserts, be judged by ordinary academic standards. Moreover, "their commonsense knowledge cannot be dismissed, minimized, or 'taken away.' "

Both the black and white women interviewed appeared to accept stratification of class. They accepted a taken-for-granted distinction between common sense and intelligence. Although white working-class women described themselves, their mothers, their aunts, and sisters as exhibiting common sense, they regarded only "certain aspects" of common sense as "real intelligence"—and these were aspects associated with men's work and men's activities.

Even when referring to skilled manual work as requiring "real intelligence" they were not referring to skilled manual work required of women working in factories; they were referring to men's manual labor. One woman commented: "Now just because we're going to school and getting educated, we shouldn't forget that people, like my husband, who work with their hands, are just as important as college professors and just as smart."

The black women interviewed did not emphasize the intelligence required to do manual work, perhaps, Luttrell speculates, because black men have had, historically, "limited access to the 'crafts.'" Further, unlike the white women interviewed, the black women did claim "real intelligence" for themselves. They credited their domestic, caretaking work as requiring "real intelligence." One woman reported:

> I got a sister I think she is smart, real intelligent. All of them is smart, but this one is special and she do the same kind of work I do but she's smart. She can hold onto money better than anyone. It look like anything she want she can get it. . . . anytime she or her childrens need something, she can go and get it. But she has a husband that help her, not like my other sisters or me. Her husband is nice to her and both of them working. But even that, it take a lot of intelligence.

Further, the necessity of dealing with racism requires "real intelligence." A woman named Kate reported: "I'll tell you what takes real intelligence—dealing with people's ignorance. . . . You see a lot and watch people. It's a feeling you have to have because not all white people are the same. I sure know that 'cause I worked for different ones, you know, taking care of their children, and I've seen different things." Resisting racism requires intelligence.

Luttrell concludes that differences between white and black working-class women's understandings of knowledge disclose that women do not share a single view of their identities as women. They do share a sense that the organization of knowledge— organized as academic expertise and as men's competence— undermines their power in negotiating the world. Luttrell writes: "Since women do not all experience the work of being a woman in the same way, it is impossible to identify a single mode of knowing. To understand why certain forms of knowledge appear more amenable to women, we must look more closely at the ethnic-, class-, and race-specific nature of women's experiences, as well as the values that are promoted in each context."

Luttrell's research points toward the specificity of relations between identity and knowledge, and particularly toward the nonsynchronous complexity of race, class, and gender. Her study undermines the feminist claim that women's gendered experience is more fundamental than their racial or class experience. This view is taken further in the concluding essay of the first section, "Racism and the Limits of Radical Feminism." While unfortunately presenting radical feminism as monolithic, Murphy and Livingstone's angry article does make important points pertinent to understanding identity and representation. Provocatively, they assert that "race" is a social—and economic—question; upon analysis, it falls apart as a category. The distinction between "black" women and women of "color" (a more inclusive category, including Asian, Hispanic, Native American, and Third World people generally), for example, does not hold:

> (i) Black does not designate a colour. Africans are no more black than Eskimoes are white; and people of colour may well be 'blacker' (i.e., darker) than black people. (ii) Black does not designate a culture. Black people may be of Caribbean or English culture, as may people of colour have a culture which is Indian, English, or anything else. (Not to mention the fact that never is any 'culture' homogeneous.) (iii) Black does not designate a 'race'. A black person or person of colour may be of 'mixed race'.

They point out that such efforts to differentiate racially are "products" of racism. What underlines the gradations of color is nothing biological; it is political. "Those who are the most resistant tend to be painted the blackest, and those who are more easily 'integrated' are given a lavishing of white." To whatever extent there is a black culture, they continue, it is created through the struggle against racial oppression.

The concept of ethnicity, Murphy and Livingstone insist, is a "white concept." (This view is not shared by, for instance, Alma Young; see Chapter 11.) They write: "Black culture is the culture of resistance and rebellion—whatever form this may take. . . . *ethnicity* turns what is essentially an economic question about racism into a problem of culture." In this sense, multiculturalism becomes an instance of Fanon's concept of 'cultural mummification'.

"Multi-culturalism tries to resurrect an old culture, a culture from the past, from a different setting: a mummy to mummify. It takes what it supposes to be black people's culture, separates it from its living historical context, and offers it, like a drug, to black people, to make them placid and inert." This is also a view not universally shared, as we will see in the next section.

Although extreme in tone and thesis, this article functions to summarize the first section by reiterating questions of identity, and specifically gender. Written in the United Kingdom for a British audience, the Murphy-Livingstone article also functions to remind us that issues of racial identity and representation are not exclusively American, although given the American history of slavery and racial segregation, they may prove more intractable for us than for many other nationalities.

The Murphy and Livingstone article not only functions as summary. Additionally, it functions as a transition to the second section, wherein issues of difference within identity and their curricular representations become paramount. The concept of curriculum as racial text is a complex one. One issue—as we have seen—is that of representation, including how images of racial identity are portrayed in curricular materials such as textbooks and instructional films. Obviously, these can function to convey racial stereotypes, despite the intentions of their producers. The complexity of racial identity, its singularity, diversity, and historicity, was illustrated via a focus upon gender. Issues of "breaking the silence" within the African American community, issues between and within white and black working-class women as well as vignettes of fictional and historical figures, all speak to this complexity and suggest, most elementally, that representations of racial identity might be most progressively produced from within racialized communities. Representation becomes important not only because it reflects identity at a particular historical conjuncture; it is important because it also creates that identity. Understanding curriculum as racial text implies, in part, that we teach ourselves when we teach textbooks. The identities we represent to children are those we wish (as a nation) to become and to avoid as well as those which we are. The complexity of these issues makes it unsurprising that representations of difference have led to difficult curriculum politics. To these subjects we turn in the second part.

Curriculum Politics and Representations of Difference

In this part we sample several kinds of curriculum arguments. Concepts of cultural diversity and ethnicity organize the opening statements, well posed by Roger Collins and Alma Young. After these essays we will interrupt our movement, as it were, and review these and those related efforts characterized as multiculturalism, efforts Cameron McCarthy will succinctly organize and summarize. (We shall see that these efforts cannot be reduced to "mummification.") After this review we shall read two strong analyses of curriculum politics relating to African American history, by Joe Kincheloe and Beverly Gordon. We conclude with Peter Taubman's reflection on issues of representation, identity, and difference.

Cultural Pluralism and Ethnicity   In the opening essay Roger Collins points out that during the decade of the 1980s the United States absorbed the second-largest wave of immigration in the nation's history. During previous waves of immigration—primarily European—there was consensus upon the assimilation model. For other ethnic and racial groups—Collins lists blacks, Hispanics, and Native Americans—this model has not functioned. Despite efforts to assimilate, significant segments of these populations met and continue to meet discriminatory mistreatment. Because of insufficient rewards, relinquishing the group's cultural identity came to seem unwarranted.

A related issue concerns the nature of integration with mainstream culture. Collins employs the term *culture of power*

> to draw attention to the premise that certain ways of self-presentation, certain ways of talking, interacting, writing, and so on, can serve to facilitate or hinder an individual's chances for success within "mainstream" institutions. When an institution is dominated by individuals from the majority culture, facility with that culture, the culture of power, can contribute to a minority person's chances for success. Often, the failure of culture-of-home advocates to acknowledge the importance of minority students' access to the culture of power leads to minority parents' resistance to a curriculum and instruction that promotes, exclusively, the culture of home. Cultural pluralism, however, does not view the cultures of power and of home as mutually exclusive.

Collins then describes various curricular and instructional practices which honor the concept of cultural pluralism.

In the Collins chapter we observe a notion of American identity in which the integrity of its marginal cultural elements is honored. At the same time, the expediency of acquiring modes of self-presentation palpable to the mainstream culture—the "culture of power" in Collins's essay—is accepted. Identity here becomes a mediation between native and acquired cultures. There is the notion that assimilation can occur without sacrifice of native cultural integrity. Certainly there is here a different representation of difference than Murphy and Livingstone posit. That is, in the Collins chapter and in the Young chapter which follows we read representations of race that have cultural referents, not simply political or economic ones. Additionally, in the Collins piece we note curriculum and instruction conceived as mediating the difference between native and acquired (dominant) culture, a version of curriculum as racial text.

Alma Young focuses on the concept of ethnicity. For her the distinguishing characteristic is not racial (in a biological sense) but behavioral. "An ethnic group may well include people of differing phenotype; and a recognized phenotype may create an identity that has marked behavioral consequences." For Young, then, ethnicity is "*conscious* togetherness." In part, this sense of solidarity derives from racism, from others' prejudices. She quotes Kilson: "so much of what it means to be black in America is intricately linked to white society, and the formation of black ideas, values and institutions occurs in complex dialectical interaction with this society." Like Edgerton, Young discusses marginality, emphasizing economic as well as cultural marginality. In response to this marginality, Young reaffirms the tradition of "self-help" in the African American community. "We must continue to draw upon our own resources, the most basic of which is the special value structure that has sustained us. Those values include the primacy of the family, the importance of education, and the necessity for individual enterprise and hard work. We need to renew our commitment to those historical values as a basis for action today."

Self-help, Young adds, is not enough. She recalls the definition of ethnicity as "learned behavior," behavior not only learned internally within African American society, but as responses to others outside that society. She argues that racism must be interrupted by governmental policies and programs for job creation, restoration of the physical infrastructure of black neighborhoods, and the development of human resources (education, training, and health).

Both self-help and governmental intervention against racism will enable African Americans to compete more effectively in the marketplace. She adds: "Only then will African Americans be able to create a stronger sense of community and cultural identity. That greater sense of self will help us to struggle against the injustices to which all African Americans are exposed."

Multiculturalism Concepts of cultural pluralism and ethnicity have led to efforts to develop a multicultural curriculum. Indeed, multicultural education represents a major effort to acknowledge cultural diversity in the curriculum. Despite its noble intentions, it is problematical, as Cameron McCarthy explains in Chapter 12. McCarthy characterizes multicultural education as a "contradictory and problematic 'solution' to racial inequality in schooling." He reviews the history of multicultural education, beginning with its assimilationist antecedents and their critique during the 1950s and 1960s. Multiculturalism, McCarthy tells us, was replaced by a so-called pluralist model that advocated cultural diversity. Multiculturalism, in McCarthy's words, "disarticulated elements of black radical demands for the restructuring of school knowledge and rearticulated these elements into more reformist professional discourses around issues of minority failure, cultural characteristics, and language proficiency." Multicultural proponents emphasize (a) cultural understanding, (b) cultural competence, and (c) cultural emancipation. We focus here upon the third approach.

Like the cultural understanding and cultural competence models of multicultural education, the cultural emancipation model affirms minority identity. Like the cultural understanding model (and even like cultural deprivation models), the cultural emancipation model notes the value of a positive self-concept for minority students, a state that derives from studying minority history and culture. (It should be noted that an improved self-concept does not necessarily lead to academic achievement [Castenell, Jr., 1983].) There is an additional claim associated with this model: improved academic achievement will enable minority youth to succeed in the labor market. Like the social reconstructionists Harold Rugg and George Counts, proponents of the emancipatory model believe that the profound shifts in the economic and social spheres will accrue from improved academic achievement. After Giroux, McCarthy characterizes this belief as a "language of possibility," a language not present in assimilationist discourse. Further, implicit in this model is an enlargement of the school curriculum to include the history and experience of minority and other marginalized groups. Finally, the cultural emancipation model does point to the economic and public sphere generally, well beyond the confines of the classroom. However, even this model fails to acknowledge the racial inequality of those spheres. Indeed, implicit in all models of multicultural education is the naive assumption that academic achievement guarantees economic achievement. McCarthy summarizes:

> As we saw, each of these approaches represents a subtly different inflection on the issue of what is to be done about racial inequality in schooling. Thus proponents of cultural understanding advocate sensitivity and appreciation of cultural differences—a model for racial harmony. Cultural competence proponents insist on the preservation of minority ethnic identity and language and "the building of bridges" between minority and mainstream cultures. Finally, models of cultural emancipation go somewhat further than the previous two approaches in suggesting that a reformist multicultural curriculum can boost the school success and economic futures of minority youth.

Unfortunately, McCarthy adds, these approaches to curriculum reform fail to provide explanations or "solutions" to persisting problems of racial inequality in schools. All three approaches, he believes, depend on changing values, attitudes, and, indeed, human nature. Common to these approaches is an emphasis upon the "individual."

> Schools, for example, are not conceptualized as sites of power or contestation in which differential interests, resources, and capacities determine the maneuverability of competing racial groups and the possibility and pace of change. . . In abandoning the crucial issues of structural inequality and differential power relations, multicultural proponents end up placing an enormous responsibility on the shoulders of the classroom teacher in the struggle to transform race relations in American schools and society.

Put another way, past approaches have tended to favor "building bridges" from marginalized groups to mainstream society over "a collective minority identity politics oriented toward change in the current structure of race relations in schools and society." McCarthy's review allows us to pause as it situates the cultural pluralism and ethnicity arguments of Collins and Young, respectively. Additionally, it sets the stage for the next two essays, those by Kincheloe and Gordon.

A Critical, Emancipatory Curriculum of Difference   Kincheloe argues that black history should be taught with a "critical edge." When black history is taught as a series of isolated events or organized around brief personality profiles (for instance, Booker T. Washington as a "credit to his race"), black history ignores the fundamental question: What does it mean to be an African-American? Historically, this question of identity would include, for example, a black perspective on the Age of Discovery.

> The rote-based memorization of the "discoveries" of Columbus, Cortes, Balboa, DeGama, et al. would give way to a thematic conceptualization of the reasons for European expansionism and the effect of such actions on African, Asian, and Native American peoples. . . . The study of the Age of Exploration would lead naturally into an examination of colonialism and its effect on the daily events of the late twentieth century. Thus, questions generated by black history would fundamentally change what mainstream educators and standardized test makers have labeled "basic knowledge" about Western civilization.

Like McCarthy, Kincheloe criticizes mainstream multicultural approaches as characterizing racism in a fundamental way as an attitude to be changed. Like McCarthy, Kincheloe notes that such a characterization hides the "social relations of domination in which racism is situated." A critical black history would reveal these social relations, for instance, the ways in which racism has exhibited a "tendency for viruslike mutations." From the segregation of the first half of this century racism now tends to hide in institutional policies, policies which pretend to be racially neutral but in their repudiation of affirmative action function to discriminate against African Americans.

An equally significant feature of a critical black history is its capacity to support an Afrocentric vision. He writes that those who are subjugated must establish their own visions, not copy those of dominant groups. In this respect, the power of black history is in its truth telling. Kincheloe writes: "As it removes history from the afternoon shadows cast by the dominant culture, its truth telling reshapes the present as it creates new visions of the future." Such a self-representation of the future allows knowledge to support self-generated identities, allows difference itself to support an identity with a "critical edge," rather than one experienced as a powerless, devaluated marginality. Kincheloe concludes:

> Critical black history in its essence is concerned with repressed memory, subjugated knowledge and the influence of such repression on the life of the present. The power of the memory of repression is nowhere better represented than in the Afro-American experience—among those who have been denied a useful past. Memory finds itself intimately connected to the present as its cultivation helps liberate the knowledges of peoples long separated from their pasts. With oppressed groups memory engenders consciousness, which leads to a panoply of possible futures.

As McCarthy notes, this language of "possibility" and "hope" characterizes radical approaches to a racialized or multicultural curriculum. Beverly Gordon locates these in African American cultural knowledge, "because it is born out of the African-American community's historical common struggle and resistance against the various oppressive effects of capitalism and racism." Gordon provides an abbreviated history of this knowledge. Afterward, she suggests that "a major shortcoming of the African-American intelligentsia . . . has been their failure to take the work . . . [of] Booker T. Washington, W. E. B. DuBois, Kelly Miller, Carter G. Woodson, and William T. Fontaine . . . [and] synthesize it into a body of knowledge and to make it the basis of a common intellectual heritage that would give leadership and direction to the African-American community."

African American scholars, she continues, must return to this legacy, to the whole of African American traditions, history, and cultural thought and construct an African American mode of rationality independent of Western European domination. African American knowledges need to be synthesized in what she terms an "African-American epistemology." Gordon concludes:

> Emancipatory pedagogy requires the reconceptualization of knowledge into new forms of ideology, paradigms, and assumptions that can help illuminate and clarify African-American reality. Emancipatory pedagogy also requires counter-indoctrination against the blind acceptance of the dominant culture's concepts

and paradigms. Emancipatory pedagogy is the freeing of one's mind to explore the essence and influence of the African-American race throughout the world, and the ability to pass on that information . . . as a foundation upon which to build.

Gordon insists that her argument does not represent simply another effort to justify the teaching of African American history in the schools. Instead, she is arguing that teachers and teacher educators must be knowledgeable in black scholarship and that the varieties of African American experience must be explored in classrooms utilizing an emancipatory pedagogy. "Citizenship education then ideally becomes education for informed political awareness, and in the practice of critically analyzing reality, and not simply a process of rote indoctrination."

Conclusion: Toward a Nonsynchronous Identity We return to our beginning to close the collection. In "Separate Identities, Separate Lives," Peter Taubman examines approaches to multicultural and antibias education in terms of identity. To do so he has defined three separate but intersecting registers through which the construction, function, and meaning of identity are expressed. The first register he terms *fictional* "because identity emerges here primarily as a construct of language and certain preverbal relationships and as an artifice imposed on the plenitude of the individual." This register can be explored via the so-called poststructuralism, especially the work of Lacan, Foucault, and Derrida. In this register, Taubman tells us, "occur the attempts to endlessly evoke and utter the unutterable, to map the uttered and to expose the absence under the fading presence of the word." The second register he terms the *communal;* in this register "identity is activated and given meaning by and through the group." In this register identity functions as pretext for reflection and action. The third register Taubman calls the *autobiographical,* wherein "identity emerges as a personally meaningful and continually developing aspect of one's Self, as a private center of being or as an autonomous subject capable of excavating his or her own history in the service of transcending it."

Taubman criticizes mainstream approaches to multicultural and antibias education as being frozen in the second register.

Blackness or Afro-Americanness, rather than an identity-in-motion which can be used to illuminate experience and serve as a

ground for action and reflection, becomes a fixed and sedimented identity over which may be erected a *monumentalized*
history and culture, one which in the process of memorializing
history forgets it. For example, in the monumentalizing of Martin Luther King, Jr., his possibility-in-the-present is forgotten.

When the identity-in-motion becomes frozen, it becomes severed from the fictional and autobiographical registers. The person
disappears into a Lacanian dialectic of alienation. He illustrates
this danger by recounting the widely reported dispute which occurred in New York between a Korean grocery store owner and a
Haitian customer. "The trap in this dynamic," Taubman argues,
"was that the identities-in-motion lost dialectical tension with the
other registers and became immobile." Consequently, "neither
group could possibly attain the gaze desired, nor could either
group become more than what the gaze of the other returned to
them. No member of either group could be seen as what the member wanted to be seen as, since each member embodied the group
and thus would always remain less than what he or she was, while
thinking he or she was more."

After criticizing the conservatives, Taubman turns to the radicals, those who espouse "empowerment" and who focus upon
those nonsynchronous racist, classist, and sexist dynamics which
operate in the school to produce knowledge and identity. Taubman
regards this view as incomplete. The identities implicit in radical
approaches to multiculturalism remain immobilized "because the
approach posits oppression as the origin and horizon of the identity. . . . One's identity is determined always along an axis of oppression. . . . the communal register is severed from the autobiographical register." What is absent in this approach is a creative
tension between the fictional and autobiographical registers,
which function to mobilize the identity of the oppressed and/or
oppressor, thus transforming it into an identity-in-motion "which
could be used to illuminate the dynamics of oppression and investigate one's own being as well as the relationships one has with
others."

With Taubman's analysis we are returned to our beginning, to
issues regarding racial representations of identity and difference.
When we acknowledge we are racial creatures, that we are what we
know and what we do not know, we acknowledge that the curriculum is racial text. In its representation of race, difference, and
identity, the school curriculum—included in which are those con-

versations we have about it as well as how we experience it—
communicates images of who we are, as individuals and civic creatures. As Americans we live a complex, nonsynchronous identity.
We Americans are a multicultural, multiclassed, multigendered
self. Despite this fundamental truth, various elements in the American national character continue to be devalued, in fact repressed.
Our argument in this volume has been that in the present time not
only the repressed suffer—although surely their suffering is the
greatest, the most intolerable. However, European Americans suffer as well. In their ignorance that they are racial creatures, that
their knowledge is racial knowledge, indeed, that their material
and cultural wealth is in significant measure the product of "others," especially African Americans, they forget history and
politics—and themselves. They have lost touch with reality, their
own and others. Education is the cultivation of intelligence. Understanding curriculum as racial text might enable us to begin to make
that process real.

REFERENCES

Bulhan, H. (1985). *Frantz Fanon and the psychology of oppression.* New
York: Plenum.

Castenell, Jr., Louis A. (1983). Achievement motivation: An investigation
of adolescents' achievement patterns. *American Educational Research
Journal, 20,* 503–510.

Castenell, Jr., Louis A. (1991). The new south as curriculum: Implications for understanding southern race relations. In Joe L. Kincheloe
and W. F. Pinar (Eds.), *Curriculum as social psychoanalysis: The significance of place* (155–166). Albany: State University of New York Press.

Crichlow, W., and McCarthy, C. (Eds.). (1993). *Race, identity, and representation in education.* London: Routledge & Kegan Paul.

Derrida, J. (1976). *Of grammatology.* Trans. by G. C. Spivak. Baltimore:
Johns Hopkins University Press.

Gates, Jr., Henry Louis. (1990). Critical remarks. In David Theo Goldberg (Ed.), *Anatomy of racism* (319–332). Minneapolis: University of
Minnesota Press.

Goldberg, David Theo (Ed.). (1990). *Anatomy of racism.* Minneapolis:
University of Minnesota Press.

Jordan, W. (1971). *White over black: American attitudes toward the
Negro 1500–1812.* New York: Penguin.

Kincheloe, J., and Pinar, W. F. (Eds.). (1991). *Curriculum as social psychoanalysis.* Albany: State University of New York Press.

Kovel, Joel. (1971). *White racism: A psychohistory.* New York: Vintage.

Lasch, Christopher. (1984). *The minimal self: Psychic survival in troubled times.* New York: Norton.

McCarthy, C. (1988a, August). Rethinking liberal and radical perspectives on racial inequality in schooling: Making the case for nonsynchrony. *Harvard Educational Review, 58*(3), 265–279.

McCarthy, C. (1988b, Summer). Slowly, slowly, slowly, the dumb speaks: Third world popular culture and the sociology for the third world. *JCT, 8*(3), 7–22.

McCarthy, C. (1990). *Race and curriculum.* London: Falmer.

Morrison, Toni. (1989, Winter). Unspeakable things unspoken: The Afro-American presence in American literature. *Michigan Quarterly* XXVIII, no. 1, 1–34.

Ogbu, J. V., and M. E. Matute-Bianchi. (1986). Understanding sociocultural factors in education: Knowledge, identity, and school adjustment. In California State Department of Education (Ed.), *Beyond Language: Social and Cultural Factors in Schooling Language Minority Students* (73–142). Los Angeles: Evaluation, Dissemination and Assessment Center, California State University.

O'Brien, E. (1989, November 23). Debates over curriculum expansion continues. *Black Issues in Higher Education, 6*(18), 1–26.

Omi, W., and H. Winant. (1983). By the rivers of Babylon: Race in the United States. *Socialist Review, 13*(5), 31–65.

Pinar, W. F. (Ed.). (1988). *Contemporary curriculum discourses.* Scottsdale, AZ: Gorsuch, Scarisbrick.

Pinar, W. F. (1991). Curriculum as social psychoanalysis. In J. Kincheloe and W. F. Pinar (Eds.), *Curriculum as social psychoanalysis: The significance of place* (167–186). Albany: State University of New York Press.

Pinar, W. F., and W. M. Reynolds. (Eds.). (1992). *Understanding Curriculum as Phenomenological and Deconstructed Text.* New York: Teachers College Press.

Pinar, W. F., Reynolds, W. M., Slattery, P., and P. M. Taubman. (1994). *Understanding curriculum.* New York: Longman.

Schwartz, Barry, and Disch, Robert. (1970). *White racism.* New York: Dell.

Taubman, Peter M. (1987). Notes on James Baldwin, a native son. Miles M. Kastendieck Chair of English Address, April 9, 1987, Polytechnic Preparatory Country Day School, Brooklyn, New York.

Thomas, Alexander, and Sillen, Samuel. (1979). *Racism and psychiatry.* New Jersey: Citadel.

PART 1

Race and Representations of Identity

An Opening: Identity and Curriculum Politics

CHAPTER 2

Canonical Sins

Peter M. Taubman

It seems that no matter where I turn these days, I hear about the literary canon. In my own school I was approached several times last year and have already been approached this year by teachers, all from other disciplines, who asked me why the English Department did not teach more classical British literature and why we did not have any survey courses. A particularly concerned faculty member asked, "What is wrong with concentrating on the best that has been thought and said according to the canon?"

The concern over the canon is inarguably widespread, the discourse of the debate increasingly prolix, and the influence this debate exerts on the nation's conversation about education rapidly growing. Few would dispute the observation that the debate on the canon reflects larger social issues that concern America and reencodes these issues in terms of Great Books, the core curriculum, and the canon. Concern about national, group, and individual identity, about values, about God, and about the foundations of thought itself emerges as a conversation about books and their circulation.

Because of the organizing principles within the canon, the debate over it has, at least in the larger society, been controlled by a dualism. One joins one's voice with the canonical discourse or with the oppositional discourse. One can agree, for example, with E. D. Hirsch, the author of *Cultural Literacy: What Every American Needs to Know,* who writes, "The effort to develop a standard sequence of core knowledge is, to put it bluntly, absolutely essential to effective educational reform in the U.S."[1] For Hirsch and others who articulate the canonical discourse, the core is constitu-

ted by "Western culture." Or one can join one's voice with that of
Louis Gates, Jr., who writes that the teaching of literature "has
become the teaching of an esthetic and political order in which no
person of color, no woman, was ever able to discover the reflection
or representation of his or her cultural image or voice."[2] Louis
Gates, Jr., is the editor of the new *Norton Anthology of African-
American Literature.*

One can hear in these quotes issues about race, gender, the
logos, and values, about those included and those excluded, about
the Same and the Other and about those in power and those out of
power, and one can also hear both sides moving toward consol-
idating and evaluating their own positions. Both the canonical
discourse and the oppositional discourse silently or vocally organize books around race, gender, ethnicity, and class. Thus literature, that is, all written texts, comes to be organized within, and
derives its identity from, two discourses, each of which anchors the
value of the text on the silent or vocal principles in its discourse
and collects the books according to its own discursive strategies.
From the viewpoint of the canonical discourse, such consolidation
is a function of intrinsic worth. The cream rises to the top, and
great books survive the "test of time." From the point of view of
the opposition, such a consolidation appears politically expedient
and developmentally necessary.

The public discourses on the canon form a kind of theological
literary discourse. Within the canonical discourse texts become
idols. The term *idol* is derived from the Greek *eidolon* or *eidoi,*
meaning form or image, and is associated with phantoms or the
image of God. Certainly canonical texts are treated as ideal forms.
Fixed in an ahistorical and atemporal realm, they are worshiped
for their embodiment of the Western metaphysic, for the aura
which surrounds them, and for the spirit they contain. It is in this
sense that those who worship the canon are, according to the
oppositional discourse, guilty of idolatry.

The oppositional discourse seeks to stretch the canon's boundaries to include noncanonical texts or to dissolve those boundaries
altogether. It seeks in part to dissolve those very foundations of the
canonical discourse. Its assault on the canon is rearticulated within
the canonical discourse as a kind of heresy. The etymology of
heresy suggests the Greek words for choice and for assault, but it

also points to the Latin *serum*, which means fluid, which flows and runs. It is in this sense that those who merge their voices with the oppositional discourse are, according to canonical discourse, guilty of heresy.

But perhaps both discourses are in certain ways guilty of a third canonical sin or murder. Because these discourses polarize around notions of abstract fixity and ideal form on the one hand and dissolution and dispersion on the other, the reader and the text remain groundless. Perhaps both discourses do violence to the quirky and unique ways books move through our lives, flatten out our private relationship to reading, and force us to read and hear a prior discourse in the words which meet our eyes and ears and the intentions which move our hand to pull down the volume from the shelf.

When I was sixteen, I was surrounded by books. In my parents' living room, there were bookcases lined with leather-bound volumes, all of which had been written and printed before 1930. The collected works of Dickens, Eliot, and Poe pressed up against encyclopedias of the beautiful, of the sciences, of the world's knowledge. Neatly shelved, dusted weekly, and rarely read, these classics rested peacefully, not unlike the texts Sartre described in *What Is Literature?* as "little coffins stacked on shelves along the walls like urns in a columbarium."[3]

My parents did read, though. They read every evening and in much of their free time. The bookshelf near my father's easy chair held not only magazines and the evening's newspaper, but also tomes on medicine, thin books on tennis, and contemporary best-sellers generally on World War II, Jews, detectives, or humor. *Catch-22, Call It Sleep, The Rabbi Slept Late,* and *The Devil's Dictionary* all stood at different times on that shelf. My mother's nightstand often held an Agatha Christie novel and a best-seller by perhaps Cheever, Mailer, or Updike. Behind these was a stack of older books which had been read at one time and perhaps waited for another look. *By Love Possessed, The Man on the Donkey,* and *For Whom the Bell Tolls* lay tranquilly on top of one another.

In my own room the bookshelves revealed various strata in my reading habits. The Oz books stood next to the Hardy Boys, which abutted the Landmark books, and biographies of sports heroes leaned against schoolbooks used in earlier grades. On my desk were piled the books I had to read for school. That year one could have found at different times an anthology of British literature, *Joseph Andrews, Silas Marner,* and the *The Moonstone.*

These were the books, then, that one, scanning the Taubman apartment at that time, would have seen. These were the books that revealed our public reading habits. But there were other books, texts, and reading material that existed in that apartment. These, however, led a more secret life, revealed a more surreptitious existence. Buried in the lingerie drawer of my mother's bureau, hidden beneath slips and girdles, were the forbidden books. It was there that I found at different times *The Story of O, Lady Chatterly's Lover,* and *The Frog Pond,* books that widened my eyes and dampened my palms as I breathlessly raced through them looking for the key words which would unlock the "good" passages. And stashed in my own closet were not only popular "potboilers" but also real "dirty books." *The Carpetbaggers* was frayed, as was *Fanny Hill.* Terry Southern's *Candy* was as thumbed as the pages I had hidden after ripping them from my father's volumes of Havilock Ellis's *The Psychology of Sex,* volumes which, I am sure, I was the only one in the house who read.

And in my father's wardrobe, in the sock drawer, next to the condoms and garters, was not a book or magazine but a neatly folded single sheet, carefully torn from the *Saturday Review.* The sheet listed the "Hundred Greatest Books." Only one title had a checkmark next to it: Sir Thomas Browne's *Religio Medico.* Over the years that sheet remained in the drawer, but no more books were checked off, just as none of the "classics" was removed from the living room shelves. Years later, I carried that same piece of paper in my wallet. The only one in the Taubman house who was reading what were and are considered canonical works was me, and I couldn't wait to get back to the books in the closet.

"How is it," Michel Foucault asks, "given the mass of things that are spoken, given the set of discourses actually held, a certain number of these discourses are sacralized and given a particular function? Among all these narratives, what is it that sacralizes a certain number and makes them begin to function as 'literature'?"[4] We might go on to ask how it comes to be that certain narratives deemed "literature" are elevated to the status of canonical literature while others are not; how it comes to be that certain narratives are, regardless of their market success, considered "popular" but not "serious"; and how it comes to be that certain narratives are publicly silenced or ignored and thus emerge as clandestine narratives, secreted away in bureau drawers or the back of closets.

We might ask how a situation arises in which children and young adults between the ages of twelve and nineteen are forced to read texts which were originally written for adults, but which today adults rarely read; in which many of these same students are forbidden to read what are paradoxically called "adult books"; in which adults and young people read books which are considered to be unworthy of teaching to these students; and in which texts which were originally subversive, popular, adult, or outside a discourse in which "literature" and canonical texts emerged are now presented, in the name of enculturation, to students who would have been prevented or discouraged from reading such texts had they been alive when the texts were written.

We might wonder how it comes to be that a particular canon not only is maintained but also becomes implicated in the construction of personal identity. We might ask, for example, why my father kept for so long that list of Great Books and why I carried it longer still. What was that list insurance against or protection from?

These questions are, of course, answered differently within the canonical discourse and the oppositional discourse. The former appeals to principles of intrinsic value, revelation, universality, immanence and transcendence, mimesis and cultural reproduction. The latter appeals to principles of extrinsic value, existentialism, historical contingency, and social transformation.

The canonical discourse or the discourse in which a canon emerges traces the formation of the canon to the intrinsic excellence of certain texts, an excellence established by critics and those educated to see the eternal value of such texts. Sacralized texts participate in the Beautiful, the True, and the Good. Furthermore, because they are still privileged today and are cornerstones in the canonical discourse, their very existence and fixity are evidence that they have endured the "test of time" and thus are atemporal.

Being atemporal, they are connected by nonhistorical threads such as a transcendent tradition (T. S. Eliot), an atemporal conversation among canonical authors (I. A. Richards, George Steiner), a spirit of Western civilization (Matthew Arnold, Allan Bloom), a structural pattern which, being both mythic and foundational, is ahistorical (Northrop Frye), a sensibility or sympathy (F. R. Leavis), and/or a cultural heritage (William Bennett, E. D. Hirsch).[5] Each of these threads weaves into the canonical discourse where modes of criticism, commentary, and interpretation are linked to one another according to the rules immanent within the discourse at a particular time.

The project of a canonical discourse in which emerge sacralized texts is one that seeks to establish an atemporal and ahistorical system of "homogeneous relations: a network of causality that makes it possible to derive each of them, relations of analogy that show how they symbolize one another, or how they all express one and the same central core."[6] Each text sacralized within the canon is thus both monumentalized and at the same time dissolved. It is monumentalized as a specific entity which is said to anchor the canonical discourse. As George Steiner writes, "In literature, the focused light of both interpretation and valuation lies in the work itself."[7] On the other hand, each text is dissolved within the canonical discourse that sustains it, so that the words of the text are reinscribed or rewritten in the canonical discourse itself. For instance, *The Scarlet Letter* is that which the canonical discourse says it is: an example of American Romanticism, a morality tale, a rebuttal or response to other authors, a piece of our heritage, and so on.

Texts which have not been canonized or deemed "serious literature" exist either at the border of canonical discourse in a state of beatification (one thinks of works by Dickens and Twain as having rested here) or in the realm of the secular. Secularized texts exist outside canonical discourse except when they emerge in it as loose groupings, for example, as "popular" literature, trash, or literary fads or as an undifferentiated mass. In this noncanonical realm they circulate aimlessly and chaotically, whispering and mocking, instructing and seducing, tickling and terrifying, but never speaking at length from within the discourse. Caught up in the exteriority of the canonical discourse, these texts may find their way into other discursive systems which, in turn, interacting with specific social practices, may render them information, topics of social conversation, code words in semiotic networks, or simply taboo.

The exteriority of the canonical discourse where secularized texts circulate constitutes, in part, the unconscious of that discourse. We must understand this unconscious, however, not simply or only as the repressed, nor must we see secularized texts as simply or only the return of the repressed. This is not just a question of the repression of the Other, be that Other people of color, women, the feminine, mama or papa, or the chaotic, although it is in part constituted by these. We must understand this unconscious not in the sense of some archaeological metaphor, although historical processes have shaped it. It does not exist below or in the depths of the discourse. It is unconscious in the sense that it is not commented on or discursively colonized by the canonical discourse.

That which exits exterior to the canonical discourse and beyond the realm of beatification is deemed unworthy of canonical comment because the works that emerge there are considered lacking in Truth, Beauty, and Goodness as well as universality and timelessness. And yet, the works that emerge there are the very ones cathected by the reading public, are like the slips that reveal the reader's psyche, the reader's desire, and the psychology of the reading public. Furthermore, this realm produces endless texts. I would argue that this production is fueled by Desire in the Lacanian sense. An unutterable need emerges as a demand which, never being homologous with the need, produces excess which Lacan calls Desire. The texts that pour forth in the secular realm never satisfy the need that calls them forth. One never hears someone say, "Oh, I've read all of Dickens' novels again and again but I can't keep them apart. They all blur together." Nor does one hear in the canonical discourse texts referred to as edible, Bacon notwithstanding. On the other hand, one may well hear such comments about, for example, Agatha Christie or Stephen King.

This is not to say that secularized texts do not emerge or become unified in other discourses, any more than it would be true to say the material which emerges from the individual subject's unconscious does not become spoken by other discourses, such as political or psychoanalytic discourses. Lacan could say, after all, that the unconscious was structured like a language—one, he could have added, he was fluent in.

We have learned from Freud and Lacan that the unconscious is formed by the No! which separates mother and child and introduces the paternal or patriarchal realm of language and the phallus. I am suggesting that the formation of the canon introduced a

No! into the individual's relationship to reading and thus opened the space for a canonical unconscious, one structured by the canon but not articulated by its discourse.

To return to a predivided state in which individual readers established idiosyncratic relationships to reading would risk dissolution and engulfment. Yet the need for a relationship which is constrained by the demand embodied in secular texts seeps out into Desire, driving the public to read increasing quantities of noncanonical texts.

The books hidden in the back of my closet and in my mother's bureau were, of course, caught up in discourses of taboo and transgression, but they also existed in the canonical discourse's unconscious, reminders of the need for a personal relationship to reading, the possibility of which the books on the living room shelf and the canonical discourse foreclosed. Thus, as the years went, by other books took the place of *Candy, The Carpetbaggers, The Frog Pond,* and *The Story of O,* books which, "cheap" and "trashy," blended into each other in a promiscuity of one-night reads, books which attempted to fill a need for relationship but which produced only Desire.

Not all of the canonical unconscious exists in its exteriority. Within the canonical discourse there exists also an unconscious which may be construed as the silent center of the discourse and which is constituted by the ego ideal as a superego of the discourse. It is here that the discourse is at one with itself and admits no beyond.

In 1922 in *The Ego and the Id,* Freud presented the superego or ego ideal as a product of the threat of castration, as a defense against Oedipal wishes and as a substitute for the lost Oedipal love object. As Freud wrote, behind the ego ideal "there lies hidden an individual's first and most important identification, his identification with his father—or more generally his parents—in his own personal prehistory."[8] The ego ideal or superego is the heir of the Oedipus complex and a substitute for a longing for the lost love object. According to Freud, it can "remain unconscious and inaccessible to the ego (and) is farther from consciousness than the ego is."[9]

I would suggest that the canonization of particular texts and their elevation within a canonical discourse into a sacralized hierarchy parallels the formation of an ego ideal or superego and functions in that capacity for the auditor of such a discourse. It is the very assumption, conceptually and theologically, of a list of valorized texts that constitutes the silent center or superego of the discourse. The No! that severed the reader from an idiosyncratic relationship to reading and the canon from the general field of texts not only gave rise to an exteriority that in part constituted the unconscious of the canonical discourse but also formed the superego or ideal ego within the discourse.

I would argue that the lost love object which Freud refers to is, in terms of the canonical discourse, the father. Thus the formation of the canon hearkens back not only to the killing of the primal father and the subsequent rise of monotheism, but also to the actual terror or loss of the father and his replacement by an abstraction. Freud said that "as a substitute for a longing for the father, [the ego ideal or superego] contains the germ from which all religious have evolved. The self-judgment which declares that the ego falls short of [the ego] ideal produces the religious sense of humility to which the believer appeals in his longing."[10] The primal father is replaced by the spirit of Western civilization encoded in a canon which, like a totem, must be respected and ceremoniously consumed. In *Literary Theory* Eagleton tells us that the rise of the canon paralleled the loss of God. Graf in *Professing Literature* argues that the modern canon arose out of anxiety over the loss of national identity and a sense of the fatherland and coincided with the displacement of the ancients as central to academic institutions.

I don't think it is a coincidence that George Panichas, the ex-headmaster of Deerfield Academy, in his eulogy for Western civilization is reminded of "the inscription on an ancient gravestone" which reads, "Your eyes are upon me, and I am not."[11] The primal father has become an abstraction, the Law of the Canon.

I suspect that the list of Great Books my father kept in the sock drawer next to the condoms—was there a connection? did he wish to control his own sense of loss as he controlled birth?—this list with its unread titles was a reminder of his gaps in knowledge, a kind of punishing superego as well as an ideal to which he aspired, which he cathected and with which he identified, a final signifier which bestowed both status and the right to speak. Finally, I suspect that this list was a substitution for his own father.

And I too carried the list for some time hoping those books would enlighten me or fill me up. At the same time they mocked my own sense of knowing anything. It is certainly not unusual for those who write papers to feel the need to read every book on the subject before beginning; nor is it unusual for perfectly sensible adults to scold themselves and feel guilty for not having read any or enough of the "classics."

The canonical discourse, then, has an unconscious which it does not itself discursively colonize but within which emerge Desire and its own ego ideal or superego. Created by the No! that severed the reader from a relationship to reading, the canonical unconscious hearkens back to the death of the primal father and the need for relationship.

I want now to argue that the canonical discourse and the cornerstone titles that support this discourse are analogous to the formation of the ego or, in a Lacanian register, the Imaginary. For Lacan the ego or "I" comes into being in the gaze of the Other and is thus born in alienation. In the same way the value of canonical works comes into being in the eyes of particular critics who read in them a particular discourse. Once canonized, the texts remain alienated from their potential "openness." They are monumentalized or, if you will, armored and constituted in the canonical discourse, congealed into a hierarchical mass.

Having described from a psychoanalytic perspective the structure of the canonical discourse, I can speculate about the psychic structures of those who idolize the canon. To do this I want to turn first to Klaus Theweleit's *Male Fantasies*, an analysis of the fascist mind. The study suggests that fascism is a flight from the feminine, a response to the fear of ego dissolution, a longing for fusion and a reaction to "the masses" which are encoded with a threatening femininity.

The fascist's fear of dissolution and fragmentation is defended against his desire to fuse into a unity in which he is on the top. Only then can he feel whole. The fascist or soldier-male's need to construct totality formations that are hierarchically structured arises from his desire for symbiosis and his dread of engulfment and dissolution. According to Theweleit, this need "corresponds precisely to the need for dual unity identified by Mahler in the child suffering from the symbiotic-psychotic syndrome. This 'not-yet-fully-born' child needs a totality within which it can be dominant since it needs to be able to perceive its opposite as functioning on its behalf."[12]

Because the soldier-male experienced physical punishment in the form of discipline as a child, he is unable to cathect his body's periphery or identify with it and thus acquires an enveloping ego from the outside, an ego which he fantasizes as armor. As Theweleit put it, "The not-yet-fully-born has a relatively stable ego imposed from the outside. He needs to feel dominant within hierarchical symbiotic structures—the most satisfying being the 'we.'"[13] The hardening of the soldier-male's ego armor increases as he feels more and more powerless to defend against engulfment. He works harder at damming in his internal chaos and finds himself terrified of that which suggests fluidity or liquidity since these are associated with dissolution and engulfment. The army and soldier-male ego serve as a way for the fascist to separate from threatening maternal engulfment, to defend against dissolution and to fuse in a symbiotic relationship. Finally, the fascist ego, the "I," is not seen as evolving from specific parental relations, but, in what structural anthropology calls "direct filiation," the newborn ego is seen as the son of history and culture.

I am suggesting that the psychic structure of the soldier-male parallels the structure of the canonical discourse and the psychic structure of those who idolize it. What appears most threatening to the canon as articulated by the canonical discourse is the dissolution of the canon and the infusion of the nonhierarchical mass of secular texts. This inundation is encoded as the loss of standards and the collapse of civilization. The emphasis on the whole, on a hierarchical totality, is a defense against the unconscious secular realm of the canonical discourse.

The damming in and chaoticizing of the desiring production of the soldier-male is analogous to the domesticating procedure in the canonical discourse (Theweleit, 1987). Texts are dammed in by literary criticism's discursive strategies of transcendence within the discourse. These are the strategies from which the teacher in the film *The Dead Poets' Society* was trying to free texts. He remained within the canonical discourse, however, by moving to a strategy of revelation and immanence. Finally, the canonical texts are removed from the real circumstances in which they arose and, like the soldier-male's ego, are placed in "direct filiation"—they are the products of an ahistorical culture, of civilization itself.

Those who worship the canon share a psychic structure which mirrors the structure of the canonical discourse. One hears in the words of Allan Bloom, E. D. Hirsch, George Steiner, and other idolaters a desire to merge or fuse with the canon and a fear of the secular mass of texts. Panichas in his preface to a published symposium on Bloom's *The Closing of the American Mind*, gives us a bit of poetry which captures the desire for fusion: "The old names are here, / And the old forms / Not alone of doorways, of houses. / The light falls the way light fell, / And it is not clear / In the elm shadows if it be ourselves here, / Or others who were before us."[14] In this nostalgia for people and places that never existed there is the desire to merge with those others, the Great Minds.

"Donning the robes of the Ancients"[15] is how Bloom describes the process of fusing with canonical authors. Hirsch, in a marvelous Cartesian move, suggests that when one interiorizes the canon one's very cognitive structures will become one and the same as the canonical structures and thus the individual will become his or her cultural heritage.

All these writers and other defenders of the canon and canonical discourse, like the soldier-male, "hallucinate a history of great names, great temporal unities,"[16] and defend against fears of dissolution and reengulfment by fusing into a hierarchical mass and by hardening the ego boundaries of the canon. These defensive maneuvers entail a cost.

The cost entails a sacrifice of the unique relationship that each reader could have to reading. It entails a castration in that in order for the reader to merge with the spirit of the father or the hierarchical mass, autobiography, the realm of necessity, and sense perceptions are subordinated to an abstract idea. The fetishizing of the canon acts as a denial of the very castration demanded and as a refusal to acknowledge, not in this case anatomical difference, but historical autobiographic difference and the imagined castration implied by that recognition.

Finally, the canon and its discourse may function for the individual as a defense against status anxiety, anxiety about identity or general feelings of inadequacy. As Stephen Mitchell points out in *Relational Concepts in Psychoanalysis: An Integration,* idealization is a refuge from persecutory anxiety and murderous rage; grandiosity, a manic defense against feeling small.

The canonical discourse points to certain pedagogical practices with which we are all too familiar. It is the practice of the master and tries to reproduce in students the very psychic structures I have outlined here. It is these psychic structures, this pedagogical practice, and this canonical discourse that the oppositional discourse is seeking to dismantle.

The oppositional discourses which have come of age in the last decade challenge the construction of the canon and the pedagogical methods it implies. Multicultural movements and feminism have challenged the obvious white male Eurocentrism of the canon as well as its phallocentric logic. Marxism and the new historicism have pointed out the sociopolitical and historical contexts of canon formation. The new theories in literary criticism have challenged the autonomy of the text, authorial intention, and the assumed subject-object split of the reader-text. Psychoanalytic criticism has opened up a space within the text which can be continually articulated. Thus the limit or boundary imposed by the canonical discourse is undermined. None of this is news. Anyone who has been following the hubbub in English departments around the country or who has been simply attending to the news knows the canon is under attack. As of course it should be.

My concern is that these oppositional discourses in certain ways reproduce in their discourses some of the same discursive strategies which are part of the canonical discourse they oppose and may, inadvertently, have similar implications for teaching. Furthermore, little attention has been paid to the way this oppositional discourse operates to privilege its own texts and in so doing to create its own unconscious. Finally, there may be in the oppositional discourse a fetishing of temporality and the molecular which could lead to a loss of a critical space and thus raise the possibility of an indirect complicity with fascism.

Let me address the last point first. In *Fables of Aggression: Wyndham Lewis, the Modernist as Fascist,* Fredric Jameson suggests that the elaboration of protofascism is determined in large part by "the disintegration and functional discrediting . . . of the various hegemonic and legitimating ideologies of the middle class state."[17] Jameson gives as examples liberalism, conservatism, and Catholicism, but we could also mention the canonical discourse and the canon.

Once the canon is discredited, a plethora of now decanonized texts may circulate. These may be claimed by, for example, a dis-

course which could only reconstitute them in terms of sociopolitical discourses. *The Taming of the Shrew, The Sun Also Rises,* and
Kim were desacralized and deuniversalized, that is, rendered con-
tingent, and reemerged as objects of analysis within sociopolitical
discourses. Conversely, texts which were considered noncanonical
may cohere around and find canonical status because of race or
gender and may be dissolved into the always already said of the
oppositional discourse, thus perpetuating one of the problems we
saw in the canonical discourse.

When I first started teaching, the eighth-grade students in my
class were assigned *To Kill a Mockingbird.* A particularly evocative
novel, at the time it appeared to me as a white liberal defense of
gradualism, a not so subtle condemnation of black militancy, another example of white consciousness appropriating the role of
savior of the Other, and a cartoon depiction of blacks and black
life in the south in the 1930s. What I taught, then, as *To Kill a
Mockingbird* was a sociopolitical discourse which I encoded and
decoded in the novel. God knows I spent hours trying to get those
eighth graders to understand that discourse at, I believe now, the
expense of their own relationships to reading the text.

On the other hand, those discourses within the oppositional
discourse which fetishize the molecular, which appeal to dispersion rather than unification, those oppositional discourses influenced primarily by contemporary French philosophy, run the risk
of dissolving the solid ground on which we can make a stand. I
don't wish to confuse the tactics of dispersion and guerrilla formation, which quickly dissolve and which do offer a resistance, with a
fetishized deconstruction or a Lacanian regression into ego dissolution. The latter two, it seems to me, refuse to reform and thus
cede the power of imagination and vision to more dangerous totalizations. The fetishizing of the molecular in particular is a denial of
difference. Each unique molecule is finally the same, since no identity lasts long enough for difference to exist. I suspect that such a
fetishizing of the molecular and the temporal reflects the fear of
any real relationship between reader and reading, reader and text. I
would argue Theweleit's point that the denial of some stability of
identity defeats the possibility of intimacy and engaged relationship and thus may lead to a protofascism as much as the movement
to hierarchical massification may.

The oppositional discourse, like the canonical discourse, has, I suspect, its own unconscious which emerges at the very moment it moves toward consolidation. As soon as there is a women's canon or an African American canon, both of which are politically expedient, as soon as these exist, there is created an excess, an exteriority which unlike the exteriority of the canonical discourse becomes a space for endless discursive colonization. All texts may be analyzed in terms of a discourse which is anchored in race, gender, or class. The unconscious works here as a field of emergence which can be rearticulated by a voracious analysis that produces endless interpretation. At the same time, since a splitting must occur—that is, not all work written by women or blacks can be included in canons based on these categories—there may arise within the oppositional canon particular hierarchies and a superego or ego ideal. The compulsion to discursively colonize that which would exist exterior to the oppositional canon is, I think, a defense against the possibility of, ironically, difference, since true difference immediately puts into question the foundational categories on which such oppositional canons are based.

The oppositional discourse, in its assault on the canon, in its construction of countercanons, in its flows and molecular structures, runs the risk of becoming what it opposes, dissolving all texts, secular and canonical, into an endless stream of interpretation within which a secure foothold, however tentative, is unlikely.

The question becomes, then: How do we talk about texts without joining our voices to the canonical discourse but avoiding the potential pitfalls of the oppositional discourse? How do we avoid the canonical sins of idolatry, heresy, and the murder that occur when we do violence to the rooted relationship between a reader and reading? How do we avoid the fixity of form and the dissolution of formlessness?

Some would suggest simply expanding the canon; others suggest establishing multiple canons. Some argue for a dialectics in which canonical texts are read from within the tradition but also from without. Others suggest a regrouping of texts around themes, mythic structures, ideologies, or interests. Finally, there are those who argue for a laissez-faire approach. Each will read what each chooses and we will have an ongoing conversation about books.

Whatever approach we take, excluding the last, we come up against that question much beloved of administrators: What books *are* you going to teach? As E. D. Hirsch said, "When I hear talk of pluralism and multi-culturalism and hierarchical arrangements, I say that in the end, we still must . . . make some kind of choice."[18] We still have to choose. When the teacher I mentioned at the beginning of this paper asked me why we shouldn't teach the best that has been thought and said, I should have replied, "The best that has been thought and said by, for, and to whom? When and where? For what immediate task? To what larger ends? Under what conditions?"

To answer these questions requires *each* of us not only to be sensitive to our students but also to ask these questions of ourselves in relation to the texts we do choose. It is to uncover in our own reading and help students uncover in theirs the idiosyncratic relationship they have to texts and reading. At the same time, it is to use texts for brief periods as the firm ground from which we can examine our lives and to use our own experience to examine that ground.

When my parents moved from our old apartment, I remember all the books were piled and scattered on the floor. In that chaos was my family's history of a relationship to reading. Other kinds of boundaries prevented us from ever discussing those relationships, nor did we have a common point of reference from which to reflect on them.

But in a classroom, we can talk about those relationships. We can discuss why Albert Tylis falls asleep over certain chapters in *The Scarlet Letter,* why I like the novel this year but didn't last year, why *The Awakening* evokes such rage among many boys, and why *The Women of Brewster Place* upset Asaki Johnson or why Nowar only reads fantasy. We can discuss how Karen Factor's tenth-grade reading of *Native Son* bumped up against her eighth-grade reading of *To Kill a Mockingbird* and sent her into her own past as well as into the reality of her Bensonhurst neighborhood. And we can read as a class not only the historical and social contingencies which affect our reading but also the psychodynamics of that reading.

We can go into the closets, bureaus, and wardrobe drawers, investigate the nightstand and shelves by the big easy chair, and we can explore the bookcases in the living room. Perhaps if we begin to explore the psychic structures revealed in the canonical and oppositional discourses we can keep from passing onto our students idols, heresies, and violence.

NOTES

1. E. D. Hirsch, The primal scene of education, *New York Review of Books,* March 2, 1989, p. 34.
2. Henry Louis Gates, Jr., Whose canon is it anyway? *New York Times Book Review,* February 26, 1989, p. 45.
3. Jean-Paul Sartre, *What is literature?* (New York: Harper & Row, 1975), p. 90.
4. Michel Foucault, *Foucault live,* trans. by John Johnston (New York: SEMIOTEXT(E), 1989), p. 113.
5. See Terry Eagleton, *Literary theory* (Minneapolis: University of Minnesota Press, 1983), and E. D. Hirsch, *Cultural literacy* (Boston: Houghton Mifflin, 1987), for a discussion of the various theories about "the Tradition."
6. Michel Foucault, *The archeology of knowledge* (New York: Pantheon Books, 1978), p. 15.
7. George Steiner, *Real presences* (Chicago: University of Chicago Press, 1989), p. 17.
8. Sigmund Freud, *The ego and the id* (New York: Norton, 1960), p. 21.
9. Ibid., p. 29.
10. Ibid., p. 27.
11. George Panichas, Prefatory notes from Old Deerfield, *Modern Age, A Quarterly Review,* 32(1)(Winter 1988), 5.
12. Klaus Theweleit, *Male fantasies,* vol. 1, trans. by Stephen Conway (Minneapolis: University of Minnesota Press, 1987), p. 224.
13. Ibid., p. 319.
14. Panichas, p. 5.
15. Allan Bloom, *The closing of the American mind* (New York: Simon and Schuster, 1987), p. 125.
16. Theweleit, p. 225.
17. Fredric Jameson, *Fables of aggression: Wyndham Lewis, the modernist as fascist* (Berkeley: University of California Press, 1979), p. 15.
18. E. D. Hirsch, Who needs the great works? *Harper's,* September, 1989, p. 52.

BIBLIOGRAPHY

Bloom, Allan. (1987). *The closing of the American mind.* New York: Simon and Schuster.

Eagleton, Terry. (1983). *Literary theory.* Minneapolis: University of Minnesota Press.
Foucault, Michel. (1978). *The archeology of knowledge.* New York: Pantheon Books.
Foucault, Michel. (1989). *Foucault live.* Trans. by John Johnston. New York: SEMIOTEXT(E).
Freud, Sigmund. (1960). *The ego and the id.* New York: Norton.
Gates, Henry Louis. (1989). Whose canon is it anyway? *New York Times Book Review,* February 26.
Graf, Gerald. (1987). *Professing literature: An institutional history.* Chicago: University of Chicago Press.
Hirsch, E. D. (1987). *Cultural literacy.* Boston: Houghton Mifflin.
Hirsch, E. D. (1989). The primal scene of education. *New York Review of Books,* March 2.
Hirsch, E. D. (1989). Who needs the great works? *Harper's,* September.
Jameson, Fredric. (1979). *Fables of aggression: Wyndham Lewis, the modernist as fascist.* Berkeley: University of California Press.
Mitchell, Stephen. (1988). *Relational concepts in psychoanalysis: An integration.* Cambridge: Harvard University Press.
Panichas, George. (1988). Prefatory notes from Old Deerfield. *Modern Age, A Quarterly Review,* 32:1 (Winter).
Sartre, Jean-Paul. (1975). *What is literature?* New York: Harper Touchstone Books.
Steiner, George. (1989). *Real presences.* Chicago: University of Chicago Press.
Theweleit, Klaus. (1987). *Male fantasies.* Vol. 1. Trans. by Stephen Conway. Minneapolis: University of Minnesota Press.

Race and Representation

CHAPTER 3

Love in the Margins:
Notes Toward a Curriculum of
Marginality in Ralph Ellison's Invisible
Man and Toni Morrison's Beloved

Susan Huddleston Edgerton

Marginality both as theoretical and embodied existence is a source of big trouble. It "lives" within the very language or world that makes it necessary and that it must oppose. Paradoxically, it must oppose the notion of opposition. Frequently marginality is placed in binary opposition to centrality or dominance, where it is further reduced to social categories such as race, class, and gender with little or no regard for the intersection of these categories with smaller group and individual contexts. Social theories and institutions as well as philosophical writings based on the logic of binary opposition are ill-equipped to deal with the nuances of these non-categories and their implications for the production of subjectivity. Literature is often the only written source of assistance and encouragement for one who wishes to think about these issues in a multi-dimensional way. Ralph Ellison, in his *Shadow and Act*, echoes these concerns in the context of expressing his reasons for writing fiction:

> Unfortunately many Negroes have been trying to define their own predicament in exclusively sociological terms, a situation I consider quite short-sighted. Too many of us have accepted a statistical interpretation of our lives and thus much of that which makes us a source of moral strength to America goes unappreciated and undefined. (1953, p. 16)

Probably no one would deny that literature has value far beyond that of pleasure and escape (not that those values are not inextricably linked to the others), but in many of the social sciences—and even the natural sciences (see Michel Serres, 1982), including my own field of curriculum theory—the potential power of literature to inform those fields has only recently begun to be articulated. It is in the spirit of such articulation that I inscribe "my own voice" within and between the margins of two twentieth-century North American novels: Toni Morrison's *Beloved* (1987) and Ralph Ellison's *Invisible Man* (1952). The stories both authors tell are of people who have been systematically excluded from recorded history at the same time they play key and often involuntary roles in the shaping of that history. Yet the categories of social marginalization that are implied by such exclusion are, as deterministic forces, insufficient to explain the textures disclosed in these works. Prior to dealing directly with these novels and the implications of this study for curriculum, I will explicate more fully my theoretical conceptions of marginality and love.

Marginality can be viewed from at least two perspectives or layers: social marginality and individual marginality. *The socially marginalized* refers to lives which lie outside the dominant culture (the center). Although I am aware that race, class, and gender are social, historical, and cultural constructions and not natural ones, at this particular historical juncture it seems accurate to refer to the margins of larger U.S. society (the socially marginalized) as, in part, racially identified, economically deprived, and feminist or "feminine." Still, it can be argued that everyone is marginal in at least some aspects. The way we attempt to define ourselves has a great deal to do with who or what we attempt to define as "other" to us. And it is at the frontier between this self and this other (these selves and these others) that our own individual marginality lies. For example, if I situate myself as a white, middle-class woman, then anyone whom I situate as nonwhite, nonmiddle class, and/or male would be an other to me. But I may also exhibit characteristics that are traditionally thought of as masculine. I may come from a working-class background, and my physical appearance, manner of speech, and behavior may be "racially ambiguous." Therein rests *part* of my marginality in the individual layer. This particular example of individual marginality also illustrates the interaction between social and individual layers in that the individual layer *differs* from the social layer by virtue of ambiguity around categories that *define* the social layer. In other words, there exists something beyond these two layers, an interactive space where these layers enfold one another, which reveals the leakiness of boundaries between different forms of marginality.

The problem with defining margins and, by default, centers as such is that in doing so we are stuck in a language of oppositions whereby the only option for change is to move from one pole to the other, a complete reversal, or to merge the two in dialectical synthesis, obliterating differences and flattening out the cultural landscape. Either the insidious structure of hierarchy is maintained or the integrity of individual difference and autonomy is endangered. Perhaps a more desirable state of affairs could result from deconstruction of that hierarchical system—and I speak here of deconstruction as set forth by Derrida. Gayatri Spivak explains this notion in the context of the feminist concern with the public/private split (opposition):

> The shifting limit that prevents this feminist reversal of the public-private hierarchy from freezing into a dogma [synthesis] or, indeed, from succeeding fully [reversal] is the displacement of the opposition itself. For if the fabric of the so-called public sector is woven of the so-called private, the definition of the private is marked by a public potential, since it *is* the weave, or texture, of public activity. The opposition is thus not merely reversed; it is displaced. . . . The peculiarity of deconstructive practice must be reiterated here. Displacing the opposition that it initially apparently questions, it is always different from itself, always defers itself. It is neither a constitutive nor, of course, a regulative norm. . . . It is in terms of this peculiarity of deconstruction then that the displacement of male-female, public-private marks a shifting limit rather than the desire for a complete reversal. (1987, p. 103)

As such, what I have called the "interactive layer of marginality" is *not* a synthesis of the social and individual or even of the larger social and community and individual—it is a deconstruction of those layers, which undermines claims to a "positive" stable identity for either self or other, margin or center.

According to Paulo Freire, the marginalized, or the oppressed, are the only ones who can understand the full significance of oppression and thus the only ones who will have the vision and the

strength to eliminate it. The greatest obstacle to their accomplishing this feat, he says, is that the oppressed "are at one and the same
time themselves and the oppressor whose consciousness they have
internalized. The conflict lies in the choice between being wholly
themselves or being divided" (1970, p. 32). Further, according to
Freire, once this process begins there is a danger of complete reversal due, in part, to internalization of oppression and the conse-
quent identification of oppressors as embodying what it means to
be human. Another danger comes from attempts (by whom is not
clear—perhaps, for example, by individually marginalized people
at the social center?) to facilitate the activism of the oppressed
through the use of "monologues, slogans, and communiqués"
rather than dialogue. This is an "attempt to liberate the oppressed
with the instruments of domestication" (p. 52). Although Freire's
sense of marginality as expressed here most closely corresponds to
what I have called "social marginality," his concern is similar to
Spivak's "deconstructivist" warnings about being subsumed within the very discourse being opposed. But she goes further in saying
that one can never oppose a discourse from a position *entirely*
outside it. In so doing, Spivak is able to encompass a broader sense
of marginality to include the interactive layer. That idea is illustrated (and was alluded to at the beginning of this writing) by the
very use of the word *oppose* for a "project" that wants to displace
binary oppositions (Spivak, 1987, pp. 106, 108, 110). This problem, however, is *not* a contradiction so much as it is a paradox. (A
paradox, as I use the term here, is a problem that doesn't require—
indeed, can't *have*—a solution.) Displacement is not the same as
elimination.

The two texts I examine in this writing confront the issue of
marginality from a black racial standpoint, and to different degrees
from a feminist standpoint. I use the term *confront* to emphasize
the problematic nature of marginality as it appears in the works of
Ellison and Morrison. In these texts, and as Freire notes, the marginalized are, in many senses, in a position to know more about the
culture that keeps them far from the center than members of that
culture can know about the margins. Likewise, marginal aspects of
even those who are in the center in the broadest sense are the
aspects of self through which they gain a metaperspective or distance from self. This is because the margin must "know" the center in order to survive, but the reverse is not true to the same

extent. Yet neither exists as such without the other. Hence there is an infusion of each in the other. I refer to this idea as the *"currere* of marginality."

Currere, as William Pinar explains (1975), is the Latin root of the word *curriculum,* and its study "involves investigation of the nature of the individual experience of the public" (p. 400). It is by the experiences and ideas through which I am marginalized, and/or through which I *choose* to dwell in the margins, that I experience the public as an individual (not as an indistinct member of a group). And it is from that experience that I gain multiple perspectives around notions of self, other, and society as both separate and connected. The term *currere* is appropriate in the context of this writing in another sense: curriculum theory as a field of study is itself marginalized in academia generally. And, as will be discussed further, this marginalization is at one and the same time oppressive (low funding, negligence, threats of oblitera- tion, and so on) and enlightening (there is relative freedom to explore multiple perspectives because of a sort of "benign neglect" within power structures). It provides what Czechoslovakian writer Ivan Klima calls "the unexpected merits of oppression" (1990, p. 769).

Other oppositions/displacements run parallel to that of the margin/center in the texts of Morrison and Ellison. There is self/other, bounded/fluid, inside/outside, male/female, white/ black, history/timelessness, public/private, memory/repression, love/hate, and a further breakdown of love into agapé/eros. I have put margin/center at the forefront because it seems to serve as an umbrella for the other pairs in the context of this writing. To deconstruct margin/center is to begin deconstruction of the others. Finally, I have looked more microscopically at love because I be- lieve its expression is integral to all else—certainly it is in these novels.

With regard to my positioning of feminist or "feminine" in the margins of larger society and my emphasis on love as integral to the workings of all the other oppositions operating within these texts, I would like to preface my discussion of the texts themselves with some notes about love as agapé or eros, masculine or femi- nine. Again, stressing my intent to avoid successful reversals, I should perhaps clarify my use of the term *feminine* and thus also *masculine.* I believe that probably every man and every woman possess characteristics from both of the cultural categories "feminine" and "masculine" so that what are considered "feminine" and "masculine" are not necessarily coexistent with female and male, respectively. Yet "feminine" perspectives toward love are mostly marginalized in the philosophical literature, particularly in Western philosophy and theology. It is the "feminine" conception(s) of love, therefore, on which I wish to focus.

In my search for meaning in the concept of love I have examined some of the historical discussions stemming from my own "Western Judeo-Christian" cultural heritage, a heritage in part "inherited" by black people in the United States (Plato, the disciple Paul, St. Augustine, and finally Freud were read via Donnelly, French, Kristeva, O'Donovan, Soble). As several of the sources I consulted point out, such discussions are rich with possibilities, but they are largely lacking with regard to female or "feminine" (as well as black racial) perspectives. For female or "feminine" perspectives I have turned to a contemporary feminist theological interpretation of the Christian concepts of agapé and eros (Donnelly, 1984). My thesis (and Donnelly's, as I read her) is that a "feminine" conception of love is one that doesn't hierarchicalize (and thus artificially split) agapé and eros—a hierarchy which necessitates dualistic thinking with regard to mind and body, spirituality and sexuality. Donnelly and others call it "radical love" (pp. 30–34).

Agapé refers, historically, to selfless love—especially the sort of love that is said to exist between God and human beings, but also within some forms of human friendship. It is considered to be the highest form of love in much of Christian (male) theological literature. *Eros* involves, but is not limited to, sensual, sexual, and/or romantic love between human beings. Both terms have, however, been variously interpreted over time. True to Derrida's insistence on the indeterminacy of origins, contradictory readings of early usages of these terms abound. The opposition deconstructs itself when looked at historically.

Both eros and agapé were concepts developed by men. Plato spoke of *eros;* the disciple Paul spoke of *agapé.* Erosic love for Plato was desire—to *love* was to seek and to love what is lacking. Still, Plato separated mind and body within eros, differentiating between a raving or vulgar eros (body) and a sublime eros (mind). Thus, for the philosopher, love involved lacking and seeking beauty, truth, the good. Freud's notion of the libido (which, incidentally is *only* male) is Plato's eros (Kristeva, 1987, pp. 59–82). Paul first announced agapé as a sort of three-tiered plan for moving the concept of love away from eros and desire and passively under the thumb of the Father or God who bestows it. He emphasizes, first, God's disinterested love for man, second, His sacrifice of the Son to prove it, and third, the importance of loving one's fellowman, including (especially) enemies and sinners as proof of allegiance to the Father (pp. 139–150).

Alan Soble interprets erosic love as being "property-based and reason-dependent," one in which we *appraise* the worth of the "object" to be loved, and agapic love as love which *bestows* value on the loved one regardless of prior properties (1990, p. 12). According to Soble, Eric Fromm sees mother love as agapic (unconditional) and father love as erosic, whereas Irving Singer considers all parental love erosic (p. 13). Soble's definitions point to male imagery for eros and female for agapé *if* one takes "property-based" and "reason-dependent" to be characteristics of modern patriarchy, and nurturing to be a "feminized" concept.[1]

St. Augustine, like Plato, divides love on the basis of mind (spirit) and body while introducing the notions of sin and shame (O'Donovan, 1980, p. 10). In the scheme of St. Augustine women had little to say or offer because they were viewed as virtually all body with no mind or spirituality and limited souls (French, 1985, p. 107). With woman as body and man as mind the translation in Christian thought to woman's love as erosic (erotic) and man's love as agapic was easy. Both Plato and St. Augustine saw mind and body as separate and hierarchicalized—a dualism that has since proven vicious, but which is still very much in place in what has been called "Western rational masculine discourse."

Is another hierarchy emerging with these notions of "feminine" and "masculine"? Only in a limited sense, I think, because, as stated before, I do not believe these categories are natural, let alone restricted to associations of "feminine" to female and "masculine" to male. The limited sense of hierarchy I present here is an inherently unstable one in that concepts and categories of feminine and masculine are historically and culturally defined moment to moment, and as such are synchronically, diachronically, and linguistically unstable. With this and my female status in mind, it should come as no surprise if my arguments and discussion favor a feminist standpoint. I do not claim innocence, but neither do I apologize. Spivak speaks of this issue as follows:

By pointing attention to a feminist marginality, I have been attempting, not to win the center for ourselves, but to point at the irreducibility of the margin in all explanations. That would not merely reverse but displace the distinction between margin and center. But in effect such pure innocence (pushing all guilt to the margins) is not possible, and, paradoxically, would put the very law of displacement and the irreducibility of the margins into question. (1987, p. 107)

Soble argues a case through a logic of binary oppositions (although he explicitly formulates it on the basis of neither hierarchy *nor* prior marginalization) for complete reversal of the agapé/eros hierarchy and the nonnecessity, then, of agapé, forgetting that the terms of language derive meaning from difference (if not différance), and the only difference at work in his system is that of opposition. Thus he obliterates all meaning in his "structure of love" by attempting to discredit and eliminate the term to which eros is opposed (and thereby derives its meaning).

A "feminine" complete reversal of the agapé/eros hierarchy is a fallacy no less than the "masculine" version. The problem for everyone is the same insofar as an incomplete reversal or displacement is the goal. The ways to approach that problem are different—different broadly for masculine and feminine[2] standpoints and different particularly for each individual. Still, I would argue for the existence of a certain advantage for the feminine standpoint through what I have called a *currere* of marginality. The feminine standpoint in which eros (or feeling) is often allowed to supercede agapé (rationality) is a marginalized standpoint in Western market society. (However, true agapé is marginalized as well; a kind of pseudo-agapé prevails—what Donnelley calls "sloppy agapé.") As expressed earlier, those coming from marginalized standpoints are typically more driven to deal with other more dominant standpoints and thus reach broader understandings encompassing multiple possibilities. This is why I feel *some* comfort in referring to the nonhierarchicalized yet noncontradictory conception of eros/agapé as "feminine."

It is through the multiplicitous experience of an entity, idea, or concept—both in mind and body—that we come to know it nonviolently. "True love" for anyone or anything comes from both mind and body, selflessness, and a kind of selfishness. I conceive of this selfishness as one where the lover attempts to soak up as much experience of the other, the loved, into the *self* as possible, though not in an intrusive (violent) sense, and not in a self-obliterating sense. It differs from pure agapé (altruistic, selfless love) in that it involves more of an emotional investment and risk of rejection. But in order to truly be established so that it can grow and evolve, it cannot be rejected—it must be reciprocal, the lover must receive a "return" on that emotional investment. Otherwise it never goes beyond agapé, which, by my interpretation of agapé, *need* only be a one-way affair (as in "love your enemies"). This is not to say that agapé is an inferior form of love—just that agapé is neither superior or *isolable*, nor is it all there is. I am also suggesting that displacement of these hierarchies is more easily associated with the "feminine" at this particular cultural moment, since such a standpoint could be conceived of as displacement of at least three oppositions: masculine/feminine, agapé/eros, and margin/center.

I have argued that a racialized standpoint is a marginalized one in addition to a feminine or feminist standpoint, and that a feminine or feminist standpoint is more capable of displacing at least three hierarchicalized oppositions (above) than is a standpoint at the center. In light of the novels examined here, an obvious next question is, how capable of displacement is the black racial standpoint relative to the feminist one? I have no intention of attempting to quantify such a comparison in any way, but only to entertain the notion that arguments similar to those for a feminist standpoint could be effectively employed for a racialized standpoint. In comparing two novels, one by a black male author and the other by a black female author, a point of interest will be to what extent the "nonsynchronous" nature of these two subjectivities affects their approaches to love and marginality. By "nonsynchrony" I am referring to a concept of dynamic and contradictory relations of race, class, and gender as theorized by Cameron McCarthy (1988, 1990) whereby, for instance, one's racial interests will under some circumstances come into direct conflict with one's gendered interests.[3]

THE TEXTS

Love as an explicit thought comes late in *Invisible Man*, though its expression is implicit throughout. It seems that Invisible Man approaches and touches the power of his own displaced (interactive) marginality repeatedly, but he always heads back for his nondisplaced center. Although at first reading the "feminine" or feminist standpoint seems notably absent from the text, further readings reveal female characters as more significant and mutually marginalized players. They seem to lead him into consciousness of his marginalization and victimization (invisibility). They are, according to Claudia Tate, "like the underground station masters of the American slave era [assisting him] along his course to freedom. . . . They embody the knowledge he needs to state his escape" (Tate, 1987, pp. 164–165).

In Tate's essay "Notes on the Invisible Women in Ralph Ellison's *Invisible Man*," she theorizes that the women in this novel are crucial to each major turning point in Invisible Man's growing self and social awareness. The nude "magnificent blonde" at the battle royal "provides . . . his first lesson in invisibility" as he recognizes their mutual objectification and exploitation and her "Kewpie Doll mask" response to it (p. 167). The second major breakthrough occurs, according to Tate, after Mary Rambo emotionally and physically nurtures him back to a state of greater self-esteem so that he can "depart from the world of 'Keep This Nigger-Boy Running'" at least for a while (p. 168). His third and fourth lessons come from the women of the Brotherhood. He is able to overcome the anxiety of confronting the taboo around sexual encounters between black men and white women with Emma and the anonymous rich white woman as well as to identify somewhat with their common exploitation. Finally, with Sybil he comes not only to recognize invisibility but also to appreciate the potential power in it.

> But before he can clearly see his relationship with the magnificent blonde, Emma, and the anonymous seductress and acknowledge their respective marginality, alienation, and ultimately their respective invisibility, he must dance his third and final dance, in which his partner is Sybil. . . . Sybil, like Mary, is another surrogate mother who comes to deliver the young protagonist from the deception of his false identity with the Brotherhood. She is also another symbolic blonde, who ushers him to the threshold of the final battle royal. In addition, she is his last teacher, who propels him along the course to freedom by making him aware that invisibility is not necessarily a liability but possibly a valuable asset. (pp. 169–170)

And it is this recognition of mutual marginalization that finally brings Invisible Man to an appreciation for the necessity of love of life and to action—love, but not to the exclusion of justifiable and motivating anger; love, but not self-obliterating or self-submerging love.

> So why do I write, torturing myself to put it down? Because in spite of myself I've learned some things. Without the possibility of action, all knowledge comes to one labeled "file and forget," and I can neither file nor forget. Nor will certain ideas forget me; they keep filing away at my lethargy, my complacency. . . . I denounce because though implicated and partially responsible, I have been hurt to the point of abysmal pain, hurt to the point of invisibility. And I defend because in spite of all I find that I love. In order to get some of it down I *have* to love. (*IM*, pp. 566–567)

When Ellison writes of love at this time I do not feel that he means it in terms only of agapé or "brotherly love." Indeed, it was his encounter with Sybil, which was simultaneously sexually, emotionally, and intellectually moving for him, that seemed to trigger thoughts of love and the connections between love and social action. Further, he displaces the "masculine" hierarchy of thinking/feeling in the following passage: "There is, by the way, an area in which a man's feelings are more rational than his mind, and it is precisely in that area that his will is pulled in several directions at the same time" (*IM*, p. 560).

Listening is love. Or at least that might be what Kristeva is saying when she calls transference love "optimum"—optimum because it "avoids the chaotic hyperconnectedness of fusion love as well as the death-dealing stabilization of love's absence" (1987, p. 15). Sybil *listened*. It was an agapic listening without judgment, an erosic listening with her body, and there was exchange of those between them. Invisible Man seemed to be shocked into awareness that this mass of human beings outside consisted of individuals who love and listen and are loved and listened to. Listening, like engagement with a text, effects a dissolution of the boundaries of self, as does love. Simultaneously frightening and exhilarating, it allows the "outside" "inside," opening up channels of possibility, sharing languages, inspiring action. Love conceived in this way could become part of what Guattari calls a "mental ecology"—one that can "face up to the logic of the ambivalence of desire [eros], . . . re-evaluate the ultimate goal of work and human activities in terms of criteria other than those of profit and productivity [relationality], acknowledge the need to mobilize individuals and social segments in ways that are always diverse and different [difference]" (1990, p. 9). It is schizophrenic—"his will is pulled in several directions at the same time" (*IM*, p. 560)—leaping into difference and otherness. But this schizophrenia can become a "positive schizophrenic line of escape" (Deleuze and Guattari, 1983, p. 363), or it can become "neuroticized" (p. 363) as narcissistic "fusion love" (pure eros) and as in other manifestations of codes relinquished to institutions (Kristeva, 1987). I should add that, in Kristeva's terms, as for Lacan, *narcissism* is not used pejoratively, but as an inescapable condition of human love and life.

> What stands between the subject and his desire for death is narcissism. The relationship between narcissism and aggressiveness makes for the fact that narcissism, the ecstatic affirmation of one's being alive, is always enacted at someone's expense. The affirmation of one's life entails the exploitation of someone else's life. (Schneiderman, 1980, p. 6)

"Fusion love" is narcissistic—"its Highness the Ego projects and glorifies itself, or else shatters into pieces and is engulfed" (Kristeva, 1987, p. 6). This is eros, untempered by agapé. Fusion is what Sethe's love for Beloved (the ghost) became for a time (more on this later), but I do not believe it started that way with Beloved (the child). Love can be murderous as a result of fusion, but love—especially perhaps mother love—complicated by the ravages of the almost total social marginalization of slavery, can be cataclysmic. Killing the child to save her (and the others) from slavery might have been, as Morrison said, "the right thing to do [but] she had no right to do it" (Otten, 1989, p. 83).

Paul D is suspicious and frightened of loving too big or too much. Sethe's love seems often all-consuming and without boundaries. Paul D first becomes aware of and is alarmed by Sethe's seemingly boundless mother love when she attempts to apologize for Denver's rudeness to Paul D, and then to disallow him to confront Denver directly about it. He feels that it is "very risky [for] a used-to-be-slave woman to love anything that much," given the fate of so many relationships under slavery. One must "love . . . everything, just a little bit [so that] maybe you'd have a little love left over for the next one" (Morrison, 1987, p. 45). Later, upon discovering that Sethe had murdered her baby girl, Paul D is horrified and uncomprehending of the source, meaning, and implications of such love.

> This here Sethe talked about love like any other woman, . . . but what she meant could cleave the bone. This here Sethe talked about safety with a handsaw. This here new Sethe didn't know where the world stopped and she began. . . . [M]ore important than what Sethe had done was what she claimed. It scared him.
> "Your love is too thick" . . .
> "You got two feet, Sethe, not four," he said, and right then a forest sprang up between them; trackless and quiet. (pp. 164–165)

The murderous spectacle put on for the white inquisitors (the masters from whom Sethe ran away) was indeed sufficient to save herself and other children from returning to slavery. (Spectacular expressions such as the woman who responded to her first bidder at the slave auction by chopping off her own hand with a hatchet were not so uncommon to slave women [Fox-Genovese, 1988, p. 329].) Finally, she is heard. But the incident was permanently inscribed in the memory of herself, her sons, and the community as a horrifying reminder of the tenuousness of their integrity as a community, as loving individuals, as families. She buried the memory with the child, purchasing a headstone with yet another indignity—selling her body to another white exploiter.

With the unexpected arrival of Paul D the task for Sethe and him and Denver becomes that of dealing somehow with this repressed past that interferes with their ability to feel for themselves and one another. Paul D had always "dealt" with his own past by moving around, effectively denying it. But now he wanted to stop and settle with the person who had known him longer than anyone else.

The ghost (proper) of Beloved, who had earlier been maintaining Sethe and Denver without serious challenges, had now been run off by Paul D. Sethe, Denver, or both had to bring her back in a form that could not be denied by Paul D. Beloved's reappearance at a crucial point in the development of the love relationship between Sethe and Paul D has the effect of stopping the painful process of love and analysis. Paul D and Sethe had been serving as one another's analysts, but a new analyst had to enter the picture for the cure to be effected.

The analysis proceeds pathologically. Paul D participates in exhuming this past by impregnating the ghost, the analyst, Sethe's past. This act of his could be seen as a response to *fear of love*— fear, indeed, of the object of Sethe's love, knowing what her love can lead to. On the other hand, he provided her past, her ghost, with possibilities (pregnant with possibilities), but in doing so the ghost almost consumed Sethe. With Beloved as analyst, Sethe's transference love quickly escalates out of control. As the boundaries between Sethe and the one she loves obsessively (Beloved) are further diminished by this love of hers, her "self" declines mentally and physically to a dangerously marginal place. Boundaries dissolve to the point that Sethe's love must be a kind of self-love, narcissism.

But what is Denver's stake in all this? She is fascinated with the ghost (Sethe made?). Why? Sethe, the one Denver loves, is afraid of her own love, understandably, and that fear or love takes the form of the ghost. Denver is *fascinated* with the "abject"—the object of her mother's fear and love. Kristeva writes that the abject is at the margins of life and death, "the edge of non-existence," and is signified by waste, corpses (ghosts?) (Kristeva, 1982, pp. 1–11).

Meanwhile, Paul D is plowing through an emotional crisis of his own. It is when their respective crises of love reach a climax (the analysis is complete when the pregnancy "ends") that both Paul D and Sethe together find a place for love that could be characterized as displacement of the agapé/eros or of the (self-obliterating love)/(fear and distance) hierarchy. Much of this work is done via Stamp Paid and Denver through the legacy of love left behind by Baby Suggs, who had arrived upon a "deconstruction" of those dualisms long ago. Suggs preached love of body, love of self, and, in the "same breath," Christian love (pp. 88–89).

Whereas in *Beloved*'s conclusion the possibility for love not based on opposition seems imminent, the fate of Invisible Man is less clear. He has become aware of his invisibility and marginality and what that can do for him. But his notion of love is still quite vague and undeveloped and he has yet to sustain an intimate relationship in the context of this new self-awareness.

Recognition of marginality and allusions to its paradoxical nature and its "usefulness" are sprinkled throughout the experience of Invisible Man as represented by Ellison. Invisibility can be used synonymously with marginality at the social level in the sense that it means invisible to "others." At the individual level invisibility is synonymous with marginality in the sense of its being a self-awareness that is most difficult to come by—it is hidden from the self. Invisible Man begins his journey blind to his own invisibility, but by the end of this text he insists that he is "invisible, not blind" (p. 563).

In the beginning he is unable to draw on the power that his marginality can provide. He is baffled and plagued by his grandfather's dying words about what it means to "yes them to death," and he participates in his own exploitation and display in order to attend a school where he is "named . . . and set running with one and the same stroke of the pen" (p. 555). This pattern continues far beyond the point at which he has caught the first glimpses of his invisibility on into his work for the Brotherhood, where he thought he could lead a "historically meaningful life." It seems significant that the most explicit and clearly articulated verbal lessons he was given about invisibility were from a "fat man" (also black) who was committed to an insane asylum and was formerly a physician—one who seems to embody "order out of chaos" (or vice versa).[4] Speaking of Invisible Man, he says, "Already he's learned to repress not only his emotions but his humanity. He's invisible, a walking personification of the Negative, the most perfect achievement of your dreams sir! The mechanical man!" (p. 92). And then later, on the train to New York: "You're hidden right out in the open—that is, you would be if you only realized it. They wouldn't see you because they don't expect you to know anything, since they believe they've taken care of that." (p. 152).

To merely hear it said was not enough because it did not yet name his experience sufficiently. Invisible Man had to experience more. If *naming* experience is the first step to forming a sense of autonomy, as Paulo Freire claims, then "claiming ownership of that freed self" (*Beloved*, p. 95) is one step beyond that. Upon finally realizing the true agenda of the Brotherhood, Invisible Man is flooded with the realizations that

> they had set themselves up to describe the world. . . . It was as though I'd learned suddenly to look around corners; images of past humiliations flickered through my head and I saw that they

were more than separate experiences. They were me; they defined me. I was my experiences and my experiences were me, and no blind men, no matter how powerful they became, . . . could take that. . . . Here I had thought they accepted me because they felt that color made no difference, when in reality it made no difference because they didn't see either color or men . . . I now recognized my invisibility. (pp. 496–497)

This is the point at which Sybil becomes instrumental in Invisible Man's "loss of illusions." Allusions throughout the book to loss of eyes, a glass eye, blindness, and castration begin to coalesce into a network of symbolism. Houston Baker (1983) claims that black male sexuality is a key theme of the novel and that it is rarely dealt with by literary critics (p. 329). Trueblood, as object of fascination for whites, merges with Norton's phrase "casting out the offending eye," the imagery of blindness and illusion, the threat of castration at the factory hospital, and finally Invisible Man's dream of having been castrated by Jack—his testicles at times described more like eyes. Confronting the repression of black male sexuality with regard to white women becomes a crucial interconnected symbolic expression of freedom, marginality, and love. White woman represents

the means by which black people in general were penalized for exercising the freedom of choice, in that the penalty was translated into the accusation of rape and the sentence was death. The symbolic linkage between the white woman and freedom, therefore, finds its origin in hundreds of years of southern race relations. (Tate, 1987, p. 166)

Returning to his grandfather's dying advice, Invisible Man asks the question again, what did he mean by saying "yes"? As he explores the possibilities, more capable of imagination now, he stumbles upon a "*currere* of marginality":

Was it that we of all, we, most of all, had to affirm the principle [upon which the country was built], the plan in whose name we had been brutalized and sacrificed—not because we would always be weak nor because we were afraid or opportunistic, but because we were older than they, in the sense of what it took to live in the world with others and because they had exhausted in us, some—not much, but some—of the human greed and smallness, yes, and the fear and superstition that had kept them run-

ning. (Oh, yes, they're running too, running all over themselves.)
(p. 561)

And he further captures the notion of the paradox of marginality
both in a Freirian sense and in the more subtle sense of Spivak's
deconstructivist thought.

Like Ellison, Morrison uncovers a paradoxical *currere* of marginality in *Beloved*. The carnival, which allowed for a "Colored
Thursday," was a chance unbeknownst to the white carnival folk
for black people to "see the spectacle of whitefolks making a spectacle of themselves" (p. 48). Another example of black "signifying"
on white is Paul D's "chain-gang":

> With a sledge hammer in his hands and Hi Man's lead, the men
> got through. They sang it out and beat it up, garbling the words
> so they could not be understood; tricking the words so their
> syllables yielded up other meanings. . . . They killed a boss so
> often and so completely they had to bring him back to life to pulp
> him one more time. (pp. 108, 109)

The power of marginality in the external world is dampened in
Beloved compared to *Invisible Man* because of the difference in the
larger social situation of the time settings. Nor is it a given—it is
problematic and paradoxical. The "meanness" of the black community toward Sethe resonates with Invisible Man's recognition
that only "some—not much, but some—of the human greed and
smallness, . . . and the fear and superstition" had been exhausted
in blacks relative to whites (*IM*, p. 561).

Boundaries between social categories that are represented as
natural ones are exposed as fraudulent in *Beloved*, as they are in
Invisible Man ("a part as well as apart"). This displacement also
arises in the blurring of self/other for black/white, but Morrison
approaches it from a different perspective than Ellison—namely,
she sees black in white, whereas Ellison sees white in black.

> Whitepeople believed that whatever the manners, under every
> dark skin was a jungle. Swift unnavigable waters, swinging
> screaming baboons, sleeping snakes, red gums ready for their
> sweet white blood. In a way, he thought, they were right. The
> more coloredpeople spent their strength trying to convince them
> how gentle they were, how clever and loving, how human, the
> more they used themselves up to persuade whites of something

Negroes believed could not be questioned, the deeper and more tangled the jungle grew inside. But it wasn't the jungle blacks brought with them to this place from the other (livable) place. It was the jungle whitefolks planted in them. And it grew. It spread. In, through and after life, it spread, until it invaded the whites who had made it. Touched them every one. Changed and altered them. Made them bloody, silly, worse than even they wanted to be, so scared were they of the jungle they had made. The screaming baboon lived under their own white skin; the red gums were their own. (*B*, pp. 198–199)

Ultimately, for Sethe it is the love she negotiates with Paul D that allows her the awareness that she is indeed her own "best thing." Like Invisible Man, this negotiated, "deconstructed" love provides the turning-around place for a more autonomous life. The difference between the two novels with regard to love that is most pronounced is the different directions from which the deconstruction is approached. For Morrison, Sethe has come from an almost complete reversal of the agapé/eros hierarchy in her mother love for first Denver and the Beloved (as ghost). For Ellison, Invisible Man seems to begin with very little self-definition for the concept of love. But in those situations, dominant oppositions tend to win by default. These different starting places affect approaches to other oppositions as well. Blurred boundaries in *Beloved* become more distinct, and clear distinctions became more fluid in *Invisible Man*—more fluid in spite of his wary tendency to keep things divided.

Difference is approached in different, though not *distinct*, ways for different historical periods. For *Beloved*'s characters the difference between takes on a greater urgency and/or less subtlety in terms of survival than for Invisible Man—the difference *between* being social categories of difference that determine historical exclusion and oppression of marginal groups. Still, for people who live within (and in spite of) such systems to have lives that include love, pleasure, and so on, other levels and layers of difference had to come into play. Barbara Johnson's (1987) "difference within" is useful but limited. According to this theory, differences between are often illusions created by repression and projection of differences within. Both difference between and difference within connote a negativity to differences—either I have an identity foisted upon me from without and I am excluded *or* I am repressing parts of myself and thus excluding some ones or some things from my consideration. These connotations belie the *positive* potential of difference and of marginality. Already I have discussed the *currere* of marginality which begins to reveal causes for celebration in difference (without ignoring historically oppressive consequences). I would like to offer the suggestion that there is another way of thinking about difference that is *neither* purely within *nor* between, that is not based on repression or exclusion in any life-denying senses of those terms, and that is conducive to action in the ethico-aesthetic realms, where action is so badly needed now. *Invisible Man*'s invisibility-becoming glimpses this, I think.

The dual or perhaps paradoxical sense of marginality whereby it serves as both a force that excludes and includes—excludes one from power and yet includes one by promoting forms of knowledge that can be translated into forms of power—seems to parallel Ellison's usages of "leaping outside history." Leaping out in search of a kind of psychic relief from the pressures of invisibility and marginality can be viewed as an act of hopelessness, of abandoning social and political action and retreating into self—an ultimately conservative move much like those of the hysteric and the sorceress as described by Catherine Clement and Helene Cixous (1975). On the other hand, it can be viewed as leaping outside *recorded* or official history and self-consciously into the more compelling, *un-written* history. In this sense it might be thought of as taking "the ultimate" political action of rejecting systems that forbid joy; a way of converting the hysterical laughter into the "god-laugh," ("the god-laugh always seems frivolous" [Robbins, 1987, p. 232]), and searching out and acting out the *marginality* within. It seems to me that Ellison is attempting to find a way of taking this leap outside history while continuing to maintain a level of realism in which sociopolitical action is more outwardly and materially manifested. After his leap to embrace invisibility he is no less concerned for the evicted elderly couple and the other displaced and dispossessed of Harlem than he was before that leap. Perhaps he even cares more.

That simultaneous sense of difference and connection, I think, can be theorized through love and learning that takes place through a kind of "translation." Translation and its significance to this project will be briefly discussed in the following section. First it will be necessary to return to the significance of literature in the context of this writing.

LOVE, LITERATURE, AND THE *CURRERE* OF MARGINALITY

Early on in this love letter I made the claim that literature (such as the texts of Morrison and Ellison) can extend theorizing in the social sciences in ways that social science discourses cannot typically do for themselves. This thought needs elaboration. The contemporary ecological call to "think globally, but act locally" hits a certain mark while missing another in the context of literary studies in the social sciences. Literature highlights the significance of *particular* places, times, and voices, and in doing that (that is, in the sense of the particularistic), *may* connect to the universal. To think *globally* in the sense of finding solutions, now, and for everyone, is, however, problematic. That is, global thinking in this sense can be terroristic to the margins. Works of literature are *not* global. Literature as "method" (for understanding the margins, particularities) does not offer global solutions. The principles, assumptions, and methodologies of the social sciences, on the other hand, are rooted in prior notions of the possibility for global thinking and problem solving.[5] Literature resists and often subverts such assertions. The following passage from George Konrad's *The Caseworker* (1974) is an ironic example.

> I question, explain, prove, disprove, comfort, threaten, grant, deny, demand, approve. . . . The order I defend is brutal though fragile, it is unpleasant and austere; its ideas are impoverished and its style is lacking in grace. . . . I repudiate the high priests of individual salvation and the sob sisters of altruism, who exchange commonplace partial responsibility for the aesthetic transports of cosmohistorical guilt or the gratuitous slogans of universal love. I refuse to emulate these Sunday-school clowns and prefer—I know my limitations—to be the sceptical bureaucrat that I am. My highest aspiration is that a medium-rank, utterly insignificant civil servant should, as far as possible, live with his eyes wide open. (cited in Greene, 1988, p. 123)

Through the *literary* voice of a Hungarian social worker wherein social science as practice and way of life is privileged over "the aesthetic," one is able to glimpse a world that is unlikely to be so richly described in social science discourse (text).

At this, one might justifiably protest that social science writings are attempting to do more than description and cannot do what they do without globally conceived empirical and scientific methods *not* found in literature. I do not intend to pit one against the other in simple hierarchical fashion. I merely wish to question the global claims of the social sciences (to which the curriculum field has been largely devoted) and to suggest the possibilities for multiple ways of thinking about the social in the contexts of social sciences by way of literary studies (though I should note that Michel Serres, for one, thinks that scientific *discoveries are* found in literature [1982]). Indeed, Felix Guattari says that the best of Freud's works read like novels, and the best novels provide the greatest psychoanalytic insight, or "the best cartographies of the psyche" (1990, p. 5).

It is the *translation* that takes place between literary and social science works, and between different literary works, that produces learning that is attuned to the tremendous power of difference and marginality. The term *translation* is preferred here to more common terms relating to communication because it connotes a partiality, an incompleteness, and at the same time the effort to recognize differences as significant is understood. Translation, given that it is always partial, can serve as an approach to communication that is not based in a desire to eliminate the noise of otherness. The notion that translation can take place presupposes some common meaning—some "common sense." Philosopher John Rajchman advises, "If it is sense that translation preserves, where there is translation, there can be no *altogether* new sense. There is always some sense in common" (1991, p. 6). Yet too often the translation that takes place between dominant and subordinant groups in institutions called schools is such that the "common sense" ("common culture") is attributed only to a single dominant cultural identity. This is certainly true of any form of "cultural deprivation" theory. But it is also, more subtly, true of any curricular models or approaches that fail to recognize the complexity of difference and the production of subjectivity. "Conversely," Rajchman continues, "translation without a master would be the art of breaking with those with whom one nevertheless identifies, while exposing oneself to the *singularities* of those one nevertheless tries to understand" (p. 7, emphasis added).

Again, translation without a master is a two- or multiway process. As David Murray points out with regard to early encounters between aboriginal Americans and whites in the United States,

In a situation of dominance, the cultural translation is all one-
way, and the penalty to the subordinant group for not adapting
to the demands of the dominant group is to cease to exist.
Knowledge of the *processes* of this translation, though, must be
repressed by the dominant side, in favour of a reassuring image of
mutual intelligibility which does not register as significant who
has had to "translate." (1991, p. 6)

This assumption of the transparency of language, this "unspoken
belief in the isomorphic relationship between language and reality" (Greenblatt, 1976, p. 572), is precisely the trouble with an
ideology of positivism which has such a firm grip on current theory
and practice in the curriculum field and in education generally.
Rajchman asks,

> Can there exist a common sense, a public, or public space—*a
> glasnost*—which is not identified with a single tradition, or with
> a single way of classifying the plurality of traditions, but which is
> so divided up that each tradition remains exposed to the singu-
> larities of the others, and of those yet to come? (1991, p. 6)

Such translations within, for example, the multicultural curriculum need not succumb to the criticisms of those who fear the
"loss" of Western culture and tradition. Tradition in such a new
assemblage, contrary to accusations by conservative critics of
"multiculturalism," is not tossed out; it is rearticulated, rein-
terpreted, eventually reterritorialized (a continuous cycle); it is
translated. Encounters among positions in the margins and the
center result in such rearticulations of traditions—rearticulations
that initially deterritorialize elements of the old. Just as the margins are simultaneously advantageous and dangerous positions, so
is this deterritorialization. Deterritorialization, as explained by
Guattari, is a breaking up into singularities, it is ruptures of meaning, and it constitutes existential territories that have "always
sought refuge in art and religion" (1990, p. 6): "Each of the existential territories . . . exists . . . as a precarious, finite, finitized
entity for itself; it is singular and singularized; it may bifurcate into
stratified and death-laden reiterations; or it may open, as process,
into praxes that enable it to be rendered 'inhabitable' by human
projects" (p. 8). Such "human projects" become reterritorialized,
transformed by cross-cultural imagination.

Literature approached through such notions of translation
holds promise for the curriculum field as both a means of study

and an educational "method" for practice precisely *because* of its operations in and from the *margins*. The margins of places, times, and ideas are those spaces which are not obvious. Literature becomes "literature" by defamiliarization of the familiar, by dwelling in the not-obvious, by allowing for what Barbara Johnson calls "the surprise of otherness" (1987, p. 15).

Finally, it is *love* that brings together literature, marginality, and curriculum. As Jacques Daignault pointed out (and as I later found for myself with excursions through English language etymological dictionaries), the Latin infinitive for religion, *religere*, means to reread and to care. (*Negligere* is its Latin opposite and means negligence.) My journey through relevant words took me further still. *Curare*, different but similar in sound and spelling to *currere*, also means to care. *Cultus* (culture) means care, worship. Finally, *love* is related in my own text to both care and to religion (in the sense of spirituality) as well as desire. "*Leave* is the offspring of yet another Indo-European root, *leubh-* 'to care, to desire; to love'" (Partridge, 1983, p. 343). And this *leaves* us with crisis, Greek *krisis* (a separating, decision, dis-crimination), Latin *discrimen* (interval, intervening space, turning point, difference, risk). The *risk* of loving—caring, deciding, discriminating, and finally leaving (in any number of senses)—is common to the educational enterprise and to literature. And it is living in the midst of this *risk* (crisis) that marks the margins in all its layers.

The pedagogical and psychoanalytic risk of love—transference love—is the displacement or deconstruction of hierarchicalized love (agapé/eros or eros/agapé), and is a prerequisite for translation without a master. The implications that psychoanalysis holds for pedagogy are suggested by the significance of love to both. Henceforth in this writing love functions as an analogy for teaching and learning, and at the same time it is often, as in psychoanalysis, more than an analogy; it is a very real and necessary condition for the pedagogical situation. This (transference) love "occupies the middle spot between knowledge and ignorance" (Serres, 1982, p. 246). These assertions are detailed in the immediately following paragraphs.

Love (in the sense of "in love") effects a stifling of imagination (as in "love is blind") at the same time that it totally disrupts. It is a dangerous moment at the same time that it renews (like the margins). "One speaks [of it (one learns; imagination returns)] only after the fact" (Kristeva, 1987, p. 3). It subverts and problematizes language, providing an opening for translation. "I" becomes an "other." It makes one unique and special (particular) at the same time that it blurs boundaries between self and other. Fear shares its symptoms. Indeed, it is "fear of crossing and desire to cross the boundaries [margins] of the self" (p. 6). And, like learning, it is schizophrenic.

The experience of love ties a knot with strands made of the *symbolic,* the *imaginary,* the *real.* "Strangled within this tight knot, reality vanishes: I do not take it into account, and I refer it, if I think of it, to one of the three other realms. That means in love I never cease to be mistaken as to reality" (Kristeva, 1987, p. 7). Like learning and teaching, these are dangerous territories, disruptive, unsettling, risking blowing apart all that is official or certain. Love and learning are marginal passages. Love and learning call into question the very notion of identity. "Indeed, in the rapture of love, the limits of one's own identity vanish. . . . Do we speak of the same thing? And of which thing? The ordeal of love puts the univocity of language and its referential and communicative power to the test" (p. 2). What *do* we mean by *love?* Searching the question reveals a "linguistic profundity"—love as "solitary because incommunicable" is nonetheless translatable. Versions of love (languages of love) "commune [only] through a third party: ideal, god, hallowed group" (p. 3).

Can a classroom be one such place (Serres's "included third"; "between"), political problematics and all? "Love probably always includes a love for power. Transference love is for that very reason the royal road to the state of love; no matter what it is, love brushes us up against sovereignty" (Kristeva, 1987, p. 9). Transference takes place through a granting of authority by the analysand (student? teacher?). We ask our students to "suspend disbelief" in our competence. We ask them to grant us authority.

But it is *they* who are to listen as we tell our stories. Here lies the "swerve" in this analogy. The swerve is the surplus, the place of nonsense, the uncultivated (Serres, 1989). It is a margin (a "margin of mystery" [p. 8]). The swerve gives us time, "breathing space" (p. 11). There is still something left to do, to fill. This particular swerve means that *sovereignty is not complete.* If it is *they,* our students, who listen, are they not the analysts and we the analysands in this analogy? Yet it is we, the teachers, who are "presumed to know." And "as soon as there is somewhere a subject presumed to know, there is transference" (Lacan, cited in Felman, 1982, p. 35).

Psychoanalysis proceeds, as does teaching, through a kind of "mutual apprenticeship" (Felman, p. 33). The analyst "attempts to learn from the students his own knowledge" (p. 33). Love, then, is two-way. Lacan insists: "I deemed it necessary to support the idea of transference, as indistinguishable from love, with the formula of the subject presumed to know," and, "The question of love is thus linked to the question of knowledge," and, "Transference *is* love . . . I insist: it is love directed toward, addressed to, knowledge" (Felman, p. 35).

Listening is a love; love pays attention to listening. It occurs in an open system. Kristeva writes, "As implied in modern logical and biological theories dealing with so-called 'open systems,' *transference* is the Freudian self-organization" (1987, p. 14). With this, as Felman reminds us, "the position of the teacher is itself the position of *the one who learns,* of the one who *teaches* nothing other than *the way he learns.* The subject of teaching is interminably—a student; the subject of teaching is interminably— a learning" (p. 37).

It (learning or love) is also indefinitely deferred. A coincidence between findings of psychoanalysis and modern physics (Heisenberg's uncertainty principle) led Lacan to the following pedagogical principle: "Until further notice, we can say that *the elements do not answer in the place where they are interrogated.* Or more exactly, as soon as they are interrogated somewhere, it is impossible to grasp them in their totality" (cited in Felman, 1982, p. 29). As most dramatically evidenced by those students who return later to marvel at what they learned in a class and how little they realized it at the time, it is always after the fact—always deferred.

"Hate is the integral of all contraries," says Serres (1982, p. xxi). Is the "center" also the integral of all contraries? If so, love cannot be the opposite of hate, nor can the margins be the opposite of the center, since both would then themselves be contraries. There is no "solution." The best we can do is attempt to read well, to listen, to set ourselves up for the "surprise of otherness" (Johnson, 1987, p. 15). As such, the "integral of all contraries" is a poor reader. It reads itself into all texts, denying, repressing, and suppressing difference, denying learning, growth, and experience—yet requiring all of those for its very existence and continued domi-nance. Thus it cannot remain dominant for all situations, for all events, for all time. It moves about and around the margins, where it recuperates by appropriation, by gaining just enough insight to fling itself back to the center to rest and reatrophy—to rereify.

REFERENCES

Baker, Houston A., Jr. (1987). To move without moving: An analysis of creativity and commerce in Ralph Ellison's Trueblood episode. In K. Benston (Ed.), *Speaking for you: The vision of Ralph Ellison* (322–348). Washington, DC: Howard University Press.

Clement, Catherine, and Cixous, Helene. (1975). The newly born wom-an. Trans. B. Wing. In *Theory and history of literature* (vol. 24, 6–17). Minneapolis: University of Minnesota Press.

Deleuze, Gilles, and Guattari, Felix. (1983). *Anti-Oedipus: Capitalism and schizophrenia.* Minneapolis: University of Minnesota Press.

Donnelly, Dody H. (1984). *Radical love: An approach to sexual Spiritu-ality.* Minneapolis: Winston Press.

Ellison, Ralph W. (1952). *Invisible man.* New York: Vintage.

Ellison, Ralph. (1953). *Shadow and act.* New York: Vintage.

Felman, S. (1982). Psychoanalysis and education: Teaching terminable and interminable. *Yale French Studies, 63,* 21–44.

Fox-Genovese, Elizabeth. (1988). *Within the plantation household: Black and white women of the Old South.* Chapel Hill, NC: University of North Carolina Press.

Freire, Paulo. (1970). *Pedagogy of the oppressed.* Trans. M. B. Ramos. New York: Seabury Press.

French, Marilyn. (1985). *Beyond power: On women, men, and morals.* New York: Ballantine.

Greenblatt, S. J. (1976). Learning to curse: Aspects of linguistic colonial-ism in the sixteenth century. In F. Chiapelli (Ed.), *First images of Ameri-ca* (561–580). Berkeley: University of California Press.

Greene, Maxine. (1988). *The Dialectic of Freedom.* New York: Teachers College Press.

Guattari, Felix. (1990). The three ecologies. Paper presented at Louisiana State University.

Johnson, Barbara. (1987). *A world of difference.* Baltimore: Johns Hop-kins University Press.

Klima, Ivan. (1990, June). The unexpected merits of oppression. *The Nation, 250*(22), 769–773.

Konrad, George. (1974). *The caseworker.* New York: Harcourt Brace Jovanovich.

Kristeva, Julia. (1982). *Powers of horror: An essay on abjection.* Trans. L. S. Roudiez. New York: Columbia University Press.

Kristeva, Julia. (1987). *Tales of love.* New York: Columbia University Press.

McCarthy, Cameron. (1988, August). Rethinking liberal and radical perspectives on racial inequality in schooling: Making the case for non-synchrony. *Harvard Educational Review, 58*(3).

McCarthy, Cameron. (1990). *Race and curriculum: Social inequality and the theories and politics of differences in contemporary research on schooling.* Philadelphia: Falmer Press.

Morrison, Toni. (1987). *Beloved.* New York: Knopf.

Murray, D. (1991). *Forked tongues: Speech, writing & representation in North American Indian texts.* Bloomington: Indiana University Press.

O'Donovan, Oliver. (1980). *The problem of self-love in St. Augustine.* New Haven: Yale University Press.

Otten, Terry. (1989). *The crime of innocence in the fiction of Toni Morrison.* Columbia, MO: University of Missouri Press.

Partridge, E. (1983). *Origins: A short etymological dictionary of modern English.* New York: Greenwich House.

Pinar, William F. (1975). *Currere:* Toward reconceptualization. In William F. Pinar (Ed.), *Curriculum Theorizing: The Reconceptualists* (396–413). Berkeley, CA: McCutchan.

Pinkerton, Edward C. (1982). *Word for word.* Essex, CT: Verbatim Books.

Rajchmann, J. (1991). *Philosophical events: Essays of the 80's.* New York: Columbia University Press.

Robbins, Tom. (1987). Interview by L. McCaffery and S. Gregory (Eds.). In *Alive and writing: Interviews with American authors of the 1980s.* Chicago: University of Illinois Press.

Schneiderman, S. (Ed.). (1980). *Returning to Freud: Clinical psychoanalysis in the school of Lacan.* New Haven, CT: Yale University Press.

Serres, Michel. (1982). In J. V. Harari and D. F. Bell (Eds.), *Hermes: Literature, science, philosophy.* Baltimore: Johns Hopkins University Press.

Serres, Michel. (1989). *Detachment.* Minneapolis: University of Minnesota Press.

Snitow, Ann. (1987, September). Death duties: Toni Morrison looks back in sorrow. *VLS, 58,* 25–26.

Soble, Alan. (1990). *The structure of love.* New Haven: Yale University Press.

Spivak, Gayatri C. (1987). Explanation and culture: Marginalia. In her *In other worlds: Essays in cultural politics* (103–117). New York: Routledge.

Tate, Claudia. (1987). Notes on the invisible women in Ralph Ellison's *Invisible Man*. In K. Bensten (Ed.), *Speaking for you: The vision of Ralph Ellison* (163–172). Washington, DC: Howard University Press.

NOTES

1.   Such characterizations are, of course, essentialist. I point them out here only to reemphasize my earlier noting of the nondeterminancy (the self-deconstructing nature) of these terms when looked at historically. Also, this essentialist dichotomy is a common one among certain feminist perspectives.

2.   I realize that I have not been consistent with my use of quotation marks around feminine and masculine. This has been done self-consciously, in part to call attention to the instability of these terms, and in another part as a (tiny) rebellion against the discourse of consistency!

3.   For example, Invisible Man is concerned with his own invisibility and that of black people in general. At the same time, his gendered standpoint makes it difficult at times for him to identify his own victimization with that of the women characters, such as the nude "magnificent blonde" at the battle royal. He feels simultaneous, contradictory urges to "caress her and destroy her" (Ellison, 1952, p. 19; hereafter referred to as *IM*).

4.   This character is reminiscent of Paul D's going "crazy so he would not lose his mind" in *Beloved* (p. 41).

5.   Although I do not wish to claim mutual agreement or understanding of notions of the global and universal, and so on, I *do* wish to acknowledge Jacques Daignault with providing the initial ideas and inspiring my thoughts on these matters. Our conversations were simply too abbreviated for me to claim to be paraphrasing him. Still, maybe I am.

CHAPTER 4

Photographic Images of Blacks in Sexuality Texts

Mariamne H. Whatley

ABSTRACT

In current human sexuality textbooks, photographs of "real people" have become a major form of illustration. I examined 16 college-level sexuality textbooks, published from 1980 to 1987, to see what images of Blacks were presented in these photographs. Visual images of individuals have the potential to represent a group to which the individual belongs, especially when there is little diversity in the images presented; every portrayal of Blacks carries more weight than that of whites, since whites are allowed more diversity in representation. In addition, the photograph itself has more impact than a drawing would, since it is *seen* as an objective representation of reality, rather than as an artist's construction. While it is a mistake to attribute a single meaning to an image, it is possible to speak of predictable ways in which the photograph may be read, based on dominant meanings in our culture. In examining the photographs in these texts, though individual images of Blacks are often positive, I found a problematic pattern to the photographs of Blacks that appeared. I have grouped these into the following recurrent themes: Blacks as "exotics," Blacks as "sexually dangerous," Blacks as asexual, and Blacks and paternal re-

I wish to thank Nancy A. Worcester, Julie D'Acci, Michael Apple, and Elizabeth Ellsworth for their critical readings of the manuscript. I also greatly appreciate valuable suggestions received from Susan Smith.

sponsibility. This article, which raises issues about the impact of the photographic image and the subtle ways in which the most well-intended antiracist message can be subverted by the images presented, provides the theoretical framework to examine representations of other nondominant groups.

> But despite the presumption of veracity that gives all photographs authority, interest, seductiveness, the work that photographers do is no generic exception to the usually shady commerce between art and truth (Sontag, *On Photography*, 1977, p. 6).

RACISM AND THE TEXTBOOK

This paper, in which I examine photographic images of Blacks[1] in sexuality textbooks, is not meant as a definitive study, but as an exploratory essay. My interest in the topic arose when I noticed that in current textbooks there is generally an attempt to avoid overt racism in the text itself and to include photographs that indicate some racial and ethnic diversity. I also observed, however, a disturbing overall pattern in the images that are included or absent. As a white educator, I feel it is essential to examine the curricular materials produced in my field. First, it is the obligation of whites who are committed to working against racism to take an actively antiracist stance to promote change, and second, since textbook publishers define their market as the teacher or professor, rather than the reader (Coser, Kadushin, and Powell 1982), there is some potential for faculty to exert economic, as well as critical, pressure.

Recognizing that textbooks are not objective and factual but instead are social products, critics have examined the content of school textbooks (Wexler 1982). The view that these texts reflect an ideology of dominant groups in society may be too mechanistic and simplistic, since the text, as well as other cultural products, is a result of complex interactions mediated by economics and social structure (Apple 1985). The production of textbooks in the United States is predominantly controlled by a white male establishment. Women actually outnumber men in publishing, but are generally in "lower paying, replaceable jobs, with less possibility for advancement." Though more women have moved into important editorial positions in recent years, it is still largely men who control the "goals and policy of publishing" (Apple 1985, p. 153). Because publishing is controlled by a dominant group, as it would be in most, if not all, countries, it is tempting to view this industry as a monolithic machine for reproducing dominant ideologies. However, rather than trying to impose an educational agenda, editors are more interested in high profit margins and financial capital (Apple 1985; Coser, Kadushin, and Powell 1982). Generally, in the United States, the market for college textbooks, comprised of college professors, would not permit overt racism or sexism. Furthermore, as the authors above have pointed out, editors from most publishing houses tend to be overwhelmingly liberal. Therefore, as Apple (1985) states:

> If texts were totally reliable defenders of the existing ideological, political, and economic order, they would not currently be such a contentious area. Industry and conservative groups have made an issue of what knowledge is now taught in schools precisely because there *are* progressive elements within curricula and texts (p. 157).

These progressive elements have, in fact, created changes in textbooks. There has been a noticeable improvement in the representation of racial and ethnic minority groups, as well as of women, though substantial efforts are still needed. The extent to which the representations in textbooks of nondominant groups in a culture (whether of Maoris in New Zealand, Native North Americans in Canada, Aborigines in Australia, or Pakistanis and Indians in Great Britain) are positive is partially a reflection of the progressiveness of those who make decisions about texts. Another important factor is the activism of particular groups. For example, where the women's movement has had influence on publishing, there may be a reduction in overt sexism. For example, in response to the sexism of introductory psychology texts, a series of psychology of women texts has been generated. Many of these, however, have essentially defined women's experience as that of white, middle-class North American women (Brown et al. 1985). Of 28 psychology of women textbooks reviewed by Brown and her coauthors, 18 contained only token or no references to Afro-American women. There may be little or no overt racism in those texts, but the omission of material is a message in itself. Throughout the textbook industry there have been significant gains in the surface messages presented on gender and race issues, while covert messages in many forms may contradict or subvert the outward intent.

Though not produced by a conspiracy of dominant groups, the textbook does present a knowledge in part determined by interactions of ideology and economics. The text itself must be analyzed in this context. Anyon (1979), in her discussion of school history textbooks, writes:

> The expression of group interest in textbooks can be in the form of obvious distortions or hidden assumptions. Ideological selection can take the form of omitting a fact or of subtle distinctions or emphases. If an ideological perspective governs school history textbooks, it can acquire the status of truth, and the information will be less likely to be subjected to scrutiny in classrooms or compared with other points of view (p. 363).

In addition to critical content analysis, it is crucial to examine the form and "the symbolic methods which create in a knowledge or text an appearance of completeness and, hence, of matter-of-factness" (Wexler 1982, p. 282). As part of the form in which knowledge is presented and because they help the text "acquire the status of truth," visual images appearing in a textbook must be included in a critique. Examination of photographs is particularly important since these may have more impact than other visual images.

THEORETICAL BACKGROUND

The Message of the Text Photograph

In an essay in his book, *Image-Music-Text,* Roland Barthes (1977) examines the press photograph and the process of meaning production. Much of the same theory can be applied to the textbook photograph as well. Although, according to Barthes, the photograph, as distinct form other visual representations, professes to be a "mechanical analogue of reality" (Barthes 1977, p. 18), it must be remembered that "the press photograph is an object that has been worked on, chosen, composed, constructed, treated according to professional, aesthetic or ideological norms" (p. 19). It is, therefore, both "objective" *and* "invested." For Barthes, the ethical paradox which emerges when employing photographs is that "when one wants to be 'neutral,' 'objective,' one strives to copy reality meticulously, as though the analogical were a factor of resistance against the investment of values" (p. 19). In another essay, he specifically compares photographs and drawings, and discusses the perceived difference between "recording" and "trans-formation." In comparison to the drawing, which "does not repro-duce *everything*" and which has a "set of *rule-governed* transposi-tions" (p. 43), there is a "myth of photographic naturalness." Photographs, therefore, can have more impact on students reading a textbook, since, even if they are posed, they may be seen as true, objective pictures of reality. Classical European paintings and Japa-nese prints are, on the other hand, more likely to be viewed as the artists' constructions.

Barthes also points out that the press photograph is not an isolated structure, but that information is carried by both the pho-tograph and the text, including titles, captions, and articles. The "new informational totality" is based on a seemingly objective message, the photograph, while the text becomes secondary. While textbook authors may cringe to think of their text as secondary, that may often be the case. In a textbook, photographs accompany-ing a topic may be remembered more clearly than the text itself. For example, a section on transsexuals is more likely to be remem-bered as a visual image of a vulva constructed in place of a penis and scrotum rather than as a subtle discussion of issues of gender identity. Photographs no longer function merely to elucidate or illustrate the text, and the text may serve more to load meaning on to the photograph than to function independently. Captions ac-companying photographs may in fact, be more significant than the main body of the text. Since these messages seem "to share in its [the photograph's] objectivity" (Barthes 1977, p. 26), the caption becomes as "real" and "objective" as the photograph itself is be-lieved to be.

Some contemporary theorists would argue that no photograph or text can be analyzed in terms of *a* meaning. Meaning is multiple since every viewer or reader produces meanings of his or her own. Meaning is not inherent in the photographic image and is, in fact, a product of viewer reception. However, given a particular histori-cal/political moment, it is legitimate to argue for the presence of certain *dominant* meanings in cultural texts and photographs. Textbook readers in similar social contexts share in similar cultural discourses and it is therefore possible to speak of predictable ways in which a text or photograph may be read. While opting for the notion of dominant meanings, I also recognize that there are many who will not share in and, in fact, contest these meanings.

Given the belief in the photograph as a representation of reality and the primary role it may have in producing meanings, the choice of photographs for a textbook carries great significance. Textbook photographs can carry messages, intentional or not, never stated in the text. In examining and critiquing textbooks, the photographs should never be dismissed as merely a way to liven up the text or to clarify visually points made in the text.

Visual Images and Stereotypes

In addition to work such as Barthes' on the photograph and the production of meaning, another point directly relevant to my argument has arisen from theoretical work on visual images: A visual image of an individual can easily be interpreted as a representative of a class to which the individual is seen to belong (Gilman 1985). Since there is a great diversity of images of whites in sexuality texts, as in the rest of the media in the United States, photographs of individual whites may be seen as individuals or as representatives of a particular subgroup, such as teenagers, gays, transsexuals, people with disabilities, rather than as representatives of whites as a group. However, since so few images of cultural or racial minorities appear, each representation bears more weight. Unless one consciously works against this, in any society the representations of nondominant groups in the media can be used as a way to perpetuate the myth of inferiority of that group (both to the dominant group and to its own members), to reinforce stereotypes, and to maintain the status quo. The use of photographs may prevent the problems inherent in drawings in which there may be either distorted physical stereotypes or "white features, browned in, [which] are as biased as grotesque caricatures" (Klein 1985, p. 7). On the other hand, since they bear the burden of presumably representing reality, photographs may create other problems.

It should be noted that the portrayals and stereotypes are not always consistent and may, in fact, be contradictory, varying with the overall needs and demands of the society (Choy 1982). These contradictory messages may be readily accepted and believed simultaneously. Klein (1985, p. 35) illustrates this notion of simultaneously held contradictory stereotypes with the following example from a British social context: "West Indians come and take all our jobs *and* are all lazy and on the dole." The images of Blacks appearing in textbooks may reflect a great deal both about the way Blacks are perceived by the majority white population and about how this dominant group might consciously or unconsciously want them to be.

ANALYSIS OF TEXT PHOTOGRAPHS

I examined the photographs in 16 college-level sexuality texts published from 1980 to 1987 in the United States (listed in the Appendix) to see what images of Blacks were presented. As part of my responsibility as an educator, I review and evaluate many of the new sexuality textbooks. The sample used for this article consisted of texts I have examined in the past several years. Since these are published by established textbook publishers, are current, and have been marketed to college/university faculty, they are a representative sample. All photographs were examined and sorted in general categories established by preliminary overviews of the textbook. Examples of categories included such labels as: heterosexual couples showing physical intimacy, lesbian and gay couples, adults with children, prostitutes, nude adults. Photographs not directly related to issues of adult sexuality are not discussed in this paper. Among these are pictures of children without adults and individuals engaging in sports, work, and recreational activities without overt sexual content. This is not to imply that those photographs are devoid of potential messages about race[2] or sexuality, but merely that my focus was on specific sexuality issues. Captions were considered as part of the photograph rather than the text. Line drawings, artistic representations, and photographs identified as stills from motion pictures were not considered. After examining patterns in differences in the photographic representations of Blacks and whites, I identified several recurring themes: Blacks as "exotics," and, under the heading of Blacks in Western society, Blacks as "sexually dangerous," blacks as asexual, Blacks and paternal responsibility. Each of these will be discussed in more detail below.

The imposition of categories on the material is problematic in that it is necessary for a critical analysis of the photographs, while at the same time arbitrarily limiting alternative interpretations. The categories were named and renamed as the images were sorted and resorted. A theme first identified as Blacks and "safe" sexuality, a prescriptive answer to "dangerous sexuality," can be seen more specifically as a prescription for paternal responsibility, so was relabeled. The photographs of Black pimps might have been isolated in a narrow category, but I chose to see these in the broader context of white fears about the dangers of Black sexuality. The extended category then included issues around disease transmission. The final decisions about categories were based on whether these helped "make sense" of the material in terms of overall patterns of photographs and the historical and cultural contexts.

Just as there are no "correct" categories for classification, there are no "definitive" interpretations or readings of the photographs. My interpretations of the photographs are grounded in readings of the literature on racism and Blacks in the United States, in contemporary and historical contexts, and the literature on racism and the media, and in an examination of popular cultural images of Blacks. The research presented is value-based and attempts to challenge the status quo in terms of race, class, and gender relations. Lather (1986) offers a reconceptualization of validity and discusses how to establish data credibility in this kind of research, which she terms "openly ideological research." She makes a number of suggestions for validity checks, some of which might prove useful approaches for this paper. It would be possible, for example, to have a number of students interpret a series of photographs in some of the textbooks I examined. However, if their interpretations differed from mine, that would not necessarily invalidate my interpretations. For example, if I presented them with all the photographs of pimps in the 16 texts, they would see four images of Black pimps and no white pimps. These images might not be read, as I read them, as reflections of white fears of powerful Black sexuality. I will not attempt to predict the range of readings (including positive ones) an audience might have. However, no matter what the reading, there is a clear bias in the representation of pimps. Given the broad cultural context, including media images and common stereotypes of Blacks, there are meanings that could be attributed to those photographs. The patterns of images, both represented and absent, that emerge can be documented or validated. The interpretations represent a set of possible meanings that could be attributed, given the cultural context, to these patterns. It would be interesting in continuing this research program, to attempt to find out students' interpretations, but the results would not alter the arguments in this paper about a set of possible meanings. In addition, work in media studies suggests that asking people to report their interpretations or readings of media does not necessarily produce valid results. The idea of rational viewers or readers who are always in touch with their perceptions ignores a number of issues, such as the role of the unconscious, the common inability to conceptualize a "gut feeling," the inability to articulate certain responses due to lack of appropriate vocabulary, and the desire to give the "right" answer. The responses given may not reflect at all the impact that the media in question actually has on the viewer.

I wish at this point to make it clear that many of these books are excellent in terms of their texts and the authors have worked at nonsexist, often nonheterosexist, presentations. The inclusion of photographs of Blacks should be seen as an attempt to be nonracist, so my questioning whether stereotyped inclusion can be as destructive as omission should be taken as a supportive antiracist evaluation, not as a condemnation of the texts or the authors. Paradoxically, those receiving the most criticism may be those that made more of an effort to represent Blacks. It also should be remembered that the context and form of textbooks is often not representative of the "views and choices of the people whose names appear on the title page" (Anyon 1979, p. 362).

To establish a sense of the changes that had occurred, I examined six college-level sexuality textbooks from the early to the late 1970s. These relied on line drawings to illustrate anatomy and sexual positions and on works of art to illustrate many other topics. Paintings, drawings, and sculpture from all over the world, from many different periods, were used for topics ranging from courtship and marriage to voyeurism, bestiality, and gang rape. Very few photographs of people appeared and those that did were often stills from motion pictures. In the sexuality texts of the 1980s, although line drawings are still used to clarify sexual positions,[3] most of the visual materials are photographs of "real" people. There are still exceptions in which few photographs are used, such as in the textbook by Richard Jones (1984). Since there are important differences between how photographs and other visual arts create meaning, this change in the form of illustration must be seen as having more than stylistic/design implications.

In the sexuality texts of the 1970s, Blacks were rarely represented in the few photographs that did appear. Although images of Blacks have become more visible, faring better in numbers than other racial minority groups, such as Asians, they are still seen in a low percentage of overall photographs. When there was a strong call for multicultural educational materials in the schools, one response was just to add a few Black faces to the illustrations, with no other changes. Making sure that every tenth photograph is of a person of color is of little use if the photograph is not selected carefully. In the sexuality texts examined, photographs of Blacks have more impact, not only because of their rarity compared to the broad range of representations of whites, but also because there is a problematic pattern to the kinds of images that appear. While this article specifically examines images of Blacks in the United States, the theoretical framework can be used to examine representations in textbooks of nondominant groups in other societies.

BLACKS AS "EXOTICS" OUTSIDE WESTERN SOCIETY

In Western white culture, there has long been a fascination with the Black as "other." In a sexual context, this "otherness" is seen as unbridled sexuality, free from the constraints of society. For example, in the nineteenth century, Western medical writings described the genitalia of the Hottentot female as different from other humans, so that "the physical appearance of the Hottentot is, indeed, the central nineteenth century icon for sexual difference between the European and the Black" (Gilman 1985, p. 212).

In modern texts, no one would consider writing about Blacks being physically or physiologically different in terms of sexuality, but the theme of otherness appears in a modified version that might be labeled the "beauty is in the eye of the beholder" approach. As noted previously in this paper, captions may seem to share the photograph's "objectivity" since they are viewed as a label of an objective representation, even though they may actually be adding meaning to the image. For example, one 1984 text captions a picture, "What is attractive? Ideas about beauty differ from culture to culture. The So of northeastern Uganda consider neckrings and a hole in the lip to be attractive" (Allgeier and Allgeier 1984, p. 179). This statement assumes that white Western viewers will see the So as unattractive. The same text has a section called "Male and Female Beauty Through the Ages" (Allgeier and

Allgeier 1985, pp. 182–183). The representations in this section, whether photographs of sculpture, paintings, or people, are all clearly white except for the Black attendant to the main figure in *Bathsheba at Her Bath* and the "Prehistoric Venus." The caption to this series of 12 photographs reads, "We humans have held varied ideas about male and female beauty at different times in our history." "We humans" implies a universal, inclusive definition of beauty that changes only with time. Since the twentieth century selection includes such figures as Clark Gable and Marilyn Monroe, hardly offering a broad range of ethnic diversity, the universal "we humans" must see whiteness as an important sign of beauty. Another text has the caption "Ideas of beauty vary from one culture to another" under the picture of an African woman wearing neckrings and a great deal of jewelry (Masters, Johnson, and Kolodny 1985, p. 622). The caption is particularly interesting since the issue is more one of choice of jewelry than of actual changes in physical appearance. Similarly, in another text, a photograph of a young African woman is captioned, "There is great diversity in the culturally-defined images of what is beautiful" (Schulz 1984, p. 86). The fact that she is wearing a large ornament on her forehead is the only "difference" that might catch the eye.

No racial or ethnic group fares particularly well in these cross-cultural sections. For example, one textbook has a photograph of three Hopi women working on pottery, with the caption, "Men and women have specific tasks within the Hopi society" (Kilman 1984, p. 11). The implication is that, unlike this particular Native American culture, white society in the United States does not have gender stereotyped tasks or sex segregated labor. If this photograph were presented in a series illustrating gender roles cross-culturally, including Western industrialized societies, there would be less of the implication of otherness. Another text has a photograph of two hijiras (men who have been castrated and assume a particular role in society in India) dressed in saris and appearing very much like women. Without an in-depth discussion of social, cultural, and economic factors that create the class of hijiras, this photograph becomes merely a representation of a seemingly bizarre custom.

On the surface, it seems that these photographs and captions are an attempt to escape ethnocentrism, encouraging students to be accepting of diversity and not to see the world only through a white Western perspective. This is the same approach that many have taken in making school texts appropriate for multicultural education and it presents some of the same problems. White, Western culture is seen as the norm and all else is an exotic variation, toward which we should learn tolerance. The problem of creating cross-cultural distance can be alleviated by use of comparative photographs or careful captioning. For example, the caption accompanying a photograph of a New Guinea man wearing a penile sheath (Maier 1984, p. 195) does make a comparison to the European Renaissance codpiece in enhancement of the size of the male genitals, but that comparison still creates distance from contemporary Western culture, though historical rather than geographic. Perhaps photographs of crotches of American football players or certain rock singers might create less of a sense of distance from what might otherwise be labeled an exotic, strange custom.

Another text has the following caption accompanying a set of three photographs:

> Sexual behaviors and customs vary widely in human cultures different from our own. a) Asmat boys from New Guinea jokingly imitate parents copulating. b) Trobriand Island girls from New Guinea sing bawdy songs and dance to attract boys. c) Bride and groom, from Asmat tribe in New Guinea, during their wedding ceremony (Hyde 1987, p. 9).

Imitations of adult sexual behaviors, including copulation, are hardly unknown in Western culture. Photographers, however, may not be as likely to document these behaviors if they do not seem to have anthropological significance. While in the Trobriand Islands the dancing and singing of bawdy songs may be more formalized, anyone attending a middle school or high school dance in the United States may see very similar behaviors to "attract boys." The lyrics of much of the music contemporary Western adolescents dance to and sing along with would certainly qualify as "bawdy." Again, rather than isolating these customs as different, an attempt could be made to identify similarities.

The "beauty in the eye of the beholder" theme clearly contains the assumption that the average readers of the text would naturally find the people pictured as strange and unattractive and would need encouragement to be tolerant of their aberrations. These representations seem to have roots in such cultural products as *National Geographic, Ripley's Believe It or Not,* and nature shows with messages about exotic animals finding each other attractive. We should consider the guidelines that have been developed for selecting books for multicultural school education: "Avoid books which equate the white man with 'civilization,' those with philanthropical approaches to other people, or which reduce all non-western societies to the exotic, the primitive or the quaint" (Klein 1985, pp. 17–18). Instead of creating more cross-cultural awareness and acceptance, these illustrations may, in fact, create more of a sense of difference, of the Black as other, with the message of tolerance tacked on.

BLACKS IN WESTERN SOCIETY

Blacks as "Sexually Dangerous"

When "exotic" sexuality is distant from Western culture or under control, it may be tolerated, but, when there is no longer geographic separation, it may be viewed as threatening. This threat may be seen in the powerful myth in the United States that rape commonly involves Black men and white women; the fact is that at least 90 percent of sexual assaults involve rapist and victim of the same race (Hirsch 1980).

Angela Davis (1983) points out both the power and the danger of this myth:

> In the history of the United States, the fraudulent rape charge stands out as one of the most formidable artifices invented by racism. The myth of the Black rapist has been methodically conjured up whenever recurrent waves of violence and terror against the Black community have required convincing justifications (p. 173).

While texts do not usually have illustrations of rape, except in artistic form (such as Greek vases), this myth has a strong enough hold to add meanings to other images.

An example of how this "dangerous" sexuality can be seen in textbooks is in sections on prostitution, which generally contain photographs of prostitutes, in case the reader cannot imagine what prostitutes look like. In the texts I examined, the prostitutes represented were predominantly white. What is of particular interest is that in all four cases in which there were pimps pictured, the pimps were Black. Even in a photograph that is labeled as a simulation (Francoeur 1982, p. 646), a Black pimp is shown with two prostitutes, one of whom is clearly white. Obviously, this is a reflection of a common media stereotype of the flashy Black pimp in a big city; one photograph of a Black man is captioned, "A street pimp with his fancy car" (Meeks and Heit 1982, p. 273). This image feeds into deeper myths in the American psyche, however, since it is an extension of the view of the Black man as representing dangerous, uncontrolled, and exciting sexuality, from which white womanhood must be protected. Because a pimp is a man who controls women's sexual lives, he is a powerful figure sexually. A Black man who controls white women sexually may become a particularly threatening figure. These photographs, accompanied by such captions as, "Many streetwalkers are managed by pimps" (Allgeier and Allgeier 1984, p. 468), reflect the fear of Black men's powerful sexuality. One caption might even be considered a warning to Black men: Under a photograph of a Black pimp with a white prostitute it states, "Prostitutes are more likely to survive the fast life than are their pimps" (Geer, Heiman, and Leitenberg 1984, p. 481).

Another variation on the realm of dangerous sexuality relates to sexually-transmitted diseases. In one text, there is a full page photograph of a crowded street scene, in which the largest foreground figures, in the lower left corner, are two Black women, Facing this is the title page for the chapter "Sexual Diseases" (Greenberg, Bruess, and Sands 1986, pp. 256–257). The viewer's gaze is drawn to the Black women in several ways. First, they are the largest figures (6.5, 7.0 cm), dominating the left foreground of the frame; the closest figure to them in both size and location is a white woman who is a little over one centimeter smaller. The rest of the figures in the crowd diminish rapidly in size. Because of the nearness of the two Black women, the details of face and dress are much clearer. In addition, the movement of these two women is across the grain of the crowd movement. One of the two Black women is three-quarters face and the other almost full face to the camera, while the white woman behind them is in profile. While this juxtaposition was surely not meant to imply anything about Black women, the image and the title can work effectively together to link Black women and sexually transmitted diseases.

If the purpose of the photograph is to imply the potential spread of disease through a population or that, among a mass of people are many carriers of disease, there is no need for any large foreground figures to be present. A different camera angle or a different cropping of the photograph could have eliminated any figures being highlighted. It is clear that the figures that stand out in crowd scenes cannot be dismissed as incidental to the meanings of the photograph. For example, it is interesting to compare this photograph to a very similar photograph of the same street scene in the same text that accompanies a paragraph entitled, "Is being a sexual person an art?" (Greenberg, Bruess, and Sands 1986, p. 9). The largest figure in the foreground is a young white man, casually dressed in light-colored trousers, shirt collar open, tie undone, hand in pocket, walking toward the camera. He is clearly the person who has mastered the art of being sexual, especially compared to the closest figure in size and location—an Asian man in a business suit. It is also important to note that the photographs facing the title pages of chapters in this textbook have been chosen to relate to the titles. The chapter, "Sexual Arousal Techniques" opens with a heterosexual couple in profile, gazing at each other in an intimate way. The "Conception, Pregnancy, and Birth" chapter is illustrated by a photograph of a number of women in a prepared childbirth class.

The fear of transmission of sexually-transmitted diseases from Blacks to whites is certainly not new, having been a recurring theme in late nineteenth century and early twentieth century medical literature in the United States. For example, Kiple and Kiple (1980) cite a 1909 article from the *Journal of the Southern Medical Association* in which syphilis among Blacks is seen as:

> A very real menace to our white boys and through them after marriage to our innocent daughters also. For despite our best efforts many boys are going to sow wild oats (p. 217).

Dangers to Blacks from sexually-transmitted diseases are ignored; it is only the risk of transmission to whites that is seen as a problem. The stereotype of the Black woman as "depreciated sex object," in this instance disease-ridden, serves to warn white men against inter-racial relationships that are potentially threatening to the status quo (King 1982).

The choice of photographs illustrating discussions of disease is even more critical as the educational focus on Acquired Immune Deficiency Syndrome (AIDS) increases. Much of the popular coverage of AIDS has been both homophobic and racist and there is potential for the same problems in textbooks. For example, an overemphasis on the origins in Africa of the virus (HIV) which causes AIDS reinforces the stereotype of Blacks as disease carriers. AIDS in Africa is often presented in the media as less of a major health issue for Africans than as a potential source of infection for Western nations. It is, unfortunately, only too easy to imagine generic photographs of African villagers or crowd scenes in African cities linked to discussions of AIDS in sexuality texts. Only the most recent texts I examined presented information on AIDS, so it may still be possible to avert these problems.

According to the myths, besides being carriers of disease, Black women are sexually promiscuous and amoral. Angela Davis (1983, p. 174) quotes Gerda Lerner (1973) on that point:

> The myth of the Black rapist of White women is the twin of the myth of the bad Black woman—both designed to apologize for and facilitate the continued exploitation of Black men and women (p. 193).

This myth may be unconsciously reinforced by a photograph appearing in one text. Accompanying a paragraph with the heading, "Should sex education teach morals?" is a photograph of female students in a classroom setting (Greenberg, Bruess, and Sands 1986, p. 10). Two are Black, one appears Hispanic, and none are white. Whatever the intention may have been, an interpretation of this juxtaposition may be that the individuals who *need* to be taught morals are women of color.

Blacks as Asexual

As stated earlier, the images presented of a minority group may be contradictory, so it is not surprising to see, along with the portrayals just discussed, a disproportionate number of images of Blacks who carry no sexual threat. Some of this presentation may be a conscious attempt to counter myths about unbridled and dangerous sexuality by desexualizing Blacks. Looking at the absence of certain images is as important as noticing patterns in those present. In the texts examined, in general, there were few examples of Black heterosexual couples showing sexual intimacy, such as hugging, kissing, holding hands, necking. In this category (which did not include photographs with children or of couples not physically touching), one text showed eight such pictures of white couples, but none of a Black couple (Jones, Shainberg, and Beyer 1985); a second had 11 white couples, one Black couple not touching, and one elderly Black couple holding hands (Maier 1985); and a third showed five white couples (including the cover picture), no Black couples, and one interracial couple (Allgeier and Allgeier 1984). One text exemplifies this most dramatically. There are 12 photographs of nude adults alone, in groups, or in couples, exhibiting a joyful, uninhibited sexuality, as they romp on nude beaches or get massages in the sunshine; not one of these individuals is Black (Nass, Libby, and Fisher 1984). The same book also has 12 photographs of clothed whites in physically intimate situations with no photographs of Black couples, but two of couples that might be Hispanic.

It is interesting to note that blacks are also denied the possibility of being homosexual. In the texts examined, there are more than 30 photographs of individuals, couples, or small groups who are identified as lesbians or gay men. All these individuals are white. The only Blacks appearing in any photographs who are identified as gay are a few in large group photographs, such as from the Stonewall Riots or Gay Pride parades. That option of expression of sexuality would seem from these illustrations to be the province of whites only. While some Blacks certainly look at homosexuality as a white person's indulgence, there is a strong history and culture of Black lesbians and gay men. Black women writers, such as Audre Lorde and Barbara Smith, have examined the interlocking oppressions of racism, sexism, and heterosexism; these textbook photographs serve to make their lives invisible.

The presentation of blacks as asexual is a particular serious form of erasure, because, in this culture, to be sexually active, desirable, and desiring is to be validated as a person. To be worthy of another person's attention and love is an acknowledgment of a person's existence. In addition, the ability to command attention and recognition and to be fully engaged and engaging is a sign of power. When Blacks are denied this kind of representation, they are denied the symbolic status and position that it carries in this culture.

The question then becomes whether this is a prescriptive message for Blacks; is the alternative to "dangerous" sexuality to have no sexuality?

Blacks and Paternal Responsibility

The intermediate ground between dangerous sexuality and asexuality is "safe" sexuality, seen in these texts in a disproportionate representation of Blacks in nuclear families and of Black men with children. One of the texts that shows no Blacks in physically intimate situations shows one Black couple being married (the other marriage represented in the text is that of a disabled white couple). In another text, the only Blacks shown are in photographs of a wedding, a nuclear family, and in two photographs of Black fathers with their children. A third text has three photographs of Black fathers with their children as compared to one of a white father and a child and only one of a Black mother with her child. Two other books have equal numbers of photographs of white and Black fathers with children, the only area in which there is parity of representation. In one text, the only Black male is in a father-child interaction, while no Black women are represented at all. The representation of Black fathers is completely out of proportion to the overall representations of Black men in these textbooks.

Each of the images is in itself a positive portrayal but the overall pattern that emerges becomes problematic. As with the asexual portrayal discussed previously, this may be an attempt to counter stereotypes, in this case of the absentee Black father and the failure of the Black family. Sometimes the message seems very direct, as in the following two examples. One text has a caption reading, "The number of men heading single families is increasing dramatically" under a photograph of a Black father and child (Greenberg, Bruess, and Sands 1986, p. 436). This caption contradictorily connotes "failure" of the Black family at the same time it connotes the "responsible" Black father. Another captions the photograph of a Black father holding an infant with: "The view that the female is primarily responsible for care and rearing of children has been replaced by a concept of mutual responsibility of both parents" (Jones, Shainberg, and Beyer 1985, p. 354).

Since Daniel Patrick Moynihan published his report for the U.S. Department of Labor, "The Negro Family: The Case for National Action" in 1965, much of the blame for Black social and economic problems was placed on the failure of the Black father to stay with and support the family, and on the strong Black matriarch who kept him from assuming his rightful place in the family. Since the Moynihan report suggested that the weakness of the Black community was due to deterioration of the Black family (Rainwater and Yancey 1967), the "case for national action" was focused away from the issues of racism and discrimination. For example, little interest has been shown in the problem of Black men having to leave their families in order for their families to qualify for Aid to Families With Dependent Children (AFDC). Instead, the focus has been on the internal problems of the Black family (Giddings 1984). Variations on this theme keep recurring in the media as the "Moynihan Thesis" currently undergoes a revival (Marable 1986).

In the sexuality texts, the preponderance of images of Black nuclear families and Black men with children (compared to images of Blacks in other situations or to whites in these same situations) may amount to a prescriptive message: The place for the Black man is at home with his family, where his sexuality can be safely contained; if Black families just pull together, they will have no problems. The issue of large numbers of young single mothers, an issue of particular concern as the government makes more budget cuts in the area of social welfare, is relegated to the domain of individual solutions, represented by images of Black men taking care of their children. The message is similar to that derived from the Moynihan report: Blacks must bear personal responsibility, while racism, structural inequalities, and other failures of society can be ignored.

Manning Marable (1986) in his discussion of the "crisis of the Black family" asserts:

> Some of the talk about the Black family's crisis is indeed accurate. Black-on-Black crime, spouse abuse and other manifestations of antisocial behavior are quite real. But at the level of national public policy, there is an attempt to attribute all of the Black community's problems to internal flaws—that Black women are promiscuous, that Black teenagers are all criminally-inclined, that Black men are lazy or nonexistent husbands, etc. (p. 2).

These texts seem to offer a simple solution to a rather complex problem: The Black father must stay with his children.

CONCLUSIONS

There have been gains made toward reducing racism in sexuality textbooks as images of Blacks have gone from nonexistent to at least a token representation. Though many of the photographs are in themselves positive images, there is a pattern that emerges that tells us a lot less about Black sexuality than about how whites view it. Blacks have gained in representation but the positive messages may be subtly undermined by these images. What we see are reflections of both a racist white dominated culture's stereotypes and fears and a prescription for what would alleviate those fears. The emphasis is on the Black man, much more than the Black woman, who becomes nearly invisible. The possibilities for the sexuality of the Black man become polarized into the dangerous pimp, or the good, loving father, without allowing for the full range of sexual expression allowed to whites. Given the potential impact of photographs that connote "objectivity" in textbooks and the small number of images of Blacks, which gives each representation more weight, decisions about the photographs to be included must be made carefully in terms of both individual images and overall patterns. As discussed in detail earlier, even crowd scenes should not be taken lightly. Authors and editors may feel caught in a bind, criticized first for underrepresenting people of color and then attacked for choosing the "wrong" images. The next step then is to question why certain kinds of photographs should even be included. If photographs of white pimps are not available, is there any real benefit to the student in knowing what a pimp might look like, especially if it may just reinforce media stereotypes? Is there any purpose to showing couples in intimate situations? If we do, should we not make sure a full diversity of possible couples is represented? If photographs are not available to express that diversity, then maybe we should use none. If the photograph is not actually clarifying the text, such as a picture of a syphilis chancre or an illustration of testicular self-exam, then we must consciously examine its value in terms of messages it may convey. Even if the photograph does clarify the text, the choices must be made carefully: It must not end up being white men who do testicular self-exams while Black men have syphilis chancres.

It appears that many of those who control decisions about textbooks in the United States have made political decisions to be "liberal" about the treatment of Blacks, that is, to undermine stereotypes and to represent Blacks more often and more "positively." However, as this article illustrates, this attempt has not always been successful. In order to address issues of racism in textbooks in any society, it is not sufficient just to add more images or even more "positive" images of nondominant groups. The selection of photographs must take into account the broader context of popular myths, stereotypes, and cultural images of these groups. The selection process is not simply a question of being "objective" or "realistic" but of actively addressing through these images issues such as audience expectations and interpretive strategies. An individual photograph may, as an isolated image, seem free of racist connotations or even positive, until it is viewed in a broader cultural context.

Both textbook authors and editors generally tend to be liberal and are likely to respond to antiracist market pressure. The difficulty may come in identifying subtle ways in which the most well-intended text becomes subverted by the images presented. This article is meant to raise issues about the impact of the photographic message. Our attempts to prepare multicultural materials should not be allowed to backfire, so that we end up reinforcing more stereotypes than we destroy.

FOOTNOTES

1.   I decided to focus on Blacks rather than on all people of color for a number of reasons. The most important reason is simply that there are not enough photographs of other groups, such as Asians or Native Americans, to discern any patterns. Also, although similar general issues around representation and stereotypes might exist for a number of different groups, I did not wish to artificially group all people of color together as if there were no major differences among them. Stereotypes of different groups may present very different problems. For example, Asians are often represented as a "model minority," an image individual Asians may have trouble living up to. This can also create resentment as whites may measure the achievements of other people of color against those of various Asian populations in the United States.

2. Messages about race certainly appear in other categories of photographs not discussed in this paper. For example, two of the textbooks use the same photograph in chapters on sex roles (Francoeur 1982, p. 77; Masters, Johnson, and Kolodny 1985, p. 277). It shows girls taking an industrial arts course in school. One white girl is using a hack saw to cut a rod held in a vise, while three Black girls hold the rod and look on. This is analogous to the kinds of photographs that have been identified as sexist in texts, which picture laboratory settings in which females watch (in awe or admiration) as the males actively conduct the experiments.

3. See Pollis, Carol A. "Sensitive drawings of sexual activity in human sexuality textbooks: An analysis of communication and bias," *Journal of Homosexuality* 13 (1986): 59–73, for an analysis of age, race, class, and sexual preference in these drawings.

REFERENCES

Anyon, Jean. "Ideology and United States history textbooks." *Harvard Educational Review* 49, no. 3 (1979): 361–386.

Apple, Michael W. "The culture and commerce of the textbook." *Journal of Curriculum Studies* 17, no. 2 (1985): 147–162.

Barthes, Roland. *Image-Music-Text.* (Heath, Stephen, trans.). New York: Hill and Wang, 1977.

Brown, Anita, Goodwin, Beverly J., Hall, Barbara A., Jackson-Lowman, Huberta. "A review of psychology of women textbooks: Focus on the Afro-American woman." *Psychology of Women Quarterly* 9, no. 1 (1985): 29–38.

Choy, Christine. Cinema as a tool of assimilation: Asian Americans, women and Hollywood. In color: *Sixty years of images of minority women in the media, 1921–1981,* edited by Pearl Bowser and Ada Gay Griffin. New York: Third World Newsreel Exhibition Program, 1982.

Coser, Lewis A., Kadushin, Charles, Powell, Walter, W. *Books: The culture and commerce of publishing.* New York: Basic Books, 1982.

Davis, Angela. *Women, race and class.* New York: Vintage Books, Random House, 1983.

Giddings, Paula. *When and where I enter: The impact of black women on race and sex in America.* Toronto: Bantam, 1984.

Gilman, Sander L. "Black bodies, white bodies: Toward an iconography of female sexuality in late nineteenth-century art, medicine, and literature." *Critical Inquiry* 12 (1985): 204–242.

Hirsch, Miriam F. *Women and violence.* New York: Van Nostrand Reinhold, 1980.

King, Mae C. "The politics of stereotypes." *The Black Scholar* 13, nos. 4–5 (1982): 2–13.

Kiple, Kenneth and Kiple, Virginia. "The African connection: Slavery, disease, and racism." *Phylon* 41, no. 3 (1980): 211–222, quoting from Sutherland, H. L. "Health conditions of the Negro in the South: With special reference to tuberculosis." *Journal of the Southern Medical Association* 6 (1909): 405.

Klein, Gillian. *Reading into racism: Bias in children's literature and learning materials.* London: Routledge and Kegan Paul, 1985.

Lather, Patti. "Issues of validity in openly ideological research: Between a rock and a soft place." *Interchange* 17, no. 4 (1986): 63–84.

Lerner, Gerda. *Black women in white America.* New York: Vintage Books, Random House, 1973.

Marable, Manning. "Thinkers' fad: Blame the black family." *The Guardian.* September 10 (1986): 2.

Rainwater, Lee and Yancey, William L. *The Moynihan Report and the politics of controversy.* Cambridge, MA: M.I.T. Press, 1967.

Sontag, Susan. *On photography.* New York: Farrar, Straus and Giroux, 1977.

Wexler, Philip. "Structure, text, and subject: A critical sociology of school knowledge." In *Culture and economic reproduction in education*, edited by Michael W. Apple. London: Routledge and Kegan Paul, 1982.

APPENDIX

The following textbooks were examined for this paper:

Allgeier, Elizabeth R. and Allgeier, Albert R. *Sexual interactions.* Lexington: MA: D. C. Heath, 1984.

Crooks, Robert and Baur, Karla. *Our sexuality.* Menlo Park, CA: The Benjamin/Cummings Publishing Company, 1987.

Francoeur, Robert T. *Becoming a sexual person.* New York: John Wiley and Sons, 1982.

Geer, James, Heiman, Julia, and Leitenberg, Harold. *Human sexuality.* Englewood Cliffs, NJ: Prentice-Hall, 1984.

Greenberg, Jerrod S., Bruess, Clint E., and Sands, Doris W. *Sexuality: Insights and issues.* Dubuque, IA: Wm. C. Brown, 1986.

Hyde, Janet Shibley. *Understanding human sexuality.* New York: McGraw-Hill, 1987.

Jones, Kenneth L., Shainberg, Louis W., and Byer, Curtis O. *Dimensions of human sexuality.* Dubuque, IA: Wm. C. Brown, 1985.

Jones, Richard E. *Human reproduction and sexual behavior.* Englewood Cliffs, NJ: Prentice-Hall, 1984.

Kelly, Gary F. *Sexuality: The human perspective.* Woodbury, NY: Barron's, 1980.

Kilman, Peter R. *Human sexuality in contemporary life*. Boston: Allyn and Bacon, 1984.

Maier, Richard A. *Human sexuality in perspective*. Chicago: Nelson-Hall, 1984.

Masters, William H., Johnson, Virginia E., and Kolodny, Robert C. *Human sexuality*, second edition. Boston: Little, Brown, and Co., 1985.

McCary, Stephen P. and McCary, James L. *Human sexuality*, third brief edition. Belmont, CA: Wadsworth Publishing, 1984.

Meeks, Linda B. and Heit, Philip. *Human sexuality: Making responsible decisions*. Philadelphia: Saunders, 1982.

Nass, Gilbert D., Libby, Roger W., and Fisher, Mary P. *Sexual choices: An introduction to human sexuality*. Monterey, CA: Wadsworth Health Sciences Division, 1984.

Schultz, Donald A. *Human sexuality*, second edition. Englewood Cliffs, NJ: Prentice-Hall, 1984.

CHAPTER 5

'Til Death Do Us Part: AIDS, Race, and Representation

Brenda G. Hatfield

INTRODUCTION

While growing up as an African American female in the South during the forties and fifties, I can recall going to movies with childhood friends and all of us becoming quite excited and mesmerized by the mere presence of a black face on the screen. No matter if the black character were a fetching "Uncle Tom," a silly maid, or a mere shadow; better, however, if the character were a rhythmic tap dancer, a singer, or an actor with a significant part. Even the smallest frame of film representation could grasp our attention and cause us to shout excitedly to each other, "Hey look, a colored man!"

We were confined to the upper balcony of a segregated movie theater, while whites were seated in the separate downstairs orchestra. Our responses to the movies offered distinct contrasts to those of our counterpoint audience seated below. Always, our minority representation on screen created within us a sort of tension, an awareness, an identification that was manifested in concentrated hushed silence, nervous giggles, boisterous laughter, or triumphant applause. Our applause, shouts, whistles, cries, silences, and laughter were so often out of sync with the white audience downstairs that one could actually discern a sort of rhythmic oppositional response pattern from above and below the balcony as the film reeled simultaneously before our eyes. We were as separate in our responses to the films as we were in our segregated seating. Yet there were moments when hegemony triumphed, our racially separated spaces collided into collective agreement, and the dominant ideology prevailed among us.

Hopefully these autobiographical reflections of cinematic experiences illustrate how individuals and groups of people differentially view or read electronic media texts, and produce a variety of meanings while interacting with the text, based on their various backgrounds and social and cultural experiences. An electronic text may be a movie, television, instructional film or videotape, or other form of electronic media. Embedded within these electronic texts are encoded signs or meanings which represent the intentions of the authors or producers of the text. Just as we interpret meanings while reading a printed text such as a book, we also create meaning in the process of viewing electronic media. These encoded texts are decoded by the viewer and read intertextually, in context with other textual and lived experiences that make up the viewer's background and cultural and social experiences. It is at the intersection of reader and text that meanings are produced and created. Yet it must be emphasized that the meanings produced by the viewer or audience are not necessarily the encoded messages embedded by the authors or producers into the texts; rather, the meanings may actually be in excess or beyond the intention of the texts, thus creating meaning that the author does not intend. Critical cultural theory, including the methodology of semiotics in the analysis of texts, can help us to better understand this process and develop a theory for understanding racial representations of minorities in electronic media.

Cultural studies are concerned with the generation and circulation of meaning in society. Cultural theorists are interested in knowing how ideological meanings are produced and circulated in society, and how audiences use them to make sense of their own experiences. Media texts are considered polysemic, containing a variety of potential meanings when they interact with viewers or audiences. Cultural theorists of media contend that communities of viewers will read or interpret a text differently, depending on the readers' social, economic, or political background and experiences. The reader is considered the active maker of meanings and not a passive recipient of the text, since it is at the intersection of reader and text that meaning is created (Hall, 1984; Fiske, and Hartley, 1978; Fiske, 1987; Allen, 1987; Masterman, 1985; Becker, 1987).

Cultural theorists approach electronic media texts as sites for ideological struggle of meanings among audiences or communities or viewers (Hall, 1984; Fiske and Hartley, 1987; Fiske, 1987; Allen, 1987; Masterman, 1987; Becker, 1987; McCarthy, 1988a; Roman, Christian-Smith, and Ellsworth, 1988; Bennett, 1982). Media texts are considered sites of struggle to determine whose culture or social experiences gain meaning through textual discourse. These struggles involve what Stuart Hall (1984) terms "preferred readings": (1) dominant, (2) negotiated, or (3) oppositional readings. In a dominant reading, the viewer is situated to agree with and accept the dominant ideology. In a negotiated reading, the reader fits into the dominant ideology but needs to inflect it for his or her own social position. In an oppositional reading, the reader is positioned in direct opposition with the dominant ideology. It is generally agreed that most readings are negotiated, since no one audience is perfectly situated in perfect dominant ideological centrality. Yet it becomes problematic when minority audiences continuously find themselves marginalized, even while making negotiated meanings. Thus it becomes incumbent upon minority critics and educators to become engaged in the critical practice of oppositional readings so that they and their students can become enlightened, transformed, and liberated people in this society.

In *Becoming Feminine: The Politics of Popular Culture* (1988) authors Roman, Christian-Smith, and Ellsworth argue that popular culture is an important site in the struggle for and against the cultural and ideological hegemony of dominant groups. Their use of the concept of popular culture as representational and lived social texts suggests a relational approach to how race, class, and gender can be signified, produced, and consumed in commercialized texts such as film, television, video, and other media. They argue for cultural analysis and textual deconstruction through ethnography, semiotics, and polysemic intertextual and politicized readings by different groups of men and women in order to find the contradictions between people's lives and their representations in commercialized popular cultural forms. The analysis of a film such as *'Til Death Do Us Part* gives recognition to the instructional film medium as a site for social and cultural struggle for textually mediated power in a classroom, as well as in the larger society. Traditional and mainstream approaches to electronic media criticism are often positivistic, based on scientific analytical theory involving empirical methodologies such as statistics and quantitative content analysis in media research. Poststructural theorists of cultural studies consider these methods limited in their ability to account for the subtleties and complexities of meanings in electronic media texts (Hall, 1984; Masterman, 1985; Fiske, 1978; Allen, 1987). These cultural theorists seek to combine the methodologies of semiotics and textual analysis with ethnography and audience research in order to understand the creation of meaning in texts and the struggles of groups to represent their own experiences and culture in the creation of meaning.

Through semiotics, we can develop a clearer understanding of the production and reproduction of racial representation and the marginalization of minorities in electronic media. Semiotics is bounded by a plethora of definitions, all related to the construct of signs, codes, and meanings in written, verbal, and visual texts. The definitions and explanations of semiotics range from the concrete to the abstract. The tenability of the very notion of signs and semiotics is described by Umberto Eco (1985) as a multiplicity of signs as codes and subcodes that are transitory couplings of expressive content units that can be differently coupled and correlated in different systems, or even within the same system in different contexts. In contrast to Eco's somewhat abstract definition of semiotics in the creation of meaning, Ellen Seiter defines semiotics concretely as the study of everything that can be used for communication, including words, images, music, medical symptoms, and so on (Seiter in Allen, 1987). It is within this latter broader context that I would approach semiotics in the analysis of electronic media, and as I have approached it in this sex education film.

John Fiske illustrates how semiotic textual analysis can be used in electronic media, in his treatise entitled *Television Culture* (1978). Television is considered a cultural agent that is the producer and circulator of meaning among social groups. Television is an electronic medium that uses a system of signs and codes to generate and circulate meanings in society. According to Fiske, these codes are categorized as (1) social codes (dress, makeup, behavior); (2) technical codes (camera angle, lighting, music, sound track, editing); (3) conventional representational codes (narrative, action, conflict); and (4) ideological codes (race, capitalism, materialism, patriarchy). Fiske describes the working of codes as links between producers, texts, and audiences that interrelate intertextuality in a network of meanings that constitute our cultural world. The social and political power of the code is described by Fiske as the power to construct meanings, pleasures, social identities, and an entire socioeconomic system. According to Fiske, semiotic analysis looks directly at the layers and structures of codes to determine how these meanings are produced, and semiotic or cultural criticism deconstructs and exposes the text as a highly ideological construct.

In her book entitled *Critical Practice*, Catherine Belsey (1980) reveals the limitations of positivism and classic realism while also exploring the possibilities for a critical practice that advances semiotics. Belsey's arguments are grounded in a conceptual framework that makes a case for critical practice and discursive criticism in the deconstruction of texts. She recognizes ideology inscribed in the signifying practices of language texts, and states that the task of new critical practice is to identify the limitations of texts, seek out the process of its production, and liberate the plurality of meanings. In this framework, semiotic analysis would attempt to reveal how layers of encoded messages are structured in electronic media to produce meanings. Through this process of critical practice, Belsey decenters the authority of the text, releases the constraints of univocal readings, and allows for new meanings or knowledge to be produced and transformed. Her arguments can also be compelling for minority critics to engage in their own critical discourse and practice in the analysis and deconstruction of electronic media texts.

Len Masterman (1985), in his *Teaching the Media*, calls semiotics the "bedrock assumption" of media education which enables us to link and make conceptual sense of the diverse range of signifying practices employed by each medium. According to Masterman, semiotic analysis reaffirms the basic theoretical framework for media education, that media are symbolic sign systems which must to be actively *read*, and not unproblematic, self-explanatory reflections of external reality. This statement is critical for media educators who are selecting materials and working with minority students. If minority and oppressed people are to be liberated from the dominant interests of society, we must understand how the dominant ideology is embedded in the process of codification in the media.

In *Pedagogy of the Oppressed*, Paulo Freire's (1970) pedagogical techniques include the use of dialogical encounters with students, thematic investigation of the language and culture, and codification processes for the transmission of knowledge. Dialogical encounters require critical thinking mediated by the student's world in order to convert that world into activism. The thematic approach requires investigation of language and culture in order to understand themes of domination, unveil the reality of ethnic consciousness, and generate critical thinking of the world toward the achievement of liberation and knowledge. Finally, through the investigation of encoding and decoding processes, Freire recommends that educators learn to decipher and record the idiom of the people, their vocabulary, and syntax in order to construct situations for the codification of information as the means of effective communication and analysis of their experiences. Indeed, Freire's pedagogical approaches to education for liberation have significant relevance to the challenges and tasks we face in large urban inner-city schools that are vastly populated by disadvantaged and oppressed African American youth. Freire's arguments support the need to evaluate and analyze instructional sex education films such as *'Til Death Do Us Part* from the perspective of relevancy to the student's culture, background, and language.

In educational media studies, there is a paucity of effort in critical research, and a vital need for discursive criticism directed toward the study and analysis of racial representations of minorities in electronic media today. Critical discourse is considered a social or political action that works to deconstruct or penetrate texts for an understanding of how they work to promote or oppose the representations of various social or racial groups in society. Through critical discursive practice, we can better understand how meanings are created or produced and then circulated to serve the interests of society. Furthermore, I shall argue that such issues must be addressed from the discursive perspectives of minorities themselves.

Examination of current media criticism reveals the marginalization and subordination of racial and language minorities as subjects and producers of critical discourse in electronic media. Yet minority critics in cultural studies are becoming more vocal and critical of "others" acting as privileged speakers for oppressed and marginalized racial, ethnic, or gendered groups (McCarthy, 1988a; Williamson, 1988; Julien and Mercer, 1988; Dyer, 1988; Gaines, 1988). These minority critics recognize that the voice of the white, male middle class has dominated critical discourse on social issues for minorities, with the exception of gender issues, which have been almost exclusively spoken by white middle-class women. Minority critics argue that these forms of marginalized representation spoken for minorities produce unitary texts of monologic discourse whose authenticity cannot be validated (Julien & Mercer, 1988; McCarthy, 1988a).

In an article entitled "Slowly, Slowly, Slowly, the Dumb Speaks . . . ," Cameron McCarthy (1988b) attacks neo-Marxist accounts of schools and society that subordinate the histories and experiences of Third World, minority, and oppressed people, in which the speaking positions are reserved for white, new middle-class male intellectuals. McCarthy considers these texts "bastardized" or "counterfeit" representations of First World societies. McCarthy sees this problematic as locating a new arena of social, cultural, and educational struggle, and as a question of who gets to generate theory about whom, whose experiences get appropriated, whose theories are considered appropriate, and who has privileged access through "old boy" or other networks to dominant journals, books, and general circulation.

McCarthy responds to the problematic of marginalized minority representation in discursive criticism with a compelling argument for nonsynchronous politics (McCarthy, 1988a). McCarthy's theory of nonsynchrony is based on the assumption that individuals or groups in their relation to economic, political, and cultural institutions such as schools do *not* share similar consciousness, needs, interests, or desires at the same points in time (1988b). According to McCarthy (1988b), nonsynchrony argues for minorities to be their own representative agents as spoken subjects of their own texts. In his arguments for nonsynchrony, McCarthy urges minorities to develop their own social and political space to deconstruct and critique texts that represent and reflect their understandings of the discursive practices of electronic media and other products of popular culture (McCarthy in Roman, Christian-

Smith, and Ellsworth, 1988). Thus, nonsynchrony repositions minorities to ground their own racial, cultural, and social histories and experiences into critical discourse, especially as it pertains to their representativeness.

It is at this juncture, and within the framework of the arguments just articulated, that I have positioned my approach to the study and analysis of this sex education film on the topic of AIDS, produced by and for an African American student audience. I would like to describe excerpts from a group of African American students' readings of the film, juxtaposed with my own readings of the text. Afterward, I shall make recommendations for a more socially conscious, critical approach to the evaluation, selection, and use of instructional film media in the classroom.

STUDENTS' RESPONSE TO FILM

Student Population

This film was presented to an audience of ninety-seven students in an inner-city high school, all African Americans, in grades 10 to 12, ages fourteen to nineteen. The students who attend this school also live in the same community, which is one of the most socially and economically disadvantaged and oppressed communities in metropolitan New Orleans. Their community is centered in the city's largest and most deteriorated public housing developments, which are characterized by poverty, high unemployment, social welfare programs, single female heads of household, high crime, high drug usage, large percentages of teen pregnancies, school dropouts, student underachievement, and the many other conditions so typical of socially, economically, and racially oppressed areas of large urban cities in this country. According to the film's producers, this group of students would be considered the film's targeted audience. Therefore this population of students was selected to explore the assumptions, meanings, and contradictions of this film.

Method

My first approach to the students' analysis of this film was through a written survey questionnaire for all student viewers to answer. Despite the limitations of positivist approaches to audience research, I included this methodology in my preliminary study to help me focus the subject matter, to raise questions with students during interview sessions, to compare written responses with verbal discussions, and to provide an alternative resource that I might later need to analyze student responses. Approximately sixty-six students answered the questionnaire.

My second approach consisted of interviews with individual students and discussions with small groups of three to four participants. A total of thirty-three students participated in the interviews. It was the interview approach that I believe provided the greater reflexivity, insight, and spontaneity in the students' responses to the film. For this essay, I shall limit my preliminary findings mainly to student interviews, and I shall limit my analysis only to the subject of African American racial representations in the film by focusing on the rap music, the role of the baby, and the racialized class and gendered positions of African Americans embedded in the film's text. Finally, I shall conclude with recommendations based on the analysis and findings.

Film Presentation

Students were presented the film in their sex education classes, in which they were studying AIDS as part of the approved curriculum in the public school district. I introduced the film to them by discussing the film's purpose, its production, and my interest in learning their response and analysis of it in relation to the film's instructional information and its social, racial, and gendered messages about AIDS. I assured them that their participation did not involve a test or exam, and that there were no right or wrong answers in response to my questions, but that their opinions would be valuable to me in making decisions about future selections of sex education films for our schools. Following my introductory remarks, we proceeded to watch the film together.

Students watched the film in rapt attention from beginning to end. They hardly turned their faces away from the television monitor, nor spoke during the entire seventeen minutes of the film. Students smiled or nudged each other during the opening love scene between the boyfriend and girlfriend. The only audible response that occurred was brief laughter during the commercial skits. Many students moved to the beat of the rap music, especially the upbeat music and rhyme at the beginning of the film; but their movements discernibly diminished as the plot developed and became more intense with scenes of death and dying, and the funeral. Finally, when the film ended with the dead baby being held by Death's grip, students remained silent and still for several seconds, in what appeared to be a stunned silence, until the end of the written messages and the lengthy credit roll.

Student Analysis—Race

In terms of race, the film is set up to show how AIDS is introduced into the black community and can destroy the future hopes and aspirations of its young. Whereas students were knowledgeable about AIDS and its threat to the community, they were critically concerned about their exclusive racialized roles as carriers and victims of AIDS in the film. They were neither impressed nor more trusting of the construction of the messages in the film simply because it was written and produced by an all–black theatrical performing group. Instead, students viewed their total inclusion as representative victims of AIDS quite negatively. This contradicts a basic assumption in the film production that an all-black cast and characters will always be appealing and accepted by a targeted audience of inner-city African American students. Instead, students remarked as follows:

> It makes it look like only black people have it. (Interview 3/10/89)
>
> If whites see it, they might say "Oh, only blacks have AIDS." (Interview 3/10/89)
>
> On TV always lots of things about black people. Like they are the only ones to get the virus, use drugs and stuff. Act like they are the only ones to have the problem. (Interview 3/22/89)
>
> They think because of the environment we live in most of the kids are involved in drugs, but that's not so. . . . It's the environment . . . not the school, not true about the school being bad . . . just because we between Almonaster and Florida [Streets]. (Interview 3/10/89)
>
> Always go in the project and show black. But not everybody like that. Always show blacks on street, but not white and make blacks feel low about themselves. (Interview 3/22/89)

The above comments are significant because they indicate that African American students recognize racial biases and myths created by media that are directed toward their representation in society. In developing sex education curricula and staff development programs on the subject of AIDS, it is important for educators to be aware that the racial representation of AIDS in the community is a matter of serious concern for African Americans because of media reports which suggest that black people suffer disproportionately from the effects of AIDS. Media reports on AIDS in this country often focus on racial minorities and ethnic groups, despite the fact that the infected population is 57 percent white, 27 percent black, 15 percent Hispanic, and 1 percent other (U.S. Department of Health and Human Services, 1989, p. 9). In New Orleans, the breakdown of the infected population is 68 percent white, 29 percent black, and 3 percent Hispanic (Louisiana Department of Health & Hospitals, 1989); yet, when the majority-owned daily newspaper in New Orleans reports AIDS statistics, the headlines locate the disease almost exclusively in the African American community (*Times Picayune*, September 27, 1989, Section B, p. 1). Thus, as we view and evaluate media concerning AIDS, it is necessary to be vigilant about the prevailing racial, social, and political connotations of the disease, particularly as these issues relate to African American and oppressed people.

Student Analysis—The Baby

The treatment of the baby in this film evoked the greatest emotional response by students. Their responses ranged from sad to angry. Many students stated that they considered the death of the baby unfair. They were disturbed by the death of the baby, and blamed "others" for this situation. Among responses to the baby's death were the following:

> Sad how they treated the baby. . . . (Interview 3/10/89)
> It was sad, he did not ask to come into this world, and suffered for something he had nothing to do with. . . . (Interview 3/22/89)
> I did not like it. I did not believe that the baby should have died. (Interview 3/22/89)
> The baby should not have died 'cause it was the mama and daddy who had sex. (Interview 3/22/89)

When asked in the questionnaire, "Did you think the baby was treated fairly in the film?" students gave the lowest response rating.

The male rating was significantly lower than that of females, indicating that it was the treatment of the baby that they liked least. I found it noteworthy, in viewing the film, that the baby was of male gender, and the final statement in the production rhetorically asked, "And what could *he* have been?" It was also noteworthy that the leading male character in the film wore a cap emblazoned with an American flag throughout the play. Could this be interpreted as a sign of patriotism, a statement that AIDS is a threat to all Americans, a message that drugs are a threat to black male survival in America, or that we as black people so desperately want to be identified as Americans? More significantly, could this statement raise the question that the African American male is the problem?

Indeed, the myth of self-determinism for African American people is an overriding theme in this film. The rainbow and white picket fence in the opening scene signifies that the middle-class American dream can be attainable for all, especially blacks. Is the underlying message in the film that African American youth can determine their own futures simply by remaining drug-free and practicing safe sex? As depicted in this film, it is only the African American youth culture, peer pressure, music, and television that seduce black youth into sex and drugs and ruin their future success and happiness. The oppressive social, economic, and racial practices actually experienced by inner-city African American youth that really block their futures are never signified in the plot or in the visual or musical discourse of this film. The social and economic structures of capitalism are omitted as contributing factors to the oppression of African Americans in this society. Instead, the myth of self-determinism blames the mother, blames the father, blames the youth. Perhaps the students recognized these myths embedded in the film and identified their own sense of futility and helplessness as signified by the baby's death. This is an aspect of the students' responses that I would like to discuss further with them.

Student Analysis—The Rap

What the students seemed to enjoy most were the rap presentations in the film. Historically, the origins of rap go back to African and Caribbean tales and fables, and rap is based on the oral tradition of African American people. In America, this oral tradition took the form of slave songs and chants, particularly in the South. Later it migrated to the street corners of northern ghettoes and housing projects and became rhythmic, rhyming, competitive, and braggadocio poetic and musical expressions of inner-city youth. Thus the rap songs and poetry in the film introduced the subject matter into a more receptive cultural context for communicating information about AIDS to the students. Several students commented that they had never seen their classmates so quiet and attentive during an entire film viewing. They attributed this attention directly to the rap music and poetry. As one student commented: "What I like about the film, I have never seen in a film like this before. They have new changes such as rap, and someone dressed represented AIDS."

Yet I considered it problematic that the film featured only male performers in the role of rappers as they conveyed words of wisdom and creativity through music, dance, and poetry. Although African American females can be creative rappers, as I have witnessed them in black communities and schools, in this film they were denied participation in the production of rap dances, music, and songs. Their subordinated gendered positions were signified by their background performances in the dance routines only. African American females were stereotyped in roles of anguish, suffering, and singing the hymns. Ironically, the strongest character in the play among all of the roles was a female, but this powerful role figure was depicted as a supernatural white female. In this case, the message of white racial domination is clearly signified above black characterizations in the film.

Rap music and poetry can deliver messages that are either positive or negative, while capturing the attention of African American youth for the music's information and entertainment value. Rap can augment instruction, especially through techniques of peer education, as it has been used by many health and disease control centers to get messages into the black community about AIDS ("Don't Get It," 1988). Although rap has been touted as an effective form of conveying positive social messages to African American students in inner-city communities, some students also recognize it as a musical conveyer to sell drugs and encourage antisocial behavior. Some of the students I talked with warned me not to be "fooled" by rap, as one stated: "They rap don't do drugs, but many are drug dealing while they rap; making money, no taxes, have sex. . . ." (Interview 3/10/89).

I have concluded that rap may be useful as a pedagogical approach to teaching inner-city students, but it is also limiting. Although most of the students stated that they liked the rap songs, they also recognized that all of the necessary information about AIDS could not be conveyed through rap presentations. Some students actually found it difficult to understand all of the language in the raps. This certainly contradicts the assumption that all inner-city youth speak the same language. Many of the students suggested that other techniques might be tried, such as skits, mini-dramas, interviews with real victims of the disease, and their own student-produced films. These students wanted straightforward information about the disease.

Finally, all the messages that students saw as information seemed to be voiced authoritatively as rules of commands. For example, when I asked students what messages or information they received from the film, they stated the following:

- Don't do drugs.
- Have safe sex.
- Use condoms.
- Don't share needles.
- Don't have sex without condoms.
- Don't do it.
- Don't have sex until you're married, and even when you marry, use condoms.

The ways in which these authoritative instructional messages were expressed by the students might be read as a silent theme of the film, or the silent curriculum, reflecting the way that instructional practices, rules, and behavioral codes are often established in the classrooms of minority students (Bowles and Gintis, 1976; Anyon, 1981; Weis, 1988).

CONCLUSIONS

In conclusion, a film that deals with AIDS, such as *'Til Death Do Us Part,* requires close critical analysis in the deconstruction of its text in order to recognize the ideology inscribed within the text, to recognize the signifying practices of the text, and to liberate a plurality of meanings read intertextually by its viewers.

Since different communities of viewers will read or interpret the text differently according to their culture, background, and experiences, it becomes necessary for educators to ensure that racial and ethnic minority voices are included in the evaluation, selection, and utilization of texts.

Teachers, media specialists, and instructional and curriculum specialists must become cognizant of the culture, language, signs, and symbols of communication used by both the producers and viewers of texts.

We must be vigilant of the silent curriculum embedded in texts and the silent messages encoded within these texts that profoundly impact students' self-images and racial identities, while these embedded codes foster the continuation of underclassed positions of oppressed racial and minority groups.

Students must be provided access to films and other instructional materials that they can relate to in the best interest of their race, class, and gendered positions in society.

School districts must also encourage and provide opportunities for students to construct their own subjectivities and racial and cultural representations in the production of texts.

Finally, remembering Freire, it is incumbent upon educators to involve disadvantaged and oppressed students in dialogical encounters with the language and culture of media texts in order to foster critical thinking mediated by the students' world, in order to convert that world into activism toward the achievement of knowledge, good health, and their liberation in this society.

REFERENCES

Allen, Robert C. (1987). *Channels of discourse: Television and contemporary criticism.* Chapel Hill: University of North Carolina Press.

Anyon, Jean. (1981). Social class and the hidden curriculum at work. In Henry A. Giroux, Anthony N. Penna, and William F. Pinar (Eds.), *Curriculum and instruction.* Berkeley: McCutchan.

Becker, Ann DeVaney. (1987). *From structuralism to post-structuralism, a personal odyssey.* Paper presented at the Visual-Verbo Symposium, Stockholm, June 9.

Belsey, Catherine. (1980). *Critical practice*. London: Methuen.

Bennett, Tony. (1982). Theories of the media, theories of society. In *Culture, society and media*. M. Gureritch, T. Bennett, et al. (Eds.), (30–55). London: Methuen.

Blonsky, Marshall (Ed.). (1985). *On signs*. Baltimore: John Hopkins University Press.

Bowles, Samuel, and Gintis, Herbert. (1976). *Schooling in capitalist America*. New York: Basis Books.

Don't get it, a rap against AIDS. (1988). *Harvard Educational Review*, 58, 343–347.

Dyer, Richard. (1988). White. *Screen*, 29 (4), 44–64.

Eco, Umberto. (1985). How culture conditions the colours we see. In Marshall Blonsky (Ed.), *On signs*. Baltimore: Johns Hopkins University Press.

Fiske, John. (1978). *Television culture*. London: Methuen.

Fiske, John, and Hartley, John. (1978). *Reading television*. London: Methuen.

Freire, Paulo. (1970). *Pedagogy of the oppressed*. (Myra Bergman, tran.). New York: Continuum, 1988. (Originally published, 1970.)

Gaines, Jane. (1988). White privilege and looking relations: Race and gender in feminist film theory. *Screen*, 29(4), 12–26.

Hall, Stuart. (1984). Encoding and decoding. In Stuart Hall, *Culture, media, language*. London: Hutchinson.

Julien, Isaac, and Mercer, Kobena. (1988). Introduction—de margin and de centre. *Screen*, 29(4), 2–10.

Louisiana Department of Health & Hospitals. (1989). Office of Public Health. Louisiana AIDS prevention & surveillance project. Surveillance report for metro New Orleans. *Seroprevalence Newsletter*, September.

McCarthy, Cameron. (1988a). Marxist theories of education and the challenge of a cultural politics of non-synchrony. In Leslie G. Roman, Linda Christian-Smith, and Elizabeth Ellsworth, (Eds.), *Becoming feminine: the politics of popular culture*. London: Falmer Press.

McCarthy, Cameron. (1988b). Slowly, slowly, the dumb speaks: Third World popular culture and the sociology of the Third World. *Journal of Curriculum Theorizing*, 8(2), 7–21.

Masterman, Len. (1980). *Teaching about television*. London: Macmillan.

Masterman, Len. (1985). *Teaching the media*. London: Comedia Publishing Group.

Roman, Leslie G., Christian-Smith, Linda, and Ellsworth, Elizabeth (Eds.). (1988). *Becoming feminine: The politics of popular culture*. London: Falmer Press.

Shoumatoff, Alex. (1988). In search of the source. *Vanity Fair*. July, 94–105, 112–117.

United States Department of Health and Human Services. (1987). *Human immunodeficiency virus infection in the United States: a review of current knowledge*. Atlanta: Center for Disease Control, December 18, 36(49), 8.

United States Department of Health and Human Services. (1989). *HIV/AIDS surveillance report*. Atlanta: Center for Disease Control, August.

Weis, Lois (Ed.). (1988). *Class, race and gender in American education*. New York: State University of New York Press.

Williamson, Judith. (1988). Two kinds of otherness: Black film and the avant-garde. *Screen*, 29(4), 106–112.

Gender, Race, and Class

CHAPTER 6

It's in Our Hands:
Breaking the Silence on Gender in
African American Studies

Patricia Hill Collins

AFRICAN AMERICAN STUDIES:
THE POLITICAL CONTEXT

African American Studies has effectively held its own in a political climate that neither welcomed its creation nor encouraged its
survival. Although resistance continues to confront African American studies programs and departments, the past fifteen years have
been marked by an institutionalization of African American studies. Black studies professionals can no longer complain that white
power structures need to let us in, for many of us are inside, albeit
in clearly circumscribed ways. In the mid-nineteenth century, Maria W. Stewart, the first American woman to lecture in public on
political issues and to leave copies of her texts, used her widow's
pension to publish her work. In the early twentieth century, the
brilliant William E. B. Du Bois pioneered ground-breaking concepts in sociology yet could not be hired at the University of Pennsylvania because of his race. Zora Neale Hurston, whose 1937
work *Their Eyes Were Watching God* has only recently been recognized as a classic of American literature, died in poverty and was
buried in an unmarked grave. Compared with the struggles of
these and countless other black intellectuals, contemporary black

academicians control substantial resources. We have offices and access to libraries, and many of us are protected by the tenure process. The issue facing us concerns how we plan to use these resources and to what end.

Breaking the silence within African American studies requires examining the links among the institutional locations of black intellectuals and their scholarship because the political context housing African American studies frames the intellectual context within the discipline (Adams, 1984; Karenga, 1988). Grappling with the issue of developing the next generation of young black scholars in predominantly white institutions is one major change in the institutional location of black intellectuals brought on by the "paradox of desegregation." A student's decision of whether or not to major in African American studies parallels a larger and more serious issue facing the black intellectual community. If we cannot pass on the vision of African American studies that has been so central to its survival to the current group of black students in predominantly white institutions, who will become the scholars of African American studies in the coming decades? The location of a sizable segment of the black intellectual community has shifted to the new institutional location of the predominantly white campus.

On such campuses, African American studies as a programmatic entity represents a new "discipline." Karenga argues that a clear distinction exists between the general study of African Americans from the perspective of one or more other disciplines, and the creation of African American studies as an academic discipline in the 1960s. Using Karenga's definition, a discipline is a "self-conscious, organized system of research and communication in a defined area of inquiry of knowledge, not simply a literature, series of courses in schools and universities, or research focus in a given area" (1988, p. 399). Davidson and Weaver propose a more politicized definition of academic disciplines as "principally self-serving professional bodies whose existence is based primarily on the coordinated exercise of power over certification and academic legitimacy" (1985, p. 341). According to both of these criteria, African American studies as an area of inquiry existed prior to the 1960s but did not achieve disciplinary status until black studies professionals were able to gain power within the academy to certify knowledge.

As a result of these political phenomena, the majority of African American studies faculty members have been trained within the diverse intellectual frameworks and political climates of the traditional disciplines of the academy (Adams, 1984). Becoming an African American studies scholar and faculty member involves breaking away from these intellectual frameworks and taking a critical posture toward one's own area of training. But since black scholars select these traditional disciplines because we value them, for many, taking the critical posture toward them can be difficult.

The political context of the campus also affects the internal dialogues within the discipline. Surviving on predominantly white campuses often requires elevating race above class and gender for reasons of political expediency—unity is maintained through uniformity, and the richness of diversity and dialogue among black intellectuals is sacrificed for the very real need to defend African American studies from external assault.

How can African American studies survive within the academy yet challenge that same academy? How can African American studies sustain the vision that stimulated its founding within the confines of political structures that denigrate that vision and that are themselves the focus of the types of changes African American studies wants to bring about? While we must maintain academic credibility by the standards of the institutions in which our programs are located, we must simultaneously challenge and transform those same standards that give us our legitimacy.

Although African American studies has survived sustained political obstacles, the future of the discipline depends on the power of our ideas. The pressures are clearly there to exclude black intellectuals, students, and faculty alike from intellectual work. But what black studies professionals must ask themselves is whether the ideas in African American studies are powerful enough to attract black intellectuals who see their scholarship as important to black community development. The diversity external to the academy must be paralleled by a corresponding paradigmatic diversity in approaching the study of black life and culture. The primary challenge facing African American studies is the need to attract people who remain visionary, who will not, as it were, destroy the discipline from within.

AFRICAN AMERICAN STUDIES:
THE INTELLECTUAL CONTEXT

Changing the discipline involves asking some hard questions. Is African American studies duplicating the type of intellectual uniformity practiced by traditional academic disciplines where some are judged theoretically and methodologically "correct" while others are relegated to the sidelines? Or can African American studies accommodate the scholarly diversity essential for producing analyses of black life and culture responsive to race, class, and gender? Has African American studies contented itself with critiquing mainstream scholarship? Or is it offering alternative models analyzing contemporary race, class, and gender oppression that will empower African American women and men?

Attracting black intellectuals with a vision, both as students and as faculty, requires examining the theoretical approaches taken *within* African American studies as a discipline. In the face of continued pressures on black people not to do intellectual work and, for those African Americans who persevere as students and scholars, the pressure to allow our intellectual work to be used against the best interests of black people, African American studies must offer a variety of alternative paradigms that explain black life and culture better than traditional scholarship.

Race versus Class: The Dominant Paradigms
in African American Studies

Two distinctive paradigms currently frame contemporary African American studies scholarship. The first, the race or cultural paradigm, emphasizes the importance of Afrocentric culture and an Afrocentric worldview. Standard scholarship on blackness and race define these concepts as being either reflections of quantifiable, biological differences among humans or as residual categories that emerged in response to institutionalized racism (Omi and Winant, 1986). In contrast, Afrocentric scholarship suggests that "blackness" and Afrocentricity reflect long-standing belief systems among African peoples (Karenga, 1982; Asante, 1987; Myers, 1988). Even though black people were forced to adapt these Afrocentric belief systems in the face of different institutional arrangements of white domination, such as slavery, imperialism, colonialism, and contemporary institutional discrimination, the continuation of an Afrocentric worldview has been fundamental to African Americans' resistance to racial oppression. Thus, being black encompasses *both* experiencing white domination *and* the existence of independent, long-standing Afrocentric consciousness and institutions.

As the dominant paradigm in African American studies, the race or culture approach has been widely used to document and interpret the Afrocentric culture of black people throughout the diaspora. But this painstaking process often overshadows the equally important process of exploring the connection between the Afrocentric worldview and various forms of domination confronting black people. "There are no 'race only' solutions to the situation of black people," suggests sociologist Robert Newby (1988, p. 77). "If there is a desire to have decent health care for all black Americans, we must know that that is not going to happen in the absence of decent health care for all Americans. If there is a desire to have all black Americans employed, that is not going to happen in the absence of employment for all Americans" (p. 77). These types of concerns are often submerged in the search for distinguishing features of Afrocentric behaviors and institutions.

The second paradigm, the political economy or class approach, promises to remedy this imbalance. Analytical class approaches investigate how global capitalism shapes the institutions and experiences of African Americans (Cox, 1948; Davis, 1981; Marable, 1983; Hogan, 1984). Such approaches are to be distinguished from descriptive class approaches which attempt to quantify and sort African Americans into selected class categories and measure how many blacks are now "middle class." Analytical class approaches consider questions of how changes in capitalism affect the politics, economics, and culture of black people. They aim to explain and prescribe, not merely describe and document.

Recent attempts by some black scholars have attempted to incorporate race as a major explanatory paradigm, and not just a descriptive variable, into existing political economy paradigms. In describing the reaction to sociologist William Julius Wilson's controversial book *The Declining Significance of Race*, Robert Newby observed that the "most important contribution made by Wilson was to place the 'race question' squarely into the context of the political economy, as opposed to such heavy reliance on the 'psyche' in understanding issues of race" (1988, p. 77). Black sociologists within sociology departments overwhelmingly condemned Wilson. But Newby supported Wilson, wryly noting "I have not heard that leadership offer any systematic criticism of what capitalism as a system does to the lives of black people" (p. 77).

In spite of the works of scholars such as Manning Marable (1983) and Angela Davis (1981), class as a major analytical paradigm remains subordinated to racial paradigms in African American studies, in part because many of the black intellectuals developing class analysis are not housed in African American studies departments or programs. Moreover, for those external to African American studies, the gap between those scholars investigating race through the lens of their traditional disciplines with the emphasis on race as interpersonal development and those scholars examining class through standard disciplinary frameworks limits analytical development. Within African American studies, overreliance on cultural approaches to black life and culture often works to stifle those wishing to further a class analysis of the black experience.

Race and class analyses are not mutually exclusive. Rather than battling for theoretical dominance within African American studies, we should actively seek ways to explore the connections between the paradigms of culture and class. Recognizing that some issues affecting black people will lend themselves better to one theoretical approach over another may defuse futile struggles for paradigmatic dominance within the discipline. The African American experience is more complex than the explanations provided by any one approach alone. African American studies would benefit from not only exploring race and class paradigms individually and the interconnections between them, but also from attending to other existing paradigms such as gender, now virtually ignored within the discipline. In the face of long-standing complaints that the scholarship produced in traditional disciplines is flawed because it excludes the ideas and experiences of black people, this standard that African American studies scholars so willingly apply to traditional disciplines must also hold true for African American studies. We must model the inclusiveness that we accuse others of being so deficient at accomplishing.

Although exceptional black women scholars have done excellent work using Afrocentric and class analyses, the experiences of black women as a group do not figure prominently in either paradigm. As a result, the race-versus-class debate for paradigmatic dominance within African American studies is primarily a male debate. Although descriptive gender categories are often applied in black studies research, their use is strangely reminiscent of the descriptive use of class in Afrocentric scholarship and the descriptive use of race in political economy approaches. Gender is often seen as an attribute possessed only by black women, and not as a fundamental paradigmatic approach that explains black women's and black men's experiences with race and class oppression. This silence on gender often generates substantial problems for African American women. "Our problem is that we do not have 'home really fitted to our needs,' " observes Barbara Christian, "for the study of women of color is itself a critique of Afro-American Studies and Women Studies, yet these groups are hardly powerful institutions in the university and their validity is still in question" (1989, p. 22).

But we must remember our student. She or he is an African American in need of an Afrocentric worldview that will help her see her family, community, and culture not through denigrated Eurocentric models, but as part of a continuum of the African experience. Afrocentric analyses provide a powerful paradigm for addressing this need. She is actively preparing for entrance into the black middle class and thus needs a class analysis that will help her see the interconnections of racism and international capitalism and the choices facing privileged African Americans concerning upholding or challenging this system. The class paradigm within African American studies offers promising insights. But our student is also a woman. Hers is a gendered existence where the workings of culture and class in her life profoundly affect her gender experiences and in turn where her gender frames her encounters with race and class. At this point, the silence within African American studies on gender becomes especially problematic.

The Missing Paradigm: Gender and African American Studies

Exploring the interconnections of race and class is vital, and gender also merits a prominent role among African American studies paradigms. Gender as an analytical category represents a critical third paradigm that promises to infuse African American studies with new meaning. Using gender as a major explanatory system suggests that being a woman or a man profoundly shapes individual experiences, opportunities, and consciousness in much the same way as do an individual's race and class.

African American women have long advanced a gendered analysis of African American women's and men's experiences, knowledge that I label "black feminist thought." Starting with Maria W. Stewart (Richardson, 1987) and moving through numerous historical and contemporary African American women thinkers, black women intellectuals have created a vital analytical foundation for a distinctive standpoint on self, community, and society and, in doing so, have created a black women's intellectual tradition (Collins, 1990). Our lack of knowledge about the longevity and richness of this tradition speaks less to its content than to the long-standing suppression of African American women thinkers and scholars.

At the core of black feminist thought lie theories created by African American women which clarify a black women's standpoint—in essence, an interpretation of black women's experiences and ideas by those who participate in them. In addition to well-known black women scholars, African American women not commonly certified as intellectuals by academic institutions have long functioned as intellectuals by representing the interests of black women as a group and by fostering black feminist thought.

Reclaiming this black women's intellectual tradition involves examining the everyday ideas of black women not previously considered intellectuals. The ideas we share with one another as mothers in extended families, as members of black churches, and as teachers to the black community's children have formed one pivotal area where African American women have hammered out a black women's standpoint. Musicians, vocalists, poets, writers, and other artists constitute another group of black women intellectuals who have aimed to interpret black women's experiences. Building on the Afrocentric oral tradition, musicians in particular have enjoyed close a association with the larger community of African American women constituting their audience. Through their words and actions, political activists have also contributed to the black women's intellectual tradition.

One characteristic feature of historical and contemporary black women intellectuals is the thematic consistency of their work. Several core themes constitute a black women's standpoint, namely, the interlocking nature of race, class, and gender oppression, the importance of self-definition in resisting oppression, and analyses of specific topics such as motherhood and political activism. Another characteristic feature is the diversity with which African American women respond to these core themes.

The process of investigating black feminist thought by reclaiming the black feminist intellectual tradition has not been without political struggle. In the 1970s and 1980s, black women interested in examining the impact of gender on black women's lives often found it easier to address racism in white women's organizations than the sexism in black organizations. As a result, black women intellectuals spent considerable time critiquing the racism in white feminist intellectual discourse in a way reminiscent of the African American studies' critique of racism in traditional academic discourse. Taking a critical posture toward the treatment of gender within the culture and class paradigms of African American studies has been more difficult.

Black Feminist Thought and African American Studies Paradigms

Using black feminist thought to infuse African American studies with gender as an analytical category raises several important questions. How would black intellectual discourse have been different, if at all, had black women intellectuals been full participating members in framing the questions that mattered? Similarly, in what ways will both Afrocentric (cultural) and political economy (class) approaches within African American studies be altered by fully including black women's angle of vision?

Black feminist thought potentially affects the intellectual context of African American studies in at least four ways. First, ideas from the black feminist intellectual tradition can function to further existing ideas of both Afrocentric and class analyses and to strengthen existing interpretations. For example, one major hypothesis of Afrocentric analyses of black life and culture is that African cultural continuities exist among blacks widely dispersed in the world. Afrocentric research on religion, music, movement, and language demonstrates not only that these cultural continuities exist but that they have been central to black people's ability to survive oppression. Exploring black women's gender definitions across the diaspora should yield additional support for this fundamental thesis of Afrocentric scholarship (see, for example, Sud-arkasa [1981] and Terborg-Penn [1986]).

Investigating black women's labor market experiences furthers some of the main ideas of class analysis concerning the workplace as a site of class conflict. Traditional class scholarship focuses on manufacturing as a site of exploitation and unionization as a primary form of political resistance. Black women's experiences have been ignored in these analyses because black women have traditionally not worked in industry. But black feminist analyses of black women's work suggest that the workplace has been a powerful site of resistance for African American women (Gilkes, 1983; Rollins, 1985; Dill, 1988a).

Second, the black feminist intellectual tradition can complement existing interpretations. In this area, both cultural and class approaches offer partial views and simply omit large categories of experience that can be vital. The works of black women writers illustrate how black women writers focus on different yet equally important themes in the Afrocentric tradition (Tate, 1983). For example, the work of novelist Zora Neale Hurston can be read as a text of black affirmation. Hurston writes of black life and culture—contact with whites does not figure into her greatest work *Their Eyes Were Watching God.* In contrast, Richard Wright, her contemporary, writes of black/white interaction, primarily among men. His is protest. Both offer valid approaches to the black experience, for as June Jordan (1981) points out, black affirmation and protest against white domination are but complementary parts of the same process. And yet one has traditionally been elevated above the other as superior. Reclaiming the ideas of Hurston and other black women writers offers African American studies the opportunity to redress these long-standing imbalances.

Examining black women's work experiences offers a substantial missing piece to political economy analyses of black labor (Davis, 1981; Higginbotham, 1983). Existing class paradigms rely heavily on models of black exploitation that focus exclusively on wage labor. This emphasis obscures the ways that black women are exploited. Although black women are exploited as workers in the same way as are black men, black women's gender has confined them to an extremely narrow range of occupations, primarily agricultural work and service work, and they have been paid wages below black men because of their gender. Moreover, the emphasis on wage labor derived from examining the male experience does not take into account black women's class exploitation as unpaid workers within African American families (Dill, 1988b). Focusing on black women's labor reveals the interconnection among systems of race, class, and gender and, in doing so, provides new analytical approaches within class analysis (Glenn, 1985).

Third, the black feminist intellectual tradition can challenge selected main ideas in the culture and class paradigms. The glorification of black women as keepers of culture and the race who have somehow escaped the effects of sexism is one cornerstone of Afrocentric thought challenged by gendered analyses of black women's experiences. Pauline Terrelonge contends that a common view within African American communities is that African American women have withstood the long line of abuses against them mainly because of black women's "fortitude, inner wisdom, and sheer ability to survive." Connected to this emphasis on black women's strength is the related argument that African American women play critical roles in keeping black families together and in supporting black men. These activities have been important in offsetting the potential annihilation of African Americans as a "race." As a result, "many blacks regard the role of uniting all blacks to be the primary duty of the black woman, one that should supersede all other roles that she might want to perform, and certainly one that is essentially incompatible with her own individual liberation" (Terrelonge, 1984, p. 557).

Afrocentric work on women's activities in traditional African societies often glosses over the effects of sexism on African women's lives. Reclaiming the black feminist tradition and listening to the voices of black women disputes this rosy view. For example, African feminist Awa Thiam's (1978) book details the tenacity of genital mutilation across a wide area of the African content. Through interviews with African women who had undergone painful operations to remove the clitoris and, in many cases, part of the vulva, Thiam documents how women in many Islamic societies are literally sewn up, to be opened with a knife upon marriage. Although there is much of value in Afrocentric analyses of black life and culture, Thiam's work certainly should make us rethink uncritical analyses that glorify everything in traditional African societies.

Black feminist thought on the causes and contours of black women's poverty challenges some main ideas in theories of the black underclass. Existing theories of the black underclass focus almost exclusively on the male experience. One underlying premise of these models is that male joblessness is the fundamental cause of black poverty for both men and women. If men become employed, then they can support their families and poverty will be minimized. Although employing black men is clearly a high priority, these approaches assume a certain relationship between capitalist development and family life, both centering on gender, that may not go far enough in addressing black women's poverty. Black women are poor for many of the same reasons that black men are poor: racial discrimination that produces higher incidences of poor education, housing, and limited job opportunities for African Americans in a class structure that requires poverty. But black women's poverty is also influenced by gender and thus has a distinctive place in political economy analyses of poverty (Burnham, 1985; Claude, 1986; Brewer, 1988).

The final question of how breaking the silence on gender might affect African American studies concerns how black feminist thought produces unique analyses that do not confirm, complement, or challenge existing African American studies paradigms but instead produce something that is entirely new. Reconceptualizations of rape, violence, and the overarching structure of sexual politics (Davis, 1981; Hall, 1983); of power, political activism, and resistance (Gilkes, 1983; Reagon, 1983; Terborg-Penn, 1986); of the relationships between work and family (Dill, 1988b); and of homophobia and its impact on the interlocking nature of race, class, and gender oppression (Lorde, 1984) are all neglected topics explored in black feminist thought.

IT'S IN OUR HANDS

African American studies must attract and keep black intellectuals—both students and faculty—by the power of its ideas. Although anticipating the continual political struggles attached to the discipline's precarious position in the academy remains essential, protecting the discipline from the enemy within requires breaking the silence on gender in African American studies. Recognizing that approaches of race, class, and gender are not mutually exclusive but instead represent overlapping and complementary paradigms promises to further the intellectual diversity essential to the discipline's survival.

This can only occur if we develop the type of intellectual community that will attract and keep students. For the moment, we are doing our job, for "she" has decided to major in African American studies. Whether she decides to stay will ultimately depend on our ability to offer her inclusive analyses of culture, class, and gender that not only explain the complexity of her life but also empower her to act. Our success at this task is critical to the future of African American studies. It's in our hands.

REFERENCES

Adams, Russell L. (1984). Intellectual questions and imperatives in the development of Afro-American studies. *Journal of Negro Education,* 53(3), 201–225.

Asante, Molefi Kete. (1987). *The Afrocentric idea.* Philadelphia: Temple University Press.

Brewer, Rose. (1988). Black women in poverty: Some comments on female-headed families. *Signs,* 13(2), 331–339.

Burnham, Linda. (1985). Has poverty been feminized in black America? *Black Scholar,* 16(2), 15–24.

Christian, Barbara. (1989). But who do you really belong to—Black studies or women's studies? *Women's Studies,* 17(1–2), 17–23.

Claude, Judy. (1986). Poverty patterns for black men and women. *Black Scholar,* 17(5), 20–23.

Collins, Patricia Hill. (1990). *Black feminist thought: Knowledge, consciousness, and the politics of empowerment.* Boston: Unwin Hyman.

Cox, Oliver. (1948). *Caste, class and race.* New York: Modern Reader Paperback.

Davidson, Douglas V., and Weaver, Frederick S. (1985). Black studies, white studies, and institutional politics. *Journal of Black Studies,* 15(3), 339–347.

Davis, Angela Y. (1981). *Women, race and class.* New York: Random House.

Dill, Bonnie Thornton. (1988a). Making your job good yourself: Domestic service and the construction of personal dignity. In Ann Bookman and Sandra Morgen (Eds.), *Women and the politics of empowerment* (33–52). Philadelphia: Temple University Press.

Dill, Bonnie Thornton. (1988b). Our mothers' grief: Racial ethnic women and the maintenance of families. *Journal of Family History,* 13(4), 415–431.

Gilkes, Cheryl Townsend. (1983). Going up for the oppressed: The career mobility of black women community workers. *Journal of Social Issues,* 39(3), 115–139.

Glenn, Evelyn Nakano. (1985). Racial ethnic women's labor: The intersection of race, gender and class oppression. *Review of Radical Political Economics,* 17(3), 86–108.

Hall, Jacqueline Dowd. (1983). The mind that burns in each body: Women, rape, and racial violence. In Ann Snitow, Christine Stansell, and Sharon Thompson (Eds.), *Powers of desire: The politics of sexuality* (329–349). New York: Monthly Review Press.

Higginbotham, Elizabeth. (1983). Laid bare by the system: Work and survival for black and Hispanic women. In Amy Smerdlow and Hanna Lessinger (Eds.), *Class, race, and sex: The dynamics of control* (200–215). Boston: G. K. Hall.

Hogan, Lloyd. (1984). *Principles of black political economy.* Boston: Routledge & Kegan Paul.

Hurston, Zora Neale. (1937) (1969). *Their eyes were watching God.* Greenwich, CT: Fawcett.

Jordan, June. (1981). *Civil wars.* Boston: Beacon Press.

Karenga, Maulana. (1982). *Introduction to black studies.* Los Angeles: University of Sankore Press.

Karenga, Maulana. (1988). Black studies and the problematic of paradigm: The philosophical dimension. *Journal of Black Studies,* 18(4), 395–414.

Lorde, Audre. (1984). *Sister outsider.* Trumansburg, NY: Crossing Press.

Marable, Manning. (1983). *How capitalism underdeveloped black America.* Boston: South End Press.

Myers, Linda James. (1988). *Understanding an Afrocentric world view: Introduction to an optimal psychology.* Dubuque: Kendall/Hunt.

Newby, Robert G. (1988). The making of a class conscious "race man": Reflections on the 1960s. *Critical Sociology,* 15(2), 61–78.

Omi, Michael, and Winant, Howard. (1986). *Racial formation in the United States, from the 1960s to the 1980s.* New York: Routledge & Kegan Paul.

Reagon, Bernice Johnson. (1983). Coalition politics: Turning the century. In Barbara Smith (Ed.), *Home girls—A black feminist anthology* (356–368). New York: Kitchen Table Press.

Richardson, Marilyn (Ed.). (1987). *Maria W. Stewart, America's first black woman political writer.* Bloomington, IN: Indiana University Press.

Rollins, Judith. (1985). *Between women, domestics and their employers.* Philadelphia: Temple University Press.

Sudarkasa, Niara. (1981). Interpreting the African heritage in Afro-American family organization. In Harriette Pipes McAdoo (Ed.), *Black families.* Beverly Hills, CA: Sage.

Tate, Claudia (Ed.). (1983). *Black women writers at work.* New York: Continuum.

Terborg-Penn, Rosalyn. (1986). Black women in resistance: A cross-cultural perspective. In Gary Y. Okhiro (Ed.), *In Resistance, studies in African, Caribbean and Afro-American history.* Amherst, MA: University of Massachusetts Press.

Terrelonge, Pauline. (1984). Feminist consciousness and black women. In Jo Freeman (Ed.), *Women: A feminist perspective* (3rd ed.). Palo Alto, CA: Mayfield.

Thiam, Awa. (1978). *Black sisters, speak out. Feminism and oppression in black Africa.* London: Pluto Press.

CHAPTER 7

Black Women Heroes:
Here's Reality, Where's the Fiction?

Jewelle Gomez

Three years ago when I began writing a collection of fiction entitled *The Gilda Stories*, I began to do research on the development of heroic or mythological characters in fiction. My stories are about Gilda, who escapes from slavery in 1850 and the tales trace her life through the next several centuries. Gilda, you see, becomes a vampire. My idea was/is to create a super heroic black woman who interprets our lives through a phenomenal perspective. While the premise falls into the fantasy fiction genre, the stories themselves, like all good fantasy or science fiction, are really about the human condition: loneliness, love, families and heroism.

I wanted to create a female character of larger-than-life proportion. I was seeking the type of character and situation that the burgeoning aesthetics of feminism had given birth to. While science and fantasy fiction have traditionally been dominated by male writers, the women's movement has encouraged a wealth of imaginative and expansive writing. Most of it falling into a kind of nurturer/utopian mold while only a small portion of it is more traditionally adventure oriented.

As I read and re-read some of this fiction I discovered that black women characters of heroic dimensions in fantasy fiction were almost impossible to find. I read and was perplexed. Where are our Marion Zimmer Bradleys, Joanna Russ? What is our *Wanderground*? Who is our *Woman on the Edge of Time*? At first I thought such a thing couldn't be true. America lives on icons—idealized figures who represent our intellectual and emotional fantasies. We all grew up with them from Captain Video to Wonder Woman. Rock stars and cartoon characters provide the sub-conscious guide to American society for almost every American regardless of race or socio-economic status.

Could it be that black women were somehow lacking in either epic experience or mythological substance? Is that why none seem to exist in the pantheon of icons of our youth? If that were not true, why do we not have fantasy fiction writers and black women heroes? And finally is it all important that they exist?

That black women could be incapable of historic, heroic be-havior seemed unlikely. We need only look as far as Sojourner Truth, clearly a larger-than-life figure in our history who might have served as a model for mythic interpretation. But perhaps this history was too immediate. The exploits of the recent century-and-a-half are familiar and might not lend themselves to fantasy fiction in our minds yet.

But ancient African civilization certainly yields numerous myth-ic figures both real and imagined. As Runoko Rashidi points out in an essay on African goddesses, the advent of Islam destroyed evi-dence of many goddesses of early Africa. But those who did survive are at least the equal of goddesses of other cultures. Many of the European goddesses have even been suspected of being direct de-scendants of African foremothers like Neith, worshipped in 4000 BC as the self-begotten mother of all who mated with the wind.

Or Hathor, the moon goddess and guardian of the Nile Delta. She was the giver of joy to all human kind as well as the guardian of the dead. And Isis the dominant goddess of Egypt. She was wor-shipped even after their domination by Rome. Her relentless pur-suit of the murderers of her husband culminates in a virgin birth of a child who ultimately avenges the husband's death. These women are certainly the stuff of heroic fantasy.

Historical fact is, as it has been reputed to be, at least as wild as fiction. The list of African warrior queens makes the comic book Superfriends look like Yale preppies on holiday in Ft. Lauderdale. These women were not the romantic black queens idealized by the male focused poets of the Black Arts Movement in the 1960s. They were more than the "Princess, the most praised, the lady of grace, sweet in her love . . . "

They may, indeed, have filled the above description but they also fit what Marie Linton-Umeh describes as an African woman hero: "One whose outstanding and admirable achievements are diverse, and one who can be defined as having leading roles assigned to her because of her superior gifts of body and mind. And who possesses a number of qualities that most members of the community lack . . . and acknowledge."

Some of the warrior queens of Africa have been immortalized by history. The Queen of Ethiopia (960 BC), Makeda, was so mythologized that her title became synonymous with regal supremacy: the Queen of Sheba. In addition to her famed love for King Solomon for whom she endured a legendary journey to learn his wisdom, she was also known as one of the greatest diplomats of her time.

Cleopatra, (87 BC) whose name also entered history as a trade mark for beauty has been painted as a lurid pursuer of Roman bed partners when in fact her political and sexual alliances (aside from being pleasurable) were made to serve Egypt. Her suicide was not the result of a broken heart but the act of an Egyptian nationalist who could not bear the lost control of her country.

Nzingha of what is now Angola formed alliances with the Dutch to repel the Portuguese slave traders: commanded a body of Dutch soldiers in 1646 and an army of women. She was called by her other generals, "a cunning and prudent virago, so much addicted to arms that she hardly uses other exercises and so generously valiant that she never hurt a Portuguese after quarter was given and commanded all her servants and soldiers to do the same."

She was a charismatic leader who regularly addressed her legions and prompted the desertion of thousands of slaves who were enlisted in the Portuguese army. She was named queen at the age of 41 because she was a shrewd military strategist and shrewd diplomat. She and her tribe were fierce enough to form a human chain to prevent the docking of Portuguese slavers.

African history has provided the role models for an expansion of our concept of what heroism can be. But few of us have taken the cue. When this store of wealth has been exploited, it has generally been by white male writers who bleach the history of Dahomean Amazons and turn them into Wonder Woman and Queen Hera. It is clear that the history of African women has many epic figures for those interested in the fantasy genre. But why have so few black women writers been intrigued by either this genre or this history? The possible reasons are numerous.

Until the broad-based Civil Rights Movement enslavement was the most significant metaphorical (and real) event in Afro-American history. Its far-reaching effects on society have yet to be fully explored by anyone, former slave or former slave owner. But one of the distinct legacies of that most peculiar institution was a perversion of the Afro-American sense of worth in our own culture and a sometimes prosaic proscription of how literature functions.

Post–Civil War depiction of fictional Afro-American women generally (with some exceptions) devoted itself to the uplift of the race. The market was saturated with delicate, educated mulattoes whose *raison d'etre* was to prove that blacks were human too. Over the years the scope of black women characters has expanded to include the now familiar roster of mammy, sex kitten, slut, long-suffering survivor or victim, matriarch and bitch. While the matri-archal or independent characters—Eva Peace, Nanny, Pilate—have provided what might be termed heroic figures, it is, interestingly enough, the last character, the bitch, who comes closest to being mythic.

WESTERN HEROISM

European/American heroism is predicated on male domi-nance, usually exemplified by some deed which serves to rescue the female object of his affection as a metaphor for wresting society from the grip of evil. But for the Afro-American woman this kind of romanticism is antithetical to our heroism. We have as fre-quently had to be the rescuer as the rescued in this society. Roman-tic heroism implies that women must be deferential and dependent, abdicating our responsibility to perform personally or politically mythic deeds. We must be appendages of men, complementary to and symbolic of their heroism.

Independent action is often depicted as that of the 'bitch,' a woman whose frustration has left her devoid of civility and ser-vility. And, to take it a step further, concurring with Barbara Christian's analysis in her book on black feminist criticism: "the stereotypic qualities associated with lesbian women: self-assertiveness, strength, independence, eroticism, a fighting spirit, are the very qualities associated with us (meaning black women in general). Qualities that we have often suffered for and been made to feel guilty about because they are supposedly 'manly' rather than 'feminine' qualities . . . " These are the charges leveled at the 'bitch' but the same words are accolades for the male hero.

This type of black woman character is close to mythic because, unlike the traditional female figures, even those black women who are strong survivors, the 'bitch' is the center of her own world. She controls her life and will stop at little to achieve her goals. Such a character is Cleo Judson in Dorothy West's *The Living is Easy* originally published in 1948.

In the story of Cleo, born of modest means, is majestic, disdainful, self-centered. She schemes to outwit anyone including her husband and wrings profits from anyone she sets her sight on. She is self-preservation run amok. Yet in spite of these extremes or maybe because of them, Cleo is one of the most compelling characters in our literary history. As I read I sit in amazement at the cleverness and ruthlessness of each deed, often hoping against hope that Cleo will repent and do something for 'the greater good.' And although she, unlike Scarlet O'Hara (another great 'bitch' figure) never does, the character has resonance certainly worthy of her name. Although her mythic deeds are largely negative Cleo lives as a quintessential, larger-than-life character.

One figure with the potential for the mythic status in our culture is the Conjur Woman. She has been tangentially explored in Afro-American literature only occasionally. Several stories by Alice Walker and others use the Conjur Woman as an otherworldly force whose magical capabilities are both fear and awe-inspiring. But the Conjur Woman has not yet become a staple in the lexicon of fantasy fiction. Marie LeVeau remains a mythic prototype awaiting the birth of her progeny.

The question still remains: why? Modern feminist literature has spawned numerous novels in the fantasy/science fiction genre. Where are the black women? Another reason for the absence may be the overwhelmingly oppressive social and economic conditions which make it difficult to focus on what *might* be. What actually *is* has loomed over us so horrifically. We have been trapped in the metaphor of slavery and its immediate ramifications and at a loss as to how to extrapolate an independent future. And, of course, the previously noted demand (whether explicit or implicit) that art serve politics is a further consequence of that history. Ironically as we serve politics our writing is also reflecting politics. The sexism in our society is also sexism in our creative thinking.

The inability to see ourselves as the center of anything, even our own lives, has, in one sense, allowed black women to be a backbone of the black community but it has also limited our perspective of the world. Frequently any expression of black female commonality has been interpreted not as a move toward the liberation of all black people but as a traitorous rejection of black men. Although it was acceptable for black nationalists in the 1960s to say that the only position for black women in the revolution was prone, our attempt to refute that is termed an insurrection.

In the July/August 1985 issue of *The Black Scholar* Calvin Hernton described the scurrilous attack mounted against Ntozake Shange after the production of her play, "For Colored Girls Who Have Considered Suicide When the Rainbow Is Enuf." She was called man-hating, a rip-off and a pawn of white people in the destruction of black malehood. But what was really infuriating to her critics was not that her poems libeled black men (which they did not).

Everyone who pointed to Beau Willie Brown as a subversive assault on black men conveniently ignored the loving portraits Shange drew of Toussaint L'Ouverture, Toussaint Jones and artists like Olive Lake, Willie Colon, Archie Shepp and Hector Lavoe. The real scandal for her detractors was that most of her poems were not really about men at all. While men may have been present, the black woman's experience was the center at all times, a heroic stance not commonly accepted in black women.

Hernton speaks out as one of the first black men to admit that brothers were resentful specifically because black women declared autonomy. He acknowledges what black women writers who participate in feminist and lesbian publishing have known all along: "The literature of contemporary black women is a dialectical composite of the unknown coming out of the known. It is an upheaval in form, style and landscape. It is the negation of the negative and it proffers a vision of unfettered human possibility."

This vision of "unfettered human possibility" is indeed what fantasy fiction is all about. And to be heroic or mythic within that context means for women in general and black women specifically having the ability to be a part of the survival of a community in the way we choose and at the same time keep one eye turned toward our own survival as black women.

This requires a clarity about responsibility to not only the whole but to the visionary possibilities of the individual. Without trying to cut through this theory with Occam's razor, I mention two pieces of fiction by black writers, Octavia Butler and Michelle Parkerson, that begin to open up this vision. These writers eschew the centuries old idea—as Barbara Christian points out—which dictates that heroism for women consists largely of being physically beautiful and overtly compliant.

FEMALE HEROISM

In Butler's 1979 novel, *Kindred,* the primary character, Dana, a black woman, mysteriously and literally vanishes from her modern urban home to reappear in a 19th century plantation in time to save the life of the plantation owner's son who is drowning. Repeatedly she is drawn involuntarily into the past to save the life of the boy who soon becomes a man. She learns that his survival is key to the birth of an ancestor of hers giving the rescues their dramatic glue.

Dana becomes an inexplicable fixture, reappearing over the years on the plantation providing the slaves with a magical, legendary character. Throughout the story Dana is distinguished by her refusal to react in any traditionally prescribed way. She consistently responds to physical danger with acuity as well as strength. She uses logic and cunning, relying only on certainties including her own intuition. She never casts others in the role of her protector.

Of course, part of her strength comes from the knowledge that there is another century to which she can return when the correct conditions exist that allow her to travel in time. She is unbowed by the punitive conditions of slavery to some extent because escape awaits her more easily than the others. But her assertiveness and wisdom are part of her personality in both worlds. As if to truly challenge Dana the author has given her several patriarchal figures to overcome: her husband, a young white writer, who in spite of his sensitivity is perpetually naive and has no real idea of what this experience does to his wife physically and psychologically. Then there is the petulant boy who grows into an egocentric and cruel slave owner; and the boy's father who remains confounded by the bewitching appearances and dangerously limited by his ignorance.

On Dana's final summoning to save the boy from a drunken accident it is clear what sort of dissolute wastrel he has become yet her response continues to be humane as long as he remembers her humanity. When he assaults her and attempts to rape her she kills him with little compunction. It is not an act of cruelty but survival—cleanly done—leaving her with sadness at the taking of life but no remorse. There is no stereotypical shrinking or shrieking, no abdication of responsibility for her own life. This is a mythic hero, traditional in her direct response to personal and social danger yet 'feminine' in her refusal to disengage her emotions from the actions.

The author is admirable in her ability to avoid the idealized concepts of heroism in her writing. Dana acknowledges her emotional needs but is not paralyzed by them. The author does not create an idyllic interracial marriage or overly sympathetic husband. Dana, the hero, acts out of both the ordinary and the extraordinary.

The second story I want to discuss is by Michelle Parkerson and is only five pages long. It is entitled "Odds and Ends, a new Amazon fable" and appears in her collection of poetry and prose, *Waiting Rooms*. It is set in 2086 when a war is raging and exists as almost a snapshot of two women warriors, Loz and Sephra, who are lovers.

In this short story Parkerson extrapolates the future from our violent past. "The race wars of earth escalated to cosmic insurrection. Colored peoples everywhere had taken enough and took up arms." The warriors here are women sustaining a pitched battle against invasion and trying to maintain some semblance of personal life.

The world at war is a traditional format for creating heroic figures although the segregation of the sexes has left women out of that picture except as nurses. Here Loz is a "reluctant warrior" who lingers in the love of her sister warrior. After returning from a three-day pass such love keeps her "dancing or killing, when all else fails." Parkerson uses her skills as a poet to make the colors of love and war vibrate for us throughout the story. She turns the familiar into mythology: the seventh sector is demarcated by Squeak's Bar-B-Q and Miss Edna's Curla Palace. And the warriors are not Rambo but women whose concern for each other is shown not just in their military responsibility but in personalized interdependence.

As Parkerson describes her, Loz's lover Sephra is the "last in a notorious line of lye throwers and lovely renegades." Although the scent of love is still fresh when the vandals break through the lines and overrun her base camp, Sephra loses no time springing into action. Sentiment is encapsulated in her final note to Loz, "I am a child of dread, born of veiled face and master number/a sable eye full of Loz and Armageddon . . . " Her message of love is transmitted while she detonates the grenade which breaks the ranks of the enemy and ends her life. Sephra takes her place as a true descendant of Cleopatra and Nzingha.

Here, just as the 'bitch' makes her own existence the center of her life, the hero makes the survival of the whole an extension of herself, the center of her being—not financial security, not men, not approval, not any of the things that traditionally relegate black women to the uncomfortable balance of the pedestal or the rearguard vantage point of the kitchen.

Having learned that such women heroes can exist why is it at all important for us to look for or create them in our fiction? It's not an accident that at moments of political upheaval fantasy or science fiction writing has taken on a greater resonance for the public. George Orwell's *1984* was the fruit of post-World War II devastation and the blood-curdling reality of the atom bomb. During the turbulence of the Civil Rights and Anti-War movements of the 1960s science fiction again re-gained popularity (*Stranger in a Strange Land*, the *Foundation* series) as those hoping to destroy oppressive traditions looked to the future for utopian visions.

And the women's movement has spawned a healthy body of fantasy fiction work, replacing the images of passive victims and strident agitators with shrewd warriors and hopeful women activists. A great many of these have been lesbian characters, rich with the 'stereotyped' qualities that Christian described: "fighting spirit, strength, eroticism." All black women hunger for that vision of independent heroics. It has more often been supplied by our poets. Writers like Alexis Deveaux, Colleen J. McElroy and Cheryl Clarke embrace the mythic forms and characters in their poetry.

It is important that our mythic figures exist because ideas do affect experience and theory can affect practice. If we can create a root system, a path to our independent action from our internal and integral sources of power we can make ourselves the center of our universe if only in our fantasies. We can then change the way in which we view ourselves in this society.

The Surrealists believed that in order to change the world you had to first change your dreams. The vampire character I've created in the *Gilda Stories* dreams of a place where death is a part of the natural order of life but not the prevailing currency with which power is acquired as it is now in our nuclear age.

She dreams of a time when the lovers she takes and the brothers she keeps are bound together by mutual respect and need and an expansionary concept of progress. I chose to make my black woman hero a vampire because no one would understand the cycles of blood and life more than a woman and because I wanted a character who had known the intimate horrors of our past and still had the capacity to dream grandly of our triumph.

While critics have often neglected to scrutinize fantasy or science fiction or place it within the context of literary and social constructs, the genre—like any other popular art form—is very intimately related to the sensibilities of the broad-based populace. It can be a barometer of our secret fears and secret dreams: dreams of solidarity, strength or heroism. And we, as a people, should be acutely aware of just how powerful dreams can be.

SELECTED BIBLIOGRAPHY

Octavia Butler, *Kindred,* Pocket Books NY, 1979.

Barbara Christian, *Black Feminist Criticism,* Pergammon Press, NY, 1985.

Cheryl Clarke, *Narratives, poems in the tradition of black women*, Kitchen Table Press, 1983.

Alexis DeVeaux, *Blue Heat,* Diva Publishing, Brooklyn, NY, 1985.

Calvin Hernton, "The Sexual Mountain and Black Women Writers," *The Black Scholar,* Vol. 16, No. 4, 1985.

Colleen J. McElroy, *Queen of the Ebony Isles,* Wesleyan Univ. Press, 1984.

Michelle Parkerson, *Waiting Rooms,* Common Ground Press, Washington, DC, 1983.

Ivan Van Sertima, *Black Women in Antiquity,* Transaction Books, New Brunswick, NJ, 1985.

Ntozake Shange, *For Colored Girls Who Have Considered Suicide When the Rainbow is Enuf,* Bantam Books, NY, 1981.

Alice Walker, *In Love and Trouble,* Harcourt Brace Jovanovich, NY, 1973.

Dorothy West, *The Living is Easy,* Feminist Press, NY, 1982 (reprint).

CHAPTER 8

Working-Class Womens' Ways of Knowing: Effects of Gender, Race, and Class

Wendy Luttrell

Well, I'm not schoolwise, but I'm streetwise and motherwise and housewifewise. I think there are two kinds of intelligence— streetwise and schoolwise. I don't know much facts about things I learned in school, but I know a lot about life on the streets. I guess I someday might be schoolwise if I stick to it long enough. But what I have now, what I know already, nobody can take away.

—Doreen

You don't need an education to be smart. I know people who can read and write and do their figures. They are smart but they just never finished school. Like me and my husband. We've learned a lot along the road—in that school of hard knocks. We've got what you call common sense.

—Beatrice

The two women just quoted come from distinctly different cultural backgrounds. Doreen, a student in a community-based adult education program, was born and raised in a white, ethnic

This article is a revised version of a paper presented at the 1988 Annual Meetings of the American Sociological Association. The author would like to thank Jean O'Barr for her encouragement and Martha Dimes Toher, Rachel Rosenfeld, Robert Shreefter, Jean Stockard, John Wilson, and Julia Wrigley for their perceptive comments on earlier versions. The author is also indebted to the women who participated in the study (whose names have been changed to protect confidentiality) for their patience, openness, and critical insights. Address all correspondence to Dr. Wendy Luttrell, Sociology Department, Duke University, Durham, North Carolina 27706.

working-class community in a northeastern city; she characterized her early school experiences as "uncomfortable" and explained that she could not wait until the day she could quit and go to work in the local box factory. Beatrice, a student in a workplace-based adult education program, was born and raised on a farm in the southeast; she described going to school as a luxury—something she could do only on rainy days, along with all the other black children she knew who worked for white farmers. Despite their differences, these women share some similar ideas about knowledge and a common framework for evaluating their claims to knowledge. They both distinguish between knowledge produced in school or in textbooks by authorities and knowledge produced through experience. They also have some similar ideas about their "commonsense" capabilities to take care of others. Their ways of knowing are embedded in community, family, and work relationships and cannot be judged by dominant academic standards. Most important, their commonsense knowledge cannot be dismissed, minimized, or "taken away."

This article describes and analyzes how black and white working-class women define and claim knowledge. It is based on participant observation in classrooms and in-depth interviews outside school with 30 women who enrolled in adult basic education programs. The article argues that although these women's conceptions about knowledge overlap, they are not the same and can be traced to differences in their lives. Both the similar and contrasting meanings that the women attached to their knowledge provide us with unique lenses through which to examine the development of gender, race, and class identities and consciousness.

The article begins with a brief discussion of the relevant literature and a description of the research methodology. It then examines the women's shared views of intelligence and common sense, exploring the conflicting working-class interests and values that are promoted through these self-perceptions. This section is followed by a description of hidden gender asymmetries and inequalities in working-class women's ways of knowing and how these asymmetries surface differently for black and white working-class women. The article ends with a discussion of how dominant ideologies of knowledge undermine women's collective identities, claims to knowledge, and power and the consequences for the adult education of working-class women.

RELEVANT LITERATURE

Although the literature has not specifically addressed working-class women's ways of knowing, several bodies of theoretical and empirical scholarship framed my study. First are ethnographic accounts that describe the schooling process as an arena of struggle in which dominant and subordinate cultures, values, and knowledge collide, producing both resistance to and compliance with dominant social relationships (Apple and Weiss 1983; Connell et al. 1982; Eisenhart and Holland 1983; Fuller 1980; Gaskell 1985; Holland and Eisenhart 1988, in press; McRobbie 1978; Valli 1983; Willis 1977). These accounts form the basis of a critical theory of education in their focus on the experiences of teenagers and young adults in secondary, vocational, or postsecondary education but do not address the issues that adults face when returning to school. This literature argues that working-class girls prepare for their future identities as wives, mothers, and workers through school. However, the women I interviewed seek to change their lives as women through education; their identities are already firmly embedded in cultural, community, family, and work relationships, yet their desire to expand, perfect, or contradict the work they do as women underlies their participation in school. An understanding of how they think they learn and know enables us to appreciate better how people negotiate external constraints and internal meanings in and outside school.

A second body of literature addresses the subjective experiences of adult learners. What is strikingly absent is a critical theory of adult learning that analyzes the production of meanings and class, racial, and gender identities through resistance to imposed knowledge and adult education practices. Although Freire (1970, 1972, 1973, 1978) outlined such a theoretical approach in his work on adult literacy, he minimized gender issues.

Only a handful of researchers have approached the issue of women's adult basic education or literacy practices from a critical perspective, exploring the dilemmas and double-binds that working-class women face as they pursue an education (Luttrell 1984; McLaren 1985; Rockhill 1987). Their accounts suggest that working-class women feel a deep conflict between self and others, placing their needs last either by choice or force. Therefore, if learning is to engage working-class women, it must be presented not only as an individual self-development process but as one that is rooted in family and community relationships (Luttrell 1984). In her study of Hispanic women learners, Rockhill (1987) argued that women participate in literacy education as part of the work of the family—a way to serve their children and husbands better and to comply with the dominant values of the middle class, femininity, and Anglo-ethnocentrism—but that women's participation in school also challenges Hispanic patriarchal family relations by threatening men's power and control. Despite her compelling analysis of what Hispanic women must risk to become literate and what is at stake when they are denied this basic right, Rockhill did not address the effects of those social, cultural, and political realities on how women learn and understand the world.

This is not to say that feminist questions have not surfaced in research on adult education. Some researchers have examined women's and men's differential access to adult education (McLaren 1981; Scott 1980), and others have explored the psychological, social, and economic impact of education on women's lives (Robinson, Paul, and Smith 1973, 1978). Although scholars generally agree that women's self-perceptions may improve as a result of adult education, some have found women's economic and occupational gains to be negligible (Lovell 1980; McLaren 1985). Still others have focused on the content and pedagogy of adult education courses, suggesting that women's lives and concerns are being minimized or neglected by adult education theory and practice, which further promote unequal gender relations (Hootsman 1980; Thompson 1983). But overall, the field has not provided a comprehensive approach to the understanding of power relations and resistance in women's learning and knowing.

Relevant to this issue is the burgeoning, yet controversial, feminist scholarship about "women's ways of knowing" (Belenky et al. 1986; Chodorow 1978; Gilligan 1982; Keller 1978, 1982), which is the third body of literature to frame my study. The literature claims that through unconscious psychodynamic processes, cognitive development, and gender-role socialization, women develop propensities toward self and knowing that are less linear, separate, and hierarchical than are men's. It also suggests that women's more continuous and connected sense of self-knowledge is embedded in their social relationships and sustained and reproduced by patriarchal Western conceptions of rationality. Both men and women internalize these concepts of rationality and knowledge that falsely dichotomize emotion and thought, objectivity and subjectivity, mind and body, masculinity and femininity (Bordo 1986; Fee 1983; Rose 1983; Smith 1979). Yet, although patriarchal impositions on knowledge may be said to exist, not all women experience them in the same way. Despite the call of feminist scholars for a more comprehensive discussion of differences among women and an examination of the construction of gender in specific historical and social contexts (Dill 1983; Jaggar 1983; Rosaldo 1980; Stack 1986; Thorne 1986), we still know little about the multiple meanings that women attach to the knowledge they have or are seeking and its relationship to the concrete conditions of their lives.

Finally, to understand the cultural and political significance of working-class women's ways of knowing, I drew on Thompson's (1963) analysis of class, culture, and consciousness as ways of living within certain relationships of power. These relationships are formed and change when people articulate and identify their class interests, capabilities, or concerns as being common to others like themselves and against those whose interests are different from (and usually opposed to) theirs. Applying Thompson's framework, I examined how black and white working-class women define their knowledge and capabilities in this way. Cognitive processes are usually understood as individual or psychological, not as part of class, racial, or gender culture and consciousness. Yet, a focus on women's claims to knowledge can help expand the parameters for explaining how consciousness develops in the context of political struggles.

METHODOLOGY

The findings reported in this article are from a study of the educational experiences and perceptions of black and white working-class women attending two programs: an urban, northeastern, community-based program serving a white ethnic working-class population and an adult basic education program serving predominantly black maintenance and housekeeping employees of a southeastern university. I chose these programs because they provide a unique access to working-class women learners. The community-based program, with its emphasis on supportive services for women, particularly day care, has made it possible for white working-class women, who otherwise would not have had or considered the opportunity, to continue their education. The workplace literacy program, with its four-hour-a-week work-release arrangement, makes adult education accessible to people whose family responsibilities and transportation problems seriously limit their participation in classes held at night. Both programs attract students who do not feel comfortable in middle-class educational settings, such as high schools or community colleges. In the classroom observations and in-depth interviews, the black women identified their workplace and the white women identified the local settlement house in which the program is housed as hospitable sites for adult learning.

I was first involved in both programs as an adult educator, teaching classes, training teachers, and developing learner-centered curriculum materials. Later, I returned to the programs to conduct research. I informed the women in each program that I was studying working-class women's experiences with and perceptions of education. I collected data in classrooms at different levels of instruction (zero to fourth-grade reading level, fifth- to eighth-grade reading level) preparatory classes for the high school equivalency examination, and community-college preparatory classes) and conducted unstructured interviews with over 200 women. I took notes openly during observations and the initial unstructured interviews. Field notes included descriptions of conversations before, during, and after classes. Notes from the unstructured interviews and classroom observations were coded on a variety of dimensions that emerged as persistent themes, including past school experiences, past and present family experiences and relations, self-concept and self-esteem, educational values, and future aspirations. These themes became the focus of the in-depth interviews.

I selected 15 women from each program to interview in depth. The stratified, selective samples represent the basic demographic profile of women in each community: their marital status, occupation, income, educational level, and religion. The samples also reflect the basic profile of women in each program: their age; past attendance and type of school; number of children living at home; and participation in a classroom, program, or community (active and inactive).

The 15 white women who were interviewed all grew up in a tightly knit, ethnic working-class urban community (mostly Polish and Irish) that has suffered from industrial relocation, inadequate social services, and neglect by officials for the past two decades. Like the subjects of other studies of white working-class communities (Kohn 1977; Rubin 1976), the majority of adults in this neighborhood drop out of or have no education beyond high school, are employed in skilled or semiskilled occupations, are paid an hourly wage, and experience periodic unemployment. All the women attended neighborhood schools (two-thirds attended public school and one-third attended Catholic schools) and since then have moved in and out of the work force as clerical workers, factory workers, waitresses, or hospital or teachers' aides. Two women were displaced homemakers when the study begin in 1980.

The black working-class women all grew up in southern rural communities and attended segregated schools. Their work histories are more homogeneous than the white women's in that they all work as housekeepers on the university campus, and some have done so for as many as 20 years. More than half have done domestic work in white people's homes either full time or to supplement their incomes, and most picked cotton or tended tobacco during their youth. Some women have split their work between service and farm labor in an effort to hold onto the land—a practice that is common among southern black working-class people (Stack and Hall 1982). Even though these women reside in different neighborhoods near the university, they share a common heritage in and identity with black rural communities.

The women in both groups shared one basic characteristic: all were mothers, aged 25-50, with children still living at home. The two groups differed, however, in which stage of the life cycle they were in, income, and marital history. Thus, black women of the same age as white women tended to be grandmothers and to have older children or grandchildren living at home. In addition, the family incomes of the white women were higher than those of the black women. And more white women were married at the time of the interviews; the proportion of never-married women with children was higher among black women than among white women, but the same number of black women and white women had dropped out of school because they were pregnant.

The final interviews took place in the women's homes, lasted from two to four hours, and were repeated over the course of a year. In the first interview, I asked each woman to tell me what she remembered about being in school—to describe what she liked and disliked and what kind of student she had been. As part of these accounts, the women also talked about their early work and family experiences. In the second interviews, I asked the women to talk about their current school experiences and what caused them to participate and to evaluate themselves as learners now. These discussions led to an exploration of the women's concepts of intelligence and knowledge. Although I had not included questions about intelligence or common sense in the original guide for the in-depth interviews, each woman inevitably brought up the issue of intelligence in response to the question, "How would you describe yourself as a student?" Definitions of intelligence and common sense, who possesses them, and how they are acquired focused the women's reflections about their capacities as learners. In the final interviews, I followed up on earlier discussions, asking the women to clarify their life histories or to respond to my interpretations of their experiences. This last interview was especially important for me because as a white middle-class researcher, I felt hesitant to interpret experiences that were so vastly different from my own.

The interviews were tape recorded and then transcribed. The interviews with the white working-class women were analyzed and written up as part of my doctoral dissertation (Luttrell 1984) before I began interviewing black women to deepen and expand my understanding and analysis of working-class women's ways of knowing. In analyzing all the interviews, I tried to balance between identifying persistent themes across the interviews and treating each woman's narrative as a unique text. Translating working-class women's ways with words into sociological analysis is problematic, but as other feminist researchers have argued, it is also the task at hand (McRobbie 1982; Oakley 1981; Smith 1987).

INTELLIGENCE AND COMMON SENSE

Individually, the women expressed diverse and wide-ranging definitions of intelligence, but as a whole, they distinguished between intelligence and common sense. Common sense was most often described as a category of "smarts" attained outside school—a form of knowledge that stems from experience and is judged by people's ability to cope with everyday problems in the everyday world:

Jim considers himself stupid. He's very good at what he does at his job, but he was never good in school. He has a kind of streetsmarts—he's the commonsense type. I don't know, I'm not sure that intelligence can be measured.

Intelligence is knowing how to use what you know—it's knowing how to do things. I think being intelligent means coping with things in life. Even people with high IQs or with college degrees don't know how to do the simplest, everyday things or cope with everyday problems—that takes *real* intelligence; it takes common sense.

"Real intelligence," or common sense, is a highly valued capacity that flourishes outside school. It is not measured by what school authorities teach you, but by what you can teach yourself or what you learn in the "school of hard knocks":

My brother is very intelligent—he's self-educated, not school educated. He reads a lot and has taught himself how to play musical instruments. I consider him one of the most intelligent people I know.

My father is *really* intelligent. He loves to read everything and is interested in all sorts of things. He graduated high school, but he did really lousy. But he's by far one of the most intelligent people around and what he knows he taught himself.

The women usually contrasted common sense with school intelligence and indicated that common sense can be ruined by too much education or formal schooling:

I don't think that intelligence has anything to do with schooling. Schools only make you know more. Education is not a sign of intelligence. But people who are well schooled always seem intelligent. I suppose they might not be any more intelligent than me. My husband has this idea that people with a lot of schooling don't have common sense. It is like the more schooling you have, the less common sense you have.

I used to beg my mother to let me go to school. She would say, "girl, you have no common sense." Or when I would want to read instead of doing my chores she would say, "You're never going to learn anything like that—you've got to have common sense in this world."

Common sense has been characterized as a cultural form of knowledge, a way to apprehend the world as familiar and knowable, and as concrete knowledge to inform action (Fingeret 1983a, 1983b; Geertz 1983). The women's definitions of common sense confirm these characterizations by identifying the knowledge that grows out of people's lived experiences. For these women, common sense is accessible; it requires no specialized training or credentials.

Common sense is a way of assessing or judging the truth on the basis of what people have seen and know to be true. The black women especially believed that you can assess the truth more reliably if you know the person or if the person is known by someone within the community. As Barbara said:

> The people I know have common sense. Like my grandmother. She knows a lot because she's seen a lot. She's seen it all and I believe what she says because she's been there. Like she knows about slavery, she didn't read about it, like all of us young folk.

In addition to its cultural base, common sense is also a class-based form of knowledge—a way that the women distinguished themselves from "professionals" and identified themselves as working class:

> INTERVIEWER: So who do you consider to be intelligent?
> DEBRA: I don't know. I know a lot of people who are very intelligent but they are fruity; I wouldn't want to be one. I have common sense. Maybe I have more intelligence than I'm aware of in some areas, but I am not an academic, learned person, and I don't think I'll ever be. I'm not the professional type. I can work with those kind of intelligent people, but I don't want to be like them.
> DOTTIE: I have just never thought about average people like myself being intelligent. People like me have common sense.

According to these women, common sense is not simply an individual characteristic or possession; it reflects working-class capabilities. Common sense affirms and validates working-class experiences and is a way to identify oneself with others who share problems and potentials, creating common bonds and a sense of community. This affirmation came across most strongly in the interviews when the women described how they solved everyday problems through common sense. To them, common sense means relying on family and friends who "know the ropes" to help you learn how to negotiate bureaucracies (schools, welfare agencies, and hospitals) and seeking advice from people who can be trusted, not because they are professional experts, but because they share the same problems. The claim of common sense recognizes and validates working-class solutions, despite the power of scientific knowledge. Common sense supports working-class judgments about what is relevant to everyday life and assessments about what one social historian referred to as "really useful knowledge" in educational practice (Johnson 1979).

Unlike common sense, which is easily defined and acquired through daily life experiences as part of working-class cultures, intelligence, which is acquired through schooling, cannot be so clearly defined and is in potential conflict with working-class cultures. For example, the women thought that although schoolwise intelligence can enhance one's life, it can also interfere with one's ability to meet the demands of working-class existence; they suggested that the *more* schooling one has, the *less* common sense she is likely to have. Similarly, "real intelligence" that is gleaned from books that people teach themselves to read can benefit working-class life, but schoolwise intelligence that is gleaned from textbooks or school authorities can come in conflict with working-class, especially black working-class, experiences and values.

By distinguishing between common sense and schoolwise intelligence, the women came to believe that a certain type of intelligence, rather than class, separates people and that intelligence, rather than class, determines a person's place in the social structure:

> Intelligence has to do with how people accept life, how life comes to them, and how they deal with it. My boys don't use their intelligence. I don't use half my intelligence. If I did, why would I be here?

The women's shared notions of intelligence embraced the dominant ideology of meritocracy in a capitalist society: people's class position is not fixed but is determined by their individual efforts and ambitions:

> There are a few people who make it. They are the ones that are blessed or that has intelligence. The rest of us just have to make do.

> The important point is that the system is not working. People's mobility is very limited. People really need education to get out of

their ruts. The system keeps people in their place, in their class. You need intelligence to get out of your place.

When I responded, "I know a lot of intelligent people living here," one woman replied:

> Yeah, but if they were more ambitious, like me—what I'm trying to do here is use my intelligence—then at least they'd have half a chance of getting out of their ruts.

The ideology of intelligence is a filter through which these women think about and express themselves as adult learners, denying the actual experience and knowledge they have in their everyday lives. The dichotomy they make between intelligence and common sense reflects the disjuncture between the world they know and experience directly and the dominant ideas and images that are fabricated externally, provide a way to understand the everyday world, and serve as a means of social control (Smith 1987). For this reason, although working-class women can claim commonsense knowledge, they are distanced from their intellectual capacities, as is Mary:

> When I was in grade school, one of my teachers said I was smart, so they put me in the advanced class. Now I didn't think of myself as smart until the teacher pointed it out. I would say I have common sense, but then maybe I am smart, maybe I'm intelligent, and I don't know it. But it's been my common sense that has gotten me by in life—how I get along with people—not my grades in school. You can bet on that.

In the end, the women accepted class stratification and relations of domination through the false dichotomy of common sense and intelligence and through class-based notions of "real intelligence."

GENDER-BASED KNOWLEDGE

When the women discussed commonsense knowledge and how it is gained, they revealed their belief that common sense is not a genderless concept. Instead, they indicated that men's claims to knowledge are superior to women's and affirmed the idea that men are more powerful by virtue of their knowledge, not the privilege they have as men. However, the pattern of this gender asymmetry and its impact on each group of women was not the same and thus requires a careful examination.

When talking about people they knew who were intelligent, the white working-class women gave only men as their examples. Although they described their mothers, aunts, or sisters as having common sense, they saw only certain aspects of common sense as "real intelligence"—those that are associated with men's work and their activities.

These differences are most evident in the women's distinction between mental and manual work and ways of knowing. Throughout the interviews, the white working-class women reiterated that intelligence is required to do manual work:

> The most intelligent person I know is my brother—he can fix anything. And when you get right down to it, what's more important than being able to make things work? Not everybody can do that, you know.

> Now just because we're going to school and getting educated, we shouldn't forget that people, like my husband, who work with their hands are just as important as college professors and just as smart.

But when the white working-class women defined manual ways of knowing as "real intelligence," they always referred to skilled manual work performed by *men*, not to the manual work required of women in factory jobs. Similarly, they equated men's physical common sense—the ability to work with their hands—with "real intelligence," never discussing women's ability to work with their hands, as in sewing.

In the same spirit, the women also equated men's self-learned activities, such as reading and playing a musical instrument, with intelligence, ignoring the wide range of activities that women teach themselves, including reading and helping children with homework. Instead, the white working-class women described themselves as "housewifewise," "motherwise," "good problem solvers," or "always balancing a lot of things, if that counts." They associated commonsense abilities with activities in the family or the community and considered them trivial.

Not only did the white women value men's common sense more than their own, they described the different ways that

working-class men and women acquire common sense. White
working-class men learn common sense that translates into "real
intelligence" through a set of collective, work-related experiences,
including apprenticeships, as sons or employees, or as participants
in vocational training programs that teach them what might be
called "craft" knowledge. This "craft" knowledge—the ability to
work with one's hands and muscles—belongs to the work group;
it is not individualized as a character trait and cannot be learned
from books. It also identifies one as masculine, capable of performing traditionally sex-stereotyped manly tasks. Men acquire
this masculinity and "craft" knowledge not by nature or instinct,
but through some public, collective experience. In contrast,
working-class women acquire common sense naturally, as intuition. They describe this knowledge as simply a part of being a
woman. As Anne explained:

> There are lots of things I know—what you might call woman's
> intuition or mother's intuition. Taking care of a child with a
> chronic disease teaches you this. You can begin to predict what
> the doctors are going to tell you and then you go home and deal
> with it on your own. That's just common sense; in the end, you
> do what you have to do as a mother.

For women, common sense stems from relational activities that
are embedded in the care and affiliation with others. They do not
recognize these activities as learned but associate them with feelings and intuition. Women's common sense comes in flashes, pre-
cipitated by an event such as childbirth or divorce. It can also
develop over the years, as women evaluate their ability to cope
with extenuating circumstances. The learning process is invisible
because this intuitive knowledge is individualized an personal. It is
not collective or public, even though it identifies women as feminine and able to fulfill sex-stereotyped roles as mothers and wives,
and is seen as affective rather than cognitive. As Cheryl explained:

> Common sense is a feeling, really. Like being a mother. You do
> things that seem right at the time. Nobody ever tells you to do
> this or do that. Although my sister, she just had a baby, drives me
> crazy always calling me up, saying "What do I do?" You'd think
> she would have a little more common sense than that.

The black working-class women also located their commonsense knowledge in a variety of caretaking and domestic skills done

for the benefit of others. Like the white working-class women, they referred to their common sense as intuitive and stemming from feelings and most often focused on the common sense that it takes to raise children:

> INTERVIEWER: Where did you get the common sense you have to raise your children?
> LOIS: I was born with it. Now I didn't always use it, like with my boys, but then I was young and running all the time. But you get older, you experience things, you know what's right to do for them and what they need. You're their mother and you stay close to them; you can just feel it.

The women's classification of their knowledge as "affective," not "cognitive"; as "intuitive," not "learned"; or as "feelings," not "thoughts" all reflect an acceptance of dominant conceptions of knowledge and ultimately diminish women's power. Feminist critics of dominant conceptions of knowledge have challenged these ideological dimensions of women's ways of knowing (Rose 1983; Smith, 1979). They have argued that just as the nature of women's domestic work makes it impossible to distinguish what is "love" from what is "labor," the nature of women's knowledge makes it impossible to distinguish what is emotional from what is objective or rational. They also noted that the false dichotomy between emotional versus objective labor promotes relations of authority and the domination of men (who are exempt from personal service work) over women (who perform unpaid domestic work as part of their gender role); this false dichotomy is translated into a distinction between feelings and thoughts. Women are then falsely associated with feelings, while men are falsely associated with thoughts (Fee 1983).

Because society does not view women as sources of official, legitimate, or rational knowledge (nor do women), the women who were interviewed associated their commonsense knowledge with feelings and intuitions. As class relations shape attitudes toward schoolwise versus commonsense knowledge, gender relations influence attitudes toward rational versus intuitive knowledge, thus constraining societal expectations of women's intellectual capabilities.

White and black working-class women are drawn to common sense and intuition because both forms of knowledge allow for subjectivity between the knower and the known, rest in women themselves (not in higher authorities), and are experienced directly in the world (not through abstractions). But both classifications (common sense and intuition) place women in less powerful positions vis-à-vis men (both black and white) and white middle-class professionals (men and women). And they do so not simply because women are fooled or seduced into believing in the ideological split between feelings and rationality, the false dichotomy of mental and manual work, or the promise of meritocracy, but because the real nature of women's knowledge and power is hidden from view and excluded from thought.

HOW RACE MAKES A DIFFERENCE

Women do not experience their exclusion in the same way, however; their daily experiences of maintaining a household, raising children, and sharing a life with men vary according to race and class and create different imperatives for women's ways of knowing. Race affects how women claim knowledge, which is reflected in how the black women differentiated common sense from "real intelligence." First, they did not make the same distinctions between mental and manual ways of knowing or emphasize the intelligence required to do manual work perhaps because black men have historically had limited access to the "crafts." Instead, they viewed common sense, most often referred to as "motherwit," as encompassing everything from solving family disputes to overcoming natural disasters. It was not uncommon for black women to identify both men and women relatives who possess common-sense capabilities that stem from keeping families together. As Lois said:

> I got my common sense from my momma and daddy. They worked real hard to keep us, and they would always be there to help anyones that needed it.

Second, unlike white women, black women did claim "real intelligence" for themselves and their experiences in doing domestic, caretaking work. This "real intelligence" is based on their ability to work hard and get the material things they and their children need and want, with or without the support of a man:

I got a sister I think she is smart, real intelligent. All of them is smart, but this one is special and she do the same kind of work I do but she's smart. She can hold onto money better than anyone. It look like anything she want she can get it. She bought her a car, this was in the 60s. Then after that she bought her a trailer. She don't buy that many cars, but anytime she or her childrens need something, she can go and get it. But she has a husband that help her, not like my other sisters or me. Her husband is nice to her and both of them working. But even that, it takes a lot of intelligence.

I would say my sister is the most intelligent person I know. She knows how to get what she wants and she has done it on her own, her kids and working; she ain't never been on welfare or nothing.

Black women are central in keeping black families together— swapping resources and child care and adapting to adverse economic constraints through extended kin networking and mutual support (Jones 1985; Ladner 1972; Stack 1974). As a result, their work as women is also the work of black survival and, therefore, is not as easily diminished or trivialized as that of the white women.

The ability to deal with racism—another type of real intelligence"—is also something black women learn through doing domestic work in the service of others.

> KATE: I'll tell you what takes real intelligence—dealing with people's ignorance. One day, I was at the department store, you know, maybe it was Belk's. I was getting on the escalator and there was this little white boy pointing at me saying to his daddy, "look there at that nigger." Now you should have seen the look on his daddy's face; he looked scared, like I was going to start a race riot or something. He pushed this boy along trying to get out of my way fast. But I know children and they don't mean what they say. He was just saying what he hears at home. But people are ignorant, and it takes real intelligence to know that it's not that little boy's fault.
>
> INTERVIEWER: And how did you get that kind of intelligence?
>
> KATE: Oh, well, you live and learn. You see a lot and watch people. It's a feeling you have to have because not all white people are the same. I sure know that 'cause I worked for different ones, you know, taking care of their children, and I've seen different things.

This "real intelligence" is acquired by virtue of being a black woman in a white world. It is also a knowledge that black women share equally with black men. It is collective, learned through extended-kin relations, and practiced in daily interactions with white people.

Class-based concepts of intelligence and common sense pit experience against schooling and working-class people against middle-class people; race-based concepts of "ignorance" and "real intelligence" pit whites against blacks. But the invisible gender-based concept that pits collectivity against individuality and autonomy against dependence is the basis for unequal power relations between working-class men and women. The craft knowledge of white working-class men, like scientific knowledge, which is acquired through collective experience and consensual agreement on what constitutes a "fact," is seen as more legitimate and therefore more powerful in the hierarchy of knowledge. White working-class women's knowledge, which is acquired through individual or private experience, seems to provide no basis for consensual agreement to legitimate the "facts" of caretaking. The particulars of meeting individual needs make it impossible to universalize this knowledge and thus make women's collective claims to the knowledge of relationships unthinkable. Therefore, women's knowledge and power are structurally excluded from thought. Similarly, because intuitive common sense comes from domestic responsibilities that are not recognized as work, it appears that white working-class women do not initiate their knowledge but must be receptive when it comes; thus, the actual hard work, mastery, and collective nature of their activities in acquiring knowledge are concealed. It also appears that white working-class men seek autonomy through their knowledge and that white working-class women preserve relationships through theirs; this false notion undermines women's claims to authority or power.

Black women, however, claim knowledge not only through gender, but through racial identity and relations. Their intuitions and claims to the knowledge of relationships are part of a collective identity as black women. This knowledge is a particular, not a universal, kind in that one must be black to have real knowledge about the world of white people, who are often "ignorant" (prejudiced). Both black men and black women collect and disseminate their knowledge within extended-kin and community relationships and through hard manual work. The result is that black women are not distanced from their knowledge and power. The daily reminder of their collective identity as working-class blacks mitigates the daily reminder of their individual identity as women.

KNOWLEDGE: PARADOX OR POWER?

The women's images, concepts, knowledge, and ways of knowing must be seen as integral to the practice of power. To understand how claims to knowledge become empowering, one can apply Thompson's (1963) analysis of how class identities and interests get defined in opposition to ruling-class interests and see that when women define and claim their knowledge, they articulate class and race relations the most clearly. All the women acquire common sense in opposition to middle-class professional people, and black women acquire "real intelligence" in opposition to white people. This "real intelligence" poses whites, who lack the knowledge of racism or who behave in racist ways, as "ignorant"—regardless of their education, status, income, or power—against blacks who "know better." In the struggle to maintain dignity and self-respect in a world that judges people according to white middle-class standards, the "real intelligence" and knowledge of blacks and the common sense of working-class people suggests the possibility of collective autonomy and power. However, women's claims to motherwise common sense do not suggest their collective autonomy and power because women's knowledge is not acquired as a group in opposition to men, but, appears to be individually intuited. Thus, the gender conflicts that exist are made invisible.

At the same time, black and white working-class women express these gender conflicts differently. White working-class women express a gender conflict when they talk about going to school to be "better" in relation to their husbands:

> I'm coming back to school to show my husband that he isn't the only one in the family who can carry on an intelligent conversation.

> I can't wait to wave my diploma in his face and say, "Listen here, I know what I'm talking about."

They also acknowledge a conflict when they identify the catalyst for enrolling in school as their separation or divorce. Ironically, white working-class women seek school knowledge to empower themselves. Since it is clear that their intuitive commonsense knowledge is valued less than is men's learned common sense, they turn to school knowledge to legitimate their opinions, voices, and needs—to be "better" in relation to their children, family members, and jobs.

Pursuing schoolwise knowledge puts white working-class women in a paradoxical situation and creates in them considerable ambivalence. Schooling puts a strain on working-class women's ties with the working-class culture—a culture that values commonsense knowledge and working-class men's "real intelligence" more than it does book learning and mental work. Yet schooling is perceived as one of the few avenues by which working-class women can achieve upward mobility. Consequently, working-class women must seek legitimation from the same source that undermines their knowledge and sense of identity (as women and as part of the working class). Nevertheless, working-class women's access to school learning and to white-collar jobs gives them an edge in the balance of power. If their common sense is inevitably valued less than is the common sense of husbands, brothers, or fathers, having schoolwise *and* motherwise intelligence is perhaps their only chance. In the end, white working-class women embrace the dominant concepts of knowledge because doing so not only promises them class mobility but gives them their sole legitimate form of power vis-à-vis working-class men.

Black working-class women express this gender conflict differently. Although they do not embrace the dominant white male value of knowledge, they attribute black men's power to black men's superior knowledge. In addition to all the many skills that black men have developed to survive, the black women mentioned that black men's "real intelligence" is getting black women to "take leave of their senses." Black men have the ability to convince black women to do the very things they have sworn they will not do. Thus, black women see black men's knowledge as the power to dominate black women and black women's lack of intelligence or common sense as their willingness to accept domination:

> I lose my common sense when it comes to men. I don't know how it happens. They're just so smart getting you to listen to them and what they want. I should have learned that lesson by now, but I haven't—it's just plain stupidity on my part.

> There's lots of kinds of intelligence. It's not so easy to say. And sometimes I have it and sometimes I don't, you know the com-

mon sense type. I can get myself into some trouble when I don't. I sure need more, but not the kind we get here in school. I mean John, you know, he can get me to do just what he wants, just like that. And that takes real intelligence, it takes something to get me to do things I know's not good for me.

In the end, unequal gender relations are concealed through the women's notion that men's power lies in their intelligence or knowledge and not in their culturally sanctioned license to dominate women in many ways, including sexually.

The paradox for black working-class women vis-à-vis adult education is complex, reflecting the multiple layers of their oppression in American society. Although black working-class women do not seem to need schoolwise knowledge to legitimate their power within black communities, they do need ways to balance and legitimate their power with black men and with white men and women. They have been denied entrance to the pathways to legitimation with whites, however, through their systematic exclusion from schooling and jobs that provide the social and economic resources for upward mobility. So black women may appear less ambivalent about their ways of knowing and less willing to embrace dominant white middle-class values of knowledge, but the arenas in which their knowledge, intelligence, and common sense can be developed and disseminated have been severely limited.

In addition to this discrimination, some "scientific studies" have suggested that blacks are genetically inferior to whites in intelligence; these studies have had devastating effects on public educational policy and practice with regard to blacks, warping the expectations of both blacks and whites about what black people can achieve. Another erroneous finding that educators commonly believe is that black women are genetically more intelligent than are black men (Reid 1975). In this context, black women's claims to schoolwise intelligence are problematic and may be destructive to the relationships of black men and women. Furthermore, although there has been a parallel system of black education, which historically has provided for the development of black identities, interests, and knowledge (Giddings 1984), black working-class women have not always been its beneficiaries.

That black women's pursuit of adult education is embedded in all these contexts necessarily casts schoolwise intelligence and book learning in a vastly different light for them than for white working-class women. White working-class women's antagonism toward schoolwise intelligence is grounded in their class consciousness, but black women's conflict stems from their "dual consciousness"—of being black and working class. Although the ways in which these multiple constraints are manifested in classroom learning are beyond the scope of this article, it should be emphasized that, ultimately, black women's claim to "real intelligence" cannot be easily translated into perceptions of academic skill or competence.

CONCLUSION

The differences between white and black working-class women's claims to knowledge reveal that women do not have a common understanding of their gender identities and knowledge. But what they *do* have in common is the organization of knowledge as a social relation that ultimately is successful in diminishing their power as they experience the world. To understand women's exclusion requires an examination of the similarities and differences in the objective conditions of women's lives, as well as an analysis of how ideologies of knowledge shape women's perceptions and claims to knowledge. Since women do not all experience the work of being a woman in the same way, it is impossible to identify a single mode of knowing. To understand why certain forms of knowledge appear more amenable to women, we must look more closely at the ethnic-, class-, and race-specific nature of women's experiences, as well as the values that are promoted in each context.

In the end, the paradox and the challenge of education for all women under patriarchy are to confront the balance of power as they pursue new and different kinds of knowledge. What is important to emphasize, however, is the *ideological nature* of the knowledge women seek. The universality and rationality of schoolwise knowledge conceal its opposite: that credentials and instrumental reason are not answers to asymmetrical and unequal social relationships. If women are to *claim* rather than simply *receive* an education—an act that "can literally mean the difference between life and death" (Rich 1979, p. 232), we feminists, sociologists, and educators must be prepared to untangle both the ideologies and objective conditions in women's lives that render our work, knowledge, and power invisible.

REFERENCES

Apple, M. W., and L. Weiss. (1983). "Ideology and Practice in Schooling." Pp. 3–33 in *Ideology and Practice in Schooling*, edited by L. Weiss. Philadelphia: Temple University Press.

Belenky, M. F., B. M. Clinchy, N. R. Goldberger, and J. M. Tarule. (1986). *Women's Ways of Knowing: The Development of Self, Voice and Mind*. New York: Basic Books.

Bordo, S. (1986). "The Cartesian Masculinization of Thought." *Signs: Journal of Women in Culture and Society* 11(3):439–456.

Chodorow, N. (1978). *The Reproduction of Mothering: Psychoanalysis and the Sociology of Gender*. Berkeley: University of California Press.

Connell, R. W., D. J. Ashenden, S. Kessler, G. W. Dowsett. (1982). *Making the Difference: Schools, Families and Social Division*. London, England: George Allen & Unwin.

Dill, B. T. (1983). "On the Hem of Life: Race, Class and Prospects for Sisterhood." In *Class, Race and Sex: The Dynamics of Control*, edited by A. Swerdlow and H. Lessinger. Boston: G. K. Hall & Co.

Eisenhart, M., and D. Holland. (1983). "Learning Gender from Peers: The Role of Peer Groups in the Cultural Transmission of Gender." *Human Organization* 42(4):321–332.

Fee, E. (1983). "Women's Nature and Scientific Objectivity." In *Women's Nature: Rationalizations of Inequality*, edited by M. Lowe and R. Hubbard. New York: Pergamon Press.

Fingeret, A. (1983a). "Common Sense and Book Learning: Cultural Clash?" *Lifelong Learning: the Adult Years* 6(8).

———. (1983b). "Social Network: A New Perspective on Independence and Illiterate Adults." *Adult Education Quarterly* 33(3):133–146.

Freire, P. (1970). *Pedagogy of the Oppressed*. New York: Seabury Press.

———. (1972). *Cultural Action for Freedom*. Harmondsworth, England: Penguin Books.

———. (1973). *Education for Critical Consciousness*. New York: Continuum.

———. (1978). *Pedagogy-in-Process*. New York: Continuum.

Fuller, M. (1980). "Black Girls in a London Comprehensive School." In *Schooling for Women's Work*, edited by R. Deem. London, England: Routledge & Kegan Paul.

Gaskell, J. (1985). "Course Enrollment in the High School: The Perspective of Working-Class Females." *Sociology of Education* 58:48–57.

Geertz, C. (1983). *Local Knowledge: Further Essays in Interpretive Anthropology*. New York: Basic Books.

Giddings, P. (1984). *When and Where I Enter: The Impact of Black*

Women on Race and Sex in America. New York: William Morrow & Co.

Gilligan, C. (1982)., *In a Different Voice: Psychological Theory and Women's Development.* Cambridge, MA: Harvard University Press.

Holland, D., and M. Eisenhart. (1988). "Moments of Discontent: University Women and the Gender Status Quo." *Anthropology and Education Quarterly* 19:115–138.

———. (In press a). "On the Absence of Women's Gangs in Two Southern Universities. In *Women in the South,* edited by H. Mathews. Athens: University of Georgia Press.

———. (In press b). "Women's Ways of Going to School: Cultural Reproduction of Women's Identities as Workers." In *Class, Race and Gender in U.S. Education,* edited by L. Weiss. Buffalo: State University of New York Press.

Hootsman, H. M. (1980). "Educational and Employment Opportunities for Women: Main Issues in Adult Education in Europe." *Convergence* 13(1–2):79–89.

Jaggar, A. (1983). *Feminist Politics and Human Nature.* Totowa, NJ: Rowman & Allenheld.

Johnson, R. (1979). " 'Really Useful Knowledge': Radical Education and Working-Class Culture, 1790–1848." In *Working Class Culture: Studies in History and Theory,* edited by J. Clarke, C. Critcher, and R. Johnson. New York: St. Martin's Press.

Jones, J. (1985). *Labor of Love, Labor of Sorrow: Black Women, Work, and the Family from Slavery to the Present.* New York: Basic Books.

Keller, E. F. (1978). "Gender and Science." *Psychoanalysis and Contemporary Thought* 1:409–433.

———. 1982. "Feminism and Science." *Signs* 7(3):589–602.

Kohn, M. (1977). *Class and Conformity.* Chicago: University of Chicago Press.

Ladner, J. (1972). *Tomorrow's Tomorrow: The Black Woman.* Garden City, NY: Doubleday Anchor Press.

Lovell, A. (1980). "Fresh Horizons: The Aspirations and Problems of Intending Mature Students." *Feminist Review* 6:93–104.

Luttrell, W. (1984). "The Getting of Knowledge: A Study of Working-Class Women and Education." Unpublished Ph.D. dissertation, University of California at Santa Cruz.

McLaren, A. T. (1981). "Women in Adult Education: The Neglected Majority." *International Journal of Women's Studies* 4(2):245–258.

———. (1985). *Ambitions and Realizations: Women in Adult Education.* London, England: Peter Owen.

McRobbie, A. 1978. "Working Class Girls and the Culture of Femininity." Pp. 96–108 in *Women Take Issue: Aspects of Women's Subor-*

dination, edited by Women Studies Group CCCS. London, England: Hutchinson.

———. (1982). "The Politics of Feminist Research: Between Talk, Text and Action." *Feminist Review* 12:46–57.

Oakley, A. (1981). "Interviewing Women: A Contradiction in Terms." In *Doing Feminist Research*, edited by H. Roberts. London, England: Routledge & Kegan Paul.

Reid, I. (1975). "Science, Politics, and Race." *Signs: Journal of Women in Culture and Society* 1(2):397–422.

Rich, A. (1979). "Claiming an Education." In *On Lies, Secrets and Silence*. New York: W. W. Norton & Co.

Robinson, J., S. Paul, and G. Smith. (1973). *Project Second Start: A Study of the Experience of a Group of Low-Income Women in Adult Programs at Brooklyn College*. New York: John Hay Whitney Foundation.

———. (1978). *Second Start Revisited*. New York: John Hay Whitney Foundation.

Rockhill, K. (1987). "Literacy as Threat/Desire: Longing to Be Somebody," Pp. 315–333 in *Women and Education: A Canadian Perspective*, edited by J. Gaskell and A. T. McLaren. Calgary, Alberta, Canada: Detselig Enterpirses Ltd.

Rosaldo, M. (1980). "The Use and Abuse of Anthropology." *Signs* 8:389–417.

Rose, H. (1983). "Hand, Brain, and Heart: A Feminist Epistemology for the Natural Sciences." *Signs: Journal of Women in Culture and Society* 9(1):73–90.

Rubin, L. B. (1976). *Worlds of Pain: Life in the Working-Class Family*. New York: Basic Books.

Scott, N. A. (1980). *Returning Women Students: A Review of Research and Descriptive Studies*. Washington, DC: National Association for Women Deans, Administrators, and Counselors.

Smith, D. (1979). "A Sociology for Women." In *The Prison of Sex: Essays in the Sociology of Knowledge,* edited by J. Sherman and E. Beck. Madison: University of Wisconsin Press.

———. (1987). *The Everyday World As Problematic: A Feminist Sociology*. Boston: Northeastern University Press.

Stack, C. (1974). *All Our Kin: Strategies for Survival in the Black Community*. New York: Random House.

———. (1986). "The Culture of Gender: Women and Men of Color." *Signs: Journal of Women in Culture and Society* 11(2):321–324.

Stack, C., and R. Hall. (1982). *Holding on to the Land and the Lord: Kinship, Ritual, Land Tenure and Social Policy in the Rural South*. Athens: University of Georgia Press.

Thompson, E. P. (1963). *The Making of the English Working-Class*. New York: Vintage Books.

Thompson, J. (1983). *Learning Liberation: Women's Responses to Men's Education*. London, England: Croom Helm.

Thorne, B. (1986). "Girls and Boys Together, But Mostly Apart: Gender Arrangements in Elementary Schools." Pp. 167–184 in *Relationships and Development*, edited by W. Hartup and Z. Rubin. Hillsdale, NJ: Lawrence Erlbaum Associates.

Valli, L. (1983). "Becoming Clerical Workers: Business Education and the Culture of Feminity." Pp. 213–234 in *Ideology and Practice in Schooling*, edited by M. Apple and L. Weiss. Philadelphia: Temple University Press.

Willis, P. (1977). *Learning to Labor: How Working-Class Kids Get Working-Class Jobs*. New York: Columbia University Press.

CHAPTER 9

Racism and the Limits
of Radical Feminism

Lindsay Murphy and Jonathan Livingstone

RADICAL FEMINISM

The modern feminist movement arose at the end of the 1960s
with the confrontation between socialism and women's liberation.
It grew out of the failures of the socialist movement to deal ade-
quately with the oppression of women, and the sometimes extreme
sexism in a movement dominated by men. Feminism started out
partly as a reaction against the socialist movement, as a radical
feminism reacting against a movement which would subordinate
women's struggle to class struggle, as though women's oppression
was merely an aspect of class oppression. Against this, feminism
emphasised the specificity of the oppression of women and the
autonomy of feminist struggle. It began to promote the development of feminist consciousness.

Juliet Mitchell wrote in 1971:

> Perhaps in the future, the biggest single theoretical battle will
> have to be that between liberationists with a socialist analysis,
> and feminists with a 'radical feminist' analysis. But that future
> has come too soon. The conflict is premature because neither
> group has yet developed a 'theory'. The 'practice' which is that
> theory's condition of production has only just begun. This is not
> an argument for 'holding our horses' . . . But it *is* an argument
> for the simultaneous necessity of radical feminist consciousness
> and of the development of a socialist analysis of the oppression of
> women.[1]

The feminist movement in Britain today is neither wholly radi-cal feminist, nor thoroughly socialist, but lies somewhere between the two, extracting principles from both. Because of this, the femi-nist movement is in a contradictory position which weakens it, setting it against itself: for socialist feminism and radical feminism lie at opposing poles and to draw from both poles simultaneously is to draw incompatible and contradictory principles.* This con-tradictory position becomes most pronounced and is seen most clearly in the feminist movement's perception of racism and of the relation of the oppression of women to the oppression of blacks, which in practice amounts to the position of black women within feminist politics. It is the issue of racism that has highlighted most clearly many of the limitations of radical feminist principles and the contradictions in its practice.

If we take radical feminism as the logical conclusion of a femi-nism not thoroughly socialist, in its strongest and most consistent expression, we can define its basic principles as follows:

1. *The oppression of women is the most fundamental oppres-sion.* Patriarchy, in other words, is the essential structure of all societies throughout history,** and thus capitalism and the op-pression of blacks (racism or 'whitearchy') are by-products of, sub-ordinate to and dependent on patriarchy. It follows from this that the oppression of women, being the fundamental or *primary* op-pression, overrides race and class oppression, which are subsumed by the oppression of women by men. Therefore *all* women, despite class or race differences, are bound to each other by their overrid-ing common interests as women. Thus:

2. *The primary commonality of women; or sisterhood.* Accor-ding to this, a woman has more in common with another woman of a different race and class than with a man of the same race and class.

3. *Patriarchy is totally independent of capitalism.* The oppres-sion of women, that is, is unrelated to the oppression of the work-ing class. The oppression of women has got nothing to do with the

---

*It will not surprise us to find that at the bottom of this contradiction lies a class antagonism.

**Kate Millet describes patriarchy as a 'universal (geographical and historical) mode of power relationships'.[2]

economic system, except in as much as patriarchy preceded capitalism and therefore participated in giving birth to it. In any case,
the conditions for getting rid of patriarchy in no way coincide with
the abolition of capitalism. If anything, it is the other way round—
get rid of patriarchy and you'll be rid of capitalism. Capitalism is a
subsidiary of patriarchy; the struggle for the liberation of women is
separate from the struggle for the liberation of the working class.
Capitalism is therefore the result of male (which is to say, biological) traits.

4. *Power is personal: of men over women*—severed from its
connection to any economic relations.* It is an end in itself. All
men, individually, have and wield this power. Thus:

5. *All men are sexist.* Which in turn implies that:

6. *There is an essence of woman and man.* Women, for example, are innately gentle, closer to the body, to nature, are natural
mothers, emotional, non-logical, etc.**—though any of these may
be deleted according to the exigencies of the moment. (It is necessary sometimes to portray women as strong, rational, aggressive;
at times, to stress that all women don't have to be mothers—
though at other times, it is claimed that women have the natural,
absolute right over their children, born or unborn.) Men are naturally aggressive, dominating, unemotional, etc. Coitus itself is seen
to be intrinsically violent, an act of man's power over woman—the
penis a weapon. Hence, radical feminism's 'extreme' slogans; 'disarm rapists', and even 'disarm men', since 'all men are potential
rapists'. It is all individualised: man is the enemy. (Some radical
feminists have even raised the problem that they don't know what
to do with their own sons.) Because men cannot, in their natures,
co-exist without conflict:

7. *Separatism is the end or goal of feminism*—and with separatism, necessarily, lesbianism (or masturbation).

It might be objected that radical feminism does not necessarily
embrace each and every tenet which we have listed, and that there
is not, anyway, such a thing as a unitary radical feminism which

---

*The economic relations of women, we believe, are not only those that take place
between men and women individually in the home, but the relation of women
(as housewives/mothers and cheap labour) in the general economic system.

**Compare the characteristics attributed to black people.

shares a set of agreed principles. This may very well be true. However, we maintain that these are the necessary conclusions of a feminism which isn't thoroughly materialist, and that for this feminism not to be contradictory, it must adhere to these principles.

All of these principles depend on one another, and the moment one thread of the argument comes undone, the whole of radical feminist ideology begins to unravel. For radical feminism to believe that women's oppression is the primary oppression, for example, it must believe that patriarchy is entirely independent of capitalism (i.e., that the oppression of women has nothing to do with the oppression of the working class). It must believe that the oppression of women is fundamental in order to believe in the primary commonality of women which overrides race and class differences; and, as a corollary, it must believe that race (and class) differences are subordinate to the sexual difference between men and women if patriarchy is to be an all-embracing structure. To believe that patriarchy is independent of capitalism, it is necessary to believe that there is some other, independent, force which is the cause of women's oppression, and this force is supplied by the notion of 'power'. But for this power to exist—whatever the mode of production and social relations—there must be some concept of essence, or human nature. If the sexism of men is due to their essence, all men must be sexist, none can be exempted. If, by nature, men and women must be waging a continual civil war, then separatism can be the only solution.

Radical feminists are often confronted with the limitations of the belief that women's oppression, and thus their unity, is fundamental, as they 'come to terms' with racism. For believing that all men are necessarily and innately sexist by virtue merely of being (biologically) men, it could equally be argued that all whites by virtue of their biological colour are racist.* (To argue that there is an essence of woman must be also to argue that there is an essence of black.) And if oppression (by men and whites) is derived from biology, what is the point of struggling against them? Radical feminism's answer is to call for separation from men.

------

*The argument that all whites are racist by virtue of being born white is exactly what Racism Awareness Training preaches. It too, like radical feminism, personalises power and asserts that all whites have power over all blacks by virtue of their colour.

If radical feminism accepts that all whites are necessarily racist, it can no longer maintain that women's oppression is the fundamental oppression overriding differences of race, since this view makes racism as fundamental as sexism and the unity of black people (men and women) as fundamental as the unity of women. But if this is allowed, the whole basis of radical feminism becomes undermined. The 'requests' of radical feminist groups and organisations for black women to join them and 'teach them' is an embodiment of this unresolvable contradiction.

ETHNICITY AND 'WOMEN OF COLOUR'

The struggles of black people in general (expressed vividly in the inner-city rebellions of 1981), and of black women within feminism, suddenly brought the oppression of black people to the fore and, with it, the crisis (of the contradictions) within feminism to a head. The white, middle-class feminist movement realised almost overnight that black women were more oppressed than they were, that black women were right at the bottom of the ladder. And suddenly blackness was everywhere.

Who is black? was the question on everybody's lips. Was black synonymous with 'Third World'? Was it a matter of self-perception? Was it a matter of skin-colour? Was it a matter of oppression? And if it was a matter of oppression, could one rank oppressions? On the ground, it meant deciding whether Turkish women could attend black women's conferences, or whether Iranian feminists could write on black women's affairs. 'The notion of "black women" as delineating the boundaries of the alternative feminist movement to white feminism', wrote Floya Anthias and Nira Yuval-Davis, 'leaves non-British non-black women (like us— a Greek-Cypriot and an Israeli-Jew) unaccounted for politically.'[3] One answer was to call such feminists 'women of colour'—a term borrowed from the United States, where it actually had a broader and all-encompassing definition.*

But what was to confound the women's movement yet further was the 'borrowing' or acceptance of the notion of ethnicity. After

---

*In this usage, the term 'women of color' includes Afro-American, Native American, Hispanic, Asian and Third World women in the US.

the 1981 rebellions, where black people overtly threatened the state, policies of ethnicity were elaborated 'to mask the problem of racism and weaken the struggle against it'.[4] And the unity of black people began to be fragmented as the state practices of ethnicity divided and even put into opposition the interests of the various 'ethnic' groups.

And nowhere was the fragmentation more stark than in feminism. The Cypriot women, the Jewish women, the Irish women, all claimed to be 'ethnic' minorities suffering oppression, all claimed to be equal victims of racism. Anthias and Yuval-Davis had already laid claim to the site of this grey area between white and black by differentiating themselves from black women, but at the same time claiming they were not white and were subjected to racial oppression (see above). They went on to say that although some struggles did concern 'all migrant women', other struggles had to be recognised as affecting only each individual ethnic group. But while accepting that racism differs in its strategies and that resistance to it likewise differs in its specificities, where would such a process of fragmentation on ethnic terms end? Along such a line of argument there is no limit to the divisions that can be made between black people, as each individual is affected (slightly) differently by racism.

Ethnicity was able to make such inroads into feminism precisely because of the dominance of radical feminist ideas in the movement. For as soon as radical feminism sets aside the entire mode of production as of no relevance, it reduces racism to a question of consciousness. And such consciousness (especially when personalised in the way typical of radical feminism) then becomes a matter of culture, colour or ethnicity. In practice, with the introduction of ethnicity into feminism, the issue of racism was confused, and even lost completely. And partly as a reaction to this, some black radical feminists have begun to assert that racism is a matter of skin-colour and that no one but Afro-Caribbeans has a right to use the term black. They demand that all other 'ethnic' women—including Asian women who have identified themselves as black—use the term 'women of colour'.

But, as Shaheen Haq, Pratibha Parmar, et al pointed out in a letter to *Spare Rib*, racism (and the definition of black) is not a question of lightness or darkness:

Statements such as 'West Indian women suffer the most because the "Blacker" a woman is the more oppressed she is,' create a hierarchy based on skin colour, rather than actual oppression and exploitation which are increased by class differences, sexuality, etc. Statistics show that Asian people are subjected to more racist attacks than Afro-Caribbean people—but again, this shows that skin tone is not a useful measure of oppression, *nor is it productive to quantify oppression* (emphasis added).[5]

Black people are united, whatever their 'colour', not by a common culture, but by their common oppression—even when that oppression differs in degree, or, as so often, seeks to divide them.

Distinguishing between black women and women of colour divides black women. On what basis is this distinction made, when: (i) Black does not designate a colour. Africans are no more black than Eskimoes are white; and people of colour may well be 'blacker' (i.e., darker) than black people. (ii) Black does not designate a culture. Black people may be of Caribbean or English culture, as may people of colour have a culture which is Indian, English or anything else. (Not to mention the fact that never is any 'culture' homogenous.) (iii) Black does not designate a 'race'. A black person or person of colour may be of 'mixed race'.

These gradations and differentiations of colour are, in fact, the *products* of racism. 'Whitearchy', or racism, has produced a hierarchy that reaches all the way up from blackness to whiteness. This hierarchy has less to do with actual skin colour or race and more to do with resistance to white domination. Those who are the most resistant tend to be painted the blackest, and those who are more easily 'integrated' are given a lavishing of white. To choose to be 'of colour' is to choose a no-man's land, or a no black-or-white-land between black and white; it is to accept the lavishing of white and to take one's place in the hierarchy.

Black culture, on the other hand, is created by and through the struggle against racial oppression. Black culture is the culture of resistance and rebellion—whatever form this may take. Black culture has nothing whatever to do with the white concept of ethnicity: it is its opposite. We have already discussed how the racist concept of *ethnicity* turns what is essentially an economic question about racism into a problem of culture caused by misunderstandings between cultures; and pointed to the divisions that ethnicity

creates between people. It is through ethnicity and the ethnic policies of successive governments that a class of collaborators has
been created, initially by means of the Community Relations Commission and its local Community Relations Councils.[6] But there is
another important aspect of ethnicity—or multi-culturalism—
which it is important to discuss and which seems to have escaped
mention.

This relates to Fanon's concept of 'cultural mummification'.
Why all this interest in (the white perception of) black culture, so
that it is not only taught to the police, social workers, black and
white children in school, but is even taken up by art and pop
culture? Why do the whites, after attacking these cultures for hundreds of years, suddenly want them resurrected—unless it is to
mummify them again? For, as Fanon says, the impact of colonialism and racism on native culture is not so much to destroy it as to
mummify it. Under that impact 'This culture, once living and open
to the future, becomes closed, fixed in the colonial status, caught
in the yoke of oppression.'[7]

Culture must be living, vital, responding to circumstances and
changing, unless it is to become a ghost. Multi-culturalism tries to
resurrect an old culture, a culture from the past, from a different
setting: a mummy to mummify. It takes what it supposes to be
black people's culture, separates it from its living historical context, and offers it, like a drug, to black people, to make them placid
and inert.

FEMINISM AND RACISM

Radical feminism, because it does not understand racism as an
oppression linked inseparably to certain economic interests (thus
personalising, ethnicising and colouring it), is threatened in its very
premises by the question of race. Are all whites racist—which
would make white women also the oppressors of black women,
and imply that racism is as fundamental as sexism; or are all
women, regardless of colour, united in sisterhood because the major division of society is the gender division? In the final analysis,
and after some contortion (see the debates in *Spare Rib* over the
past three years where attempts were made to call all whites racist
and, by virtue of skin colour, the holders of power over all black

women, regardless of other factors), radical feminism had to make racism subordinate to sexism or else cease to be radical feminism.

Once patriarchy (sexism) or, more plainly, men are posed as the root of all evil—all economic considerations put firmly out of play—the struggle against racism gets diluted, or disappears altogether. The concern is not then with racism, but with the most oppressed *women* in the struggle against, not 'whitearchy', but the rule of men. Black women, being more oppressed *women* than white women (a stipulation which ignores class differences), are ranked first in the league of oppressed women.

Much of the feminist movement's interest in black women is not a concern with racism, but a proclaiming of sisterhood with all the women of the world—validating the first principle of radical feminism: that patriarchy is the fundamental oppression. It is the same principle that underlies the radical feminist fantasy *Born in Flames*. In this film, women, regardless of their differences of race and class, were fighting together against men. Black women were fighting alongside white women against black men and white men; working-class women were fighting with middle-class women against working-class men and middle-class men. Race and class are overcome in the common and most fundamental struggle— against men.

Was there any racism in *Born in Flames?* Certainly, it contained stereotyped racist images of black women, and, as such, was a white fantasy of black women—but did it *portray* any racism? Not a jot. Black women become the heroines of the radical feminist movement—living proof of the correctness of its theories—and are granted a privileged position. Black women become more than women: they become *superwomen.*

Some feminists, however, do recognise that racism (whitearchy) is as fundamental as sexism (patriarchy). But even they (though not necessarily self-avowed radical feminists), in trying to assert some commonality between white women and black people, end up appearing to associate racism with maleness, thereby letting white women off the racist hook. Thus Hazel Carby, in a generally fine article on the boundaries of white sisterhood, uses the term 'herstory' for the writing of 'the story of women', but calumniates that same story as *his*tory when white feminists do not account for the lives of their black sisters:

> The herstory of black women is interwoven with that of white women but this does not mean that they are the same story. Nor do we need white feminists to write our herstory for us, we can and are doing that for ourselves. However, when they write their herstory and call it the story of women but ignore our lives and deny their relations to us, that is the moment in which they are acting within the relations of racism and writing history.[8]

Thus, when women are racist, they are not really being *white* (women), they are being *men*.

Susan Hemmings goes somewhat further in a key *Spare Rib* article on racism. After 'confessing' that because 'racism is so pervasive, so institutionalized', no 'white feminist can ever say in our lifetime "I'm not racist"', she suddenly turns tail and elects the white man as the problem: 'Feminists have pointed out that in our world "Man is the Prototype"—all the rest of us are measured, negatively against Him. But we might just as well say, "white Man".'[9]

A classic example of the tendency to make the white man the archetypal enemy can be taken from Beatrix Campbell. According to her, 'the feminist movement . . . is learning the hard way' that the notion of people 'dispossessed of politics'* 'cannot suppress the differences experienced by black and white, able bodied and disabled, working class and middle class women'.[10] But in the very next paragraph she says, 'There's only maybe one thing that they share and that is that they are not like white, able bodied, heterosexual men.' In the first paragraph Campbell admits to race and class differences (of experience, at any rate), only to thrust them aside in the second paragraph and reassert (in radical feminist fashion) the fundamental divide: that between men and women. So, even though white and black women may have different *experiences* (a term which suppresses the role of white women as *oppressors* of black women), they all share 'maybe' one thing, that they are not *white men*, who then, with facility, become the true oppressors (women and black men being rescued and the working-class white man thrown in with the rest).

Subsuming racism to patriarchy, as radical feminism must do, denies the autonomy of the black struggle. It seduces the struggle

---

*That is, those she considers outside 'the means of organisation, the machinery of politics' of the labour movement.

away from attacking racism and engages it in frivolous arguments and superfluous activities. White women hold a different attitude to black women than they would expect—or countenance—men to take in relation to them. White women are putting black women in positions in relation to them which they wouldn't dream of occupying in relation to men. Black women are being put forward to *explain* racism to white women! They won't talk to men about sexism, yet they *expect* black women to talk to them about racism!

Radical feminism, though interested in black women, is not really interested in racism. Nor is it interested in the working class. The working class (the class struggle) becomes identified with men. Prefacing an interview with women involved in the miners' strike, an editorial in *Outwrite* says:

> Whilst we in *Outwrite* celebrate women's participation in the strike, especially the solidarity that has been built up between women, we are distrustful of those male institutions like the N.U.M. (Arthur the born-again women's rights champion!), the Labour Party and the left in general, who are glamourising the women's action. It's all very well praising the miners' wives for being 'at the front line of the struggle' on the picket lines and keeping the homes and communities together (ie, over-exploiting themselves for the miners' cause).[11]

It is interesting to note (in a paper of generally more socialist than radical feminist tendencies) that instead of applauding women's participation in the class struggle, *Outwrite* celebrates especially the solidarity between women; it attempts to deny that the miners' cause *is* the women's cause (in the interests of their class); and it fails to understand their joint fight for their communities. Listen to the definition of *working class* given in *Spare Rib* (a magazine of predominantly radical feminist tendencies):

> All those who work with their hands. People often equate factory work with being working class but factory work isn't the worst paid or lowest status work in our society—homeworkers, farm workers and cleaners, for example, are worse off . . . the working class have a strong proud history here. But on the other hand, Black people and many women without men aren't even accepted into the working class.[12]

Radical feminism grew out of the failures of the socialist movement in relation to women's oppression. If it is to prevent further mutations, the feminist movement must return to the synthesis of feminist consciousness and socialist analysis that Juliet Mitchell spoke of in 1971. It is only when the struggle against oppression and against the capitalist system is seen as a *tri-partite* struggle—against the oppression of blacks (whitearchy), the oppression of women (patriarchy), and the oppression of the working class—that the black struggle, feminism and socialism stand together, autonomous yet inseparable, equal against the common enemy. Racism and sexism would then become irreducible to the oppression of the working class, which depends on them as they depend on each other and on it.

NOTES

1.   Juliet Mitchell, *Woman's Estate* (Harmondsworth, 1971), p. 91.
2.   Cited in Mitchell, op. cit., p. 64.
3.   Floya Anthias and Nira Yuval-Davis, 'Contextualising feminism: gender, ethnic and class divisions', *Feminist Review* (No. 15, November 1983).
4.   A. Sivanandan, 'Challenging racism: strategies for the '80s', *Race & Class* (Vol. XXV, no. 2, Autumn 1983).
5.   Letter to *Spare Rib* (No. 141, April 1984).
6.   A. Sivanandan, 'Race, class and the state', in *A Different Hunger* (London, 1982).
7.   Frantz Fanon, *Towards the African Revolution* (London, 1980), p. 34.
8.   Hazel Carby, 'Black feminism and the boundaries of sisterhood', in *The Empire Strikes Back* (London, 1982), p. 213.
9.   *Spare Rib* (No. 101, 1980).
10.   Beatrix Campbell, 'Politics, pyramids and people', *Marxism Today* (December 1984), p. 36.
11.   *Outwrite* (No. 28, August 1984).
12.   *Spare Rib* (No. 138, January 1984), p. 30.

PART 2

Curriculum Politics and Representations of Difference

Cultural Pluralism and Ethnicity

CHAPTER 10

Responding to Cultural Diversity in Our Schools

Roger L. Collins

The 1980s has been a decade in which the United States has absorbed the second-largest wave of immigrants in the nation's history. Unlike previous migrations from Europe, the increasing percentage of Hispanic and Asian immigrants signals increasing racial as well as cultural diversity among these latest arrivals. Further, group differences in birthrate increase the proportion of minority youth in our schools. Whereas minorities constitute approximately 15 percent of the total U.S. population, minority youth now make up approximately 25 percent of the nation's public school students, and that percentage is expected to rise slowly but steadily (Ascher, 1987; Hodgkinson, 1985, 1986; McCay, 1986).

The challenge of this increasing diversity for our schools can only be fully appreciated by acknowledging our past failures to provide quality education to racial and cultural minority students (see, for example, Carter and Segura, 1979; Gallimore and Boggs, 1974; Kennedy, 1969; Woodson, 1933). Whether one considers racial or cultural minority-group differences in dropout rates, expulsion or suspension rates, attainment or achievement levels, quality of instruction received, access to educational resources, and so forth, the data provide one overwhelming conclusion: most racial and cultural minority students have underachieved and have been underserved.

If we look beyond our national borders, we find interestingly similar patterns of "minority" student underachievement. From Canada, Europe, and Asia there is evidence that school failure is more frequent among the youth of castelike minorities: minority groups that are politically, economically, and culturally subordinate to a dominant majority group (Neisser, 1986; Ogbu, 1978). For instance, to cite one example of a linguistic minority, French-speaking Ontarian students in English language immersion programs perform less well in school than their French-speaking peers in French-speaking schools (Cummins, 1984). On the other hand, English-speaking, linguistic majority students in French immersion programs are not similarly disadvantaged when compared with their English-speaking peers in English schools (Cummins, 1986; Swain, 1984; Swain and Lapkin, 1981). Apparently student success in immersion programs depends on students' caste status: the English, linguistic majority students were successful in learning French as a second language, maintaining skills in English commensurate with their English-speaking peers, and attaining satisfactory academic achievement. French-speaking linguistic minority students, however, did not compare favorably with their French-speaking peers on any of these indices.

Many other examples of linguistic, cultural, or racial minority student underachievement have been identified in the work of Ulric Neisser (1986) and John Ogbu (1978). Whether considering the Franco-Ontarian students of Canada, Finnish students in Sweden, the Burakumi of Japan, or the Jews of North Africa, one discovers that the school performance of students as members of castelike minorities is far inferior to their performance as less stigmatized minorities. Several sets of barriers to educational attainment among castelike minorities have been identified in the literature. Although scholars debate the relative contribution of these barriers to the undereducation of minority students, it would appear that each is significant enough to warrant the attention of scholars and practitioners (see, for example, Ogbu [1987] and Trueba [1988]).

For members of many ethnic minorities, poverty resulting from historical discrimination reduces resources to apply toward school learning tasks and contributes sources of stress that interfere with school learning tasks (Bowles and Gintis, 1976; Glidewell, 1978; Wendling and Cohen, 1980). Discriminatory treatment in the labor market reduces the incentive value of education for many ethnic minorities in comparison with majority youth (Ogbu, 1983). There are also the problems related to racial and/or cultural differences. With the recognition that culture influences knowledge acquisition, cultural differences between home and school have become increasingly identified as barriers to learning (for example, Au and Jordan, 1981; Collins, 1988; Heath, 1983; Philips, 1983). Also, majority teachers' responses to cultural differences can include prejudices, lowered expectations, and forms of discriminatory treatment that contribute to minority student underachievement (for example, Jackson and Cosca, 1974; Marwit et al., 1978; Rist, 1970; U.S. Commission on Civil Rights, 1973; Yudof, 1975; Zucker and Prieto, 1977).

Given the breadth of these barriers to quality education, one should expect improvement in the educational attainment of minority students to result from effective responses to most, if not all, of these barriers. Focus on any one set of barriers is therefore necessarily limited. However, one particular set of barriers has long been a focus of attention and continues today as a major source of debate and disagreement among educators. That focus has been on cultural differences and the role these differences play in defining the problem of and effective responses to minority student underachievement.

During our country's earlier experiences with dramatic increases in cultural diversity among the school-age population, the general consensus was that cultural differences between European minorities and the "American" mainstream needed to be eliminated (see, for example, Carlson, 1975; Higham, 1974). Although there were pockets of resistance, most European immigrants viewed the assimilationist ideal as an acceptable demand in their pursuit of success in their new land (Bodnar, 1976; Olneck and Lazerson, 1974; Smith, 1969).

Still, there were other ethnic minorities for whom acquiescence to assimilationist demands were not sufficient for achieving success even after generations of effort. Unlike the European immigrant minorities, this latter group of ethnic *and* racial minorities, including blacks, Hispanics, and Native Americans, experienced pervasive discriminatory mistreatment regardless of their adherence to mainstream cultural expectations (Weinberg, 1977). The value of the assimilationist ideology was reduced for these racial minority-group members because of the absence of rewards and the erosion of cultural identity (Novak, 1971). Resistance to assimilationist ideology among members of racial minorities has taken many forms over the years. The cultural pluralistic perspective, however, has become recognized as a viable alternative to the assimilationist perspective toward cultural diversity.

Cultural pluralism is a broad construct or, perhaps, a cluster of constructs that share a general perspective. That general perspective is the view that ethnic minority groups maintain certain aspects of culture that are of value and deserving of being nurtured. The term *pluralism* acknowledges the multiplicity of subcultures within the society and, further, the challenge of integrating aspects of those cultures, including mainstream culture, within the schools and the students they serve (see, for example, Appleton, 1983; Epps, 1974; Stent et al., 1973).

Major areas of disagreement within this cultural pluralistic perspective, however, soon become readily apparent. First, there have been disagreements over which social groups ought to be identified within our "plural" society. Scholars have variously argued that pluralism should focus on "ethnicity" (blacks, Native Americans); "culture" (Amish, Appalachians); and "social" groups (gender, sexual identity/preference, political groups, social action groups) (see Appleton, 1976, for discussion of this debate). Further, with respect to the "cultural" component of "cultural pluralism," disagreements surface regarding what constitutes "aspects of culture" and which of these aspects are "of value." Also, there is the question of which aspects of "mainstream culture" should be acknowledged as worthy of explicit assimilation by ethnic minority youth (Delpit, 1986, 1988). Still, in comparison with the assimilationist perspective, the cultural pluralistic perspective is clearly distinguishable.

Cultural pluralism can be described metaphorically as a dynamic intertwining of the culture of home with the culture of power where the culture of home is defined as a minority group's shared ways of behaving, valuing, feeling, and thinking and the culture of power as "the mainstream" culture (Delpit, 1988). Further, within the cultural pluralistic perspective the process of intertwining the culture of home and the culture of power is made explicit for the learner in accordance with the learner's readiness for such study. Finally, the possible outcomes of intertwined cultures of home and power are also made explicit: the learner's option to perform competently within either culture, in accordance with situational demands; the option to synthesize, to amalgamate the cultures of home and of power; and the option to legitimize the culture of home within institutions dominated by the culture of power. Enabling minority students to pursue these choices is the objective of an emerging consensus among cultural pluralists.

The term *culture of power* is intended to draw attention to the premise that certain ways of self-presentation, certain ways of talking, interacting, writing, and so on, can serve to facilitate or hinder an individual's chances for success within "mainstream" institutions. When an institution is dominated by individuals from the majority culture, facility with that culture, the culture of power, can contribute to a minority person's chances for success. Often, the failure of culture-of-home advocates to acknowledge the importance of minority students' access to the culture of power leads to minority parents' resistance to a curriculum and instruction that promote, exclusively, the culture of home (Delpit, 1988). Cultural pluralism, however, does not view the cultures of power and of home as mutually exclusive.

The *culture of home* can provide a different focus for instruction than the culture of power; here, the emphasis would not be on acquisition but on making latent aspects of minority culture explicit so that, by means of instruction, those aspects become a source of pride and become a point of departure for acquiring the culture of power. For example, many black inner-city youth can apply their expertise in their culture of home in making explicit the patterns that define rap as street poetry and the criteria for evaluating that form of expression. In addition to acknowledging the legitimacy and value of their culture of home and black students' expertise in that culture, this sort of classroom activity provides a starting point for exploring patterns and evaluative criteria of poetic expression within the culture of power. Although there are many methodological questions as to how best to intertwine the cultures of home and of power, this example illustrates the basic premises of the cultural pluralistic perspective (Delpit, 1988).

Cultural pluralism goes further, however, in reevaluating both the appropriateness of instructional methods and curricular content. Recent research has identified important differences among ethnic minorities and the mainstream majority regarding preferences for the organization of instruction and participation in instruction. For example, several studies have noted that Native American children prefer and are more academically productive in classrooms that minimize the need for individual student performance and minimize direct teacher control over students (Cazden and John, 1972; Erikson and Mohatt, 1982; Philips, 1972, 1983, Ch. 7). These preferences coincide with the participatory norms of the culture of home of these Native American students.

Other studies have identified specific participatory styles as preferred by many members of other ethnic minority groups. For example, collaborative preferences for engaging in school learning tasks have been identified among Blacks, Hawaiian natives, and Hispanics. During the 1970s these preferences were identified as cognitive or motivational "styles" (Cohen, 1968, 1969; Kagan and Madsen, 1971; MacDonald and Gallimore, 1971; Ramirez and Castaneda, 1974; Ramirez and Price-Williams, 1974; Shade, 1982). More recently these preferences have been identified as "participant structures" and more closely associated with patterns of communication in the culture of home (Au, 1980; Diaz et al., 1986; Kagan, 1986; Kochman, 1981). The implication of this body of research is that classroom organization with respect to relations among students can either help or hinder the academic progress of many ethnic minority students. Specifically, classrooms that provide significant opportunities for ethnic minority students to engage in cooperative and collaborative participatory structures that parallel those of the culture of home are more likely to promote academic success among these students. Further, there is ample evidence that the performance of white students, and, by inference, the performance of ethnic minority students socialized by majority culture norms, is not impaired by their participation in collaborative learning environments (Edwards and DeVries, 1972; Edwards et al., 1972; Lucker et al., 1976; Slavin, 1977).

A cultural pluralistic perspective assumes that ethnic minority students do need to develop facility in the culture of power: at some point ethnic minority students need exposure to classroom structures that require interpersonal competition or independent work from students. However, cultural pluralists believe that classroom activity structures that diverge significantly from students' home culture expectations need to be introduced with all the care and forethought that an educator would use to introduce any new concept or new classroom structure. All of the prerequisite skills and experiences necessary for minority students' participation in these less familiar and less valued participatory structures need to be provided if the introduction of these structures is to be successful. Once again, however, the question of how to balance the culture of power and the culture of home in schooling remains open to debate. Returning to the educational goals of a cultural pluralist perspective, it would seem that sufficient exposure to the cultures of home and power needs to be provided so that students will have the option to perform competently within either culture, in accordance with situational demands; the option to synthesize or amalgamate the cultures of home and of power; and the option to struggle to legitimize the culture of home within institutions dominated by the culture of power.

Cultural pluralism also has implications for evaluating the appropriateness of curricular content studied by ethnic minority youth. Similar to the culture of power, we might conceive of a knowledge of power that provides a basis for attaining success within mainstream institutions. As with the culture of power, cultural pluralism advocates that minority students have access to that knowledge via the instructional methods previously discussed. However, because barriers to success are not equally distributed across all schoolchildren, one would expect to find different strategies for minority students' success reflected in the curriculum. Although many inner-city schools with large ethnic minority student populations have supplemented their curricula with topics on drug abuse, teenage pregnancy, and other social problems, much of this study has an aura of "extracurricular" deemphasis as compared to "regular" school. Even more distressing, however, is the fact that, for the most part, such study lacks any sort of social structural analyses of social problems.

Of course, many scholars argue that those who control the curriculum also control most of the society's institutions and utilize the curriculum to reflect their social and cultural reality (Anyon, 1979, 1981; Apple, 1979; Sharp and Green, 1975). Aspects of that reality include the rational, historical, political, and cultural bases for that social control. This would include victim-blaming accounts of social inequality that provide individualistic explanations of that inequality and avoid social structural explanations of wealth, poverty, political power, and oppression (Anyon, 1979; Brittan and Maynard, 1984, pp. 157–161). Scholars also have observed that these ideological biases of the curriculum are not shared by many poor and minority students and that this ideological conflict, in conjunction with the cultural conflict discussed previously, creates a climate of resistance to and rebellion against the school's authority among these students (Anyon, 1981, p. 33; Brittan and Maynard, 1984, pp. 173–179; Form and Rytina, 1969; Gurin et al., 1969; Huber and Form, 1973; Robinson and Bell, 1978).

A major question posed by many of these analysts, however, is whether or not the school's curriculum can ever be redesigned to eliminate ideological biases and include the conceptual tools that poor minority students need to succeed in this society. An "ideologically pluralistic" curriculum would have to acknowledge the social structural flaws in our society that maintain inequalities due to race, class, and gender and would help poor, ethnic minority students develop the skills they need to overcome and correct these flaws. Though still few, there are many more examples of cultural pluralism with respect to teaching methods than ideological pluralism reported in the professional literature (for example, Au and Jordan, 1981; Barnhardt, 1982; Campos, 1982; compare Brandt, 1986). It should be noted, however, that many current critics of the prevailing ideological biases in the curriculum do see student and teacher resistance to these biases as one basis for reform (Giroux, 1983a, 1983b).

The implications of cultural and ideological pluralism for teaching practice and teacher training are tremendous. Yet there are many barriers to overcome before reform in these directions can be realized. Of course, those who benefit from structural inequalities and who exert tremendous influence over curricular decision making are likely to resist curricular reform that reconceptualizes their historical and current role as maintaining social inequality. In addition to these political barriers there are also barriers related to the culture of power's ambivalence toward cultural differences, on the one hand, and toward social conflict, on the other. That both cultural differences and social conflict are inherent features of any pluralistic society is a perspective that remains at odds with the mainstream perspective which treats social conflict as a social disease (Appleton, 1983, pp. 155–190; Horton, 1966). Efforts to minimize and underestimate the significance of social conflict and cultural differences within our society are reflected in current debates over curriculum content from kindergarten through college (for example, Bloom, 1987; Hirsch, 1987; Thomas, 1981; cf. Simonson and Walker, 1989). Cultural pluralism as a response to the cultural diversity of those served by the schools requires not only culturally sensitive curriculum and instruction but also conflict-sensitive curriculum and instruction: schooling that reflects an appreciation for cultural differences and for social conflict as a means of promoting social progress (Boulding, 1966; Enloe, 1973).

Another major barrier to realizing a culturally pluralistic response to cultural diversity is the nascent nature of the research on home-school cultural discontinuities and the limited dissemination of the knowledge base that exists. Teacher trainees' access to research on cultural differences is limited because that research is often embedded in scholarly journals and the graduate-level curriculum. Furthermore, with the exception of many literacy programs, the knowledge base in cultural differences is more often available from departments in educational (including cultural) foundations as compared with departments of curriculum and instruction, with which teacher trainees spend significantly more time during the course of their training. What coverage of cultural differences there is in several education textbooks is not sufficient to challenge the prevailing theories and ideologies most trainees bring with them to teacher training. Yet, in the context of current teacher education reform, there are indications that teacher preparation may begin to address cultural differences from a culturally pluralistic perspective (Cazden and Mehan, 1989).

In conclusion, one would hope that the search for effective solutions to the problem of educating the growing proportion of minority students would lead educators to culturally pluralistic strategies. Whether evidence of their effectiveness can overcome cultural and political resistance to their use remains to be seen. As our society becomes increasingly aware of its dependence on the productivity of an expanding ethnic minority work force, one can assume that the search for effective responses to minority student underachievement will become more and more urgent and, hopefully, more and more informed.

REFERENCES

Anyon, J. (1979). Ideology and United States history textbooks. *Harvard Educational Review,* 49(3), 361–386.

Anyon, J. (1981). Social class and school knowledge. *Curriculum Inquiry,* 11(1), 3–42.

Apple, M. (1979). *Ideology and curriculum.* London: Routledge & Kegan Paul.

Appleton, N. (1976). Cultural pluralism: Must we know what we mean? *Philosophy of education 1976: Proceedings of the Philosophy of Education Society.* Urbana, IL: University of Illinois Press.

Appleton, N. (1983). *Cultural pluralism in education: Theoretical foundations.* New York: Longman.

Ascher, C. (1987). *Trends and issues in urban and minority education.* New York: Teachers College, Columbia University, ERIC Clearinghouse on Urban Education.

Au, K. (1980). Participant structure in a reading lesson with Hawaiian children: Analysis of a culturally appropriate instruction/event. *Anthropology and Education Quarterly,* 11, 91–115.

Au, K., and Jordan, C. (1981). Teaching reading to Hawaiian children: Finding a culturally appropriate solution. In H. Trueba, G. P. Guthrie, and K. Au (Eds.), *Culture in the bilingual classroom: Studies in classroom ethnography.* Rowley, MA: Newbury House.

Barnhardt, C. (1982). Tuning in: Athabaskan teachers and Athabaskan students. In R. Barnhardt (Ed.), *Cross-cultural issues in Alaskan education* (Vol. 2). Fairbanks: Center for Cross-Cultural Studies, University of Alaska.

Bloom, A. (1987). *The closing of the American mind.* New York: Simon & Schuster.

Bodnar, J. (1976). Materialism and morality: Slavic-American immigrants and education, 1890–1940. *Journal of Ethnic Studies,* 3, 1–19.

Boulding, K. (1966). Conflict management as a learning process. In A. de Reuch (Ed.), *Conflict in society.* London: J. & A. Churchill.

Bowles, S., and Gintis, H. (1976). *Schooling in capitalist America: Educational reform and the contradictions of economic life.* New York: Basic Books.

Brandt, G. (1986). *The realization of anti-racist teaching.* London: Falmer Press.

Brittan, A., and Maynard, M. (1984). *Sexism, racism, and oppression.* Oxford: Basil Blackwell.

Campos, J. (1982). *Evaluation report, 1982–83.* Carpinteria, CA: Carpinteria Unified School District.

Carlson, R. (1975). *The quest for conformity: Americanization through education.* New York: Wiley.

Carter, T. P., and Segura, R. (1979). *Mexican Americans in school: A decade of change.* New York: The College Board.

Cazden, C., and John, V. (1972). Learning in American Indian children.

In M. Wax, F. Gearing, and S. Diamond (Eds.), *Anthropological perspectives in education.* New York: Basic Books.

Cohen, R. (1968). The relationship between socio-conceptual styles and orientation to school requirements. *Sociology of Education,* 41, 201–220.

Cohen, R. (1969). Conceptual styles, culture conflict, and nonverbal test of intelligence. *American Anthropologist,* 71, 828–856.

Collins, J. (1988). Language and class in minority education. *Anthropology and Education Quarterly,* 19, 299–326.

Cummins, J. (1984). *Bilingualism and special education: Issues in assessment and pedagogy.* San Diego, CA: College-Hill Press.

Cummins, J. (1986). Empowering minority students: A framework for intervention. *Harvard Educational Review,* 56(1), 18–35.

Delpit, L. (1986). Skills and other dilemmas of a progressive Black educator. *Harvard Educational Review,* 56(4), 379–385.

Delpit, L. (1988). The silenced dialogue: Power and pedagogy in educating other people's children. *Harvard Educational Review,* 58(3), 280–298.

Diaz, S., Moll, L., and Mehan, H. (1986). Sociocultural resources in instruction: A context-specific approach. In California State Department of Education, *Beyond language: Social and cultural factors in schooling language minority students.* Los Angeles: Evaluation, Dissemination, and Assessment Center, California State University.

Edwards, K., and DeVries, D. (1972). *Learning games and student teams: Their effects on student attitudes and achievement.* (Technical Report No. 147). Baltimore: Center for Social Organization of Schools, The Johns Hopkins University.

Edwards, K., DeVries, D., and Snyder, J. (1972). Games and teams: A winning combination. *Simulation and Games,* 3, 247–269.

Enloe, C. (1973). *Ethnic conflict and political development.* Boston: Little, Brown.

Epps, E. (1974). *Cultural pluralism and education.* Berkeley: McCutcheon.

Erikson, F., and Mohatt, G. (1982). Cultural organization of participant structures in two classrooms of Indian students. In G. Spindler (Ed.), *Doing the ethnography of schooling.* New York: Holt, Rinehart & Winston.

Form, W., and Rytina, J. (1969). Ideological beliefs on the distribution of power in the United States. *American Sociological Review,* 34, 19–31.

Gallimore, R., and Boggs, J. C. (1974). *Culture, behavior, and education: A study of Hawaiian Americans.* Beverly Hills, Ca: Sage.

Giroux, H. (1983a). Theories of reproduction and resistance in the new sociology of education: A critical analysis. *Harvard Educational Review,* 53(3), 257–293.

Giroux, H. (1983b). *Theory and resistance in education.* South Hudley, MA: Bergin & Garvey.

Glidewell, J. (1978). The psychosocial context of distress at school. In D. Bar-Tal and L. Saxe (Eds.), *Social psychology of education: Theory and research.* New York: Wiley.

Gurin, P., Gurin, G., Lao, R., and Beattie, M. (1969). Internal-external locus of control in the motivational dynamics of Negro youth. *Journal of Social Issues, 25,* 29–54.

Heath, S. (1983). *Ways with words: Language, life, and work in communities and classrooms.* Cambridge: Cambridge University Press.

Higham, J. (1974). *Strangers in the land: Patterns of American nativism, 1860–1926.* New York: Atheneum.

Hirsch, E. (1987). *Cultural literacy: What every American should know.* Boston: Houghton Mifflin.

Hodgkinson, H. (1985). *All one system: Demographics of education, kindergarten through graduate school.* Washington, DC: Institute for Educational Leadership.

Hodgkinson, H. (1986). What's ahead for education? *Principal,* 65(3), 6–11.

Horton, J. (1966). Order and conflict theories of social problems as competing ideologies. *American Journal of Sociology,* 71, 701–713.

Huber, J., and Form, W. (1973). *Income and ideology.* New York: Free Press.

Jackson, G., and Cosca, G. (1974). The inequality of educational opportunity: An observational study of ethnically mixed classrooms. *American Educational Research Journal,* 11, 219–229.

Kagan, S. (1986). Cooperative learning and sociocultural factors in schooling. In California State Department of Education, *Beyond language: Social and cultural factors in schooling language minority students.* Los Angeles: Evaluation, Dissemination, and Assessment Center, California State University.

Kagan, S., and Madsen, M. (1971). Cooperation and competition of Mexican, Mexican American, and Anglo American children of two age levels under four instructional sets. *Developmental Psychology,* 5, 32–39.

Kennedy, E. (1969). *Indian education: A national tragedy—A national challenge.* Report of the Special Subcommittee on Indian Education of the Committee of Labor and Public Welfare, U.S. Senate. Washington, DC: U.S. Government Printing Office.

Kochman, T. (1981). *Black and white: Styles in conflict.* Chicago: University of Chicago Press.

Lucker, G., Rosenfield, D., Sikes, J., and Aronson, E. (1976). Performance in the interdependent classroom: A field study. *American Educational Research Journal,* 13, 115–123.

MacDonald, S., and Gallimore, R. (1971). *Battle in the classroom: Innovations in classroom techniques.* Soanton: Intext.

Marwit, K. L., Marwit, S. J., and Walker, E. (1978). Effects of student race and physical attractiveness on teachers' judgments of transgressions. *Journal of Educational Psychology,* 70(6), 911–915.

McCay, E. (1986). *Hispanic demographics: Looking ahead.* Washington, DC: National Council of La Raza.

Neisser, U. (Ed.). (1986). *The school achievement of minority children: New perspectives.* Hillandale, NJ: Lawrence Erlbaum Associates.

Novak, M. (1971). *The rise of the unmeltable ethnics.* New York: Macmillan.

Ogbu, J. (1978). *Minority education and caste.* New York: Academic Press.

Ogbu, J. (1983). Schooling the inner city. *Society,* 21(1), 75–79.

Ogbu, J. (1987). Variability in minority school performance: A problem in search of an explanation. *Anthropology and Education Quarterly,* 18(4), 312–334.

Olneck, M., and Lazerson, M. (1974). The school achievement of immigrant children, 1900–1930. *History of Education Quarterly,* 14, 453–482.

Philips, S. (1972). Participant structures and communicative competence: Warm Springs children in community and classroom. In C. Cazden & D. Hymes (Eds.), *Functions of language in the classroom.* New York: Teachers College Press.

Philips, S. (1983). *The invisible culture: Communication and community on the Warm Springs Indian Reservation.* New York: Longman.

Ramirez, M., and Castaneda, A. (1974). *Cultural democracy, bi-cognitive development, and education.* New York: Academic Press.

Ramirez, M., and Price-Williams, D. (1974). Cognitive styles of children of three ethnic groups in the United States. *Journal of Cross-Cultural Psychology,* 5, 212–219.

Rist, R. (1970). Student social class and teacher expectations: The self-fulfilling prophecy in ghetto education. *Harvard Educational Review,* 40(3), 411–451.

Robinson, R., and Bell, W. (1978). Equality, success, and social justice in England and the United States. *American Sociological Review,* 43, 125–143.

Shade, B. (1982). Afro-American cognitive style: A variable in school success? *Review of Educational Research,* 52, 219–244.

Sharp, R., and Green, A. (1975). *Education and social control*. London: Routledge & Kegan Paul.

Simonson, R., and Walker, S. (1989). *The Graywolf annual five: Multicultural literacy*. Saint Paul: Graywolf Press.

Slavin, R. (1977). Classroom reward structure: An analytic and practical review. *Review of Educational Research*, 47, 633–650.

Smith, T. (1969). Immigrant social aspirations and American education, 1880–1930. *American Quarterly*, 21, 523–543.

Stent, M., Hazard, W., and Revlin, H. (Eds.). (1973). *Cultural pluralism in education*. New York: Appleton-Century-Crofts.

Swain, M. (1984). A review of immersion education in Canada: Research and evaluation studies. In California State Department of Education, *Studies on immersion education: A collection for United States Educators*. Sacramento, CA: Author.

Swain, M., and Lapkin, S. (1981). *Bilingual education in Ontario: A decade of research*. Toronto: Ontario Ministry of Education.

Thomas, M. (1981). The limits of pluralism. *Phi Delta Kappan*, 62, 589, 591–592.

Trueba, H. (1988). Culturally based explanations of minority students' academic achievement. *Anthropology and Education Quarterly*, 19(3), 270–287.

United States Commission on Civil Rights. (1973). *Mexican American education study, Report V: Differences in teacher interaction with Mexican American and Anglo students*. Washington, DC: Author.

Weinberg, M. (1977). *A chance to learn: A history of race and education in the United States*. Cambridge: Cambridge University Press.

Wendlin, W., and Cohen, J. (1980). The relationship of educational resources to student achievement in New York State. Denver: Education Commission of the States.

Woodson, C. G. (1933). *Miseducation of the Negro*. Washington, DC: Associated Publishers.

Yudof, M. (1975). Suspension and expulsion of black students from public schools: Academic capital punishment and the Constitution. *Law and Contemporary Problems*, 39, 741–753.

Zucker, S., and Prieto, A. (1977). Ethnicity and teacher bias in educational decisions. *Journal of Instructional Psychology*, 4(3), 2–5.

CHAPTER 11

Toward an Understanding of African American Ethnicity

Alma H. Young

> I used to mull over the strange absence of real kindness in
> Negroes, how unstable was our tenderness, how lacking in genuine
> passion we were, how void of great hope, how timid our joy, how
> bare our traditions, how hollow our memories, how lacking we
> were in those intangible sentiments that bind man to man and
> how shallow was even our despair. . . . I saw that what had been
> taken for our emotional strength was our negative confusions, our
> flights, our fears, our frenzy under pressure.
>
> —Richard Wright in *Black Boy*

The question is often asked, Why has the African American
community been unable to harness its resources sufficiently to
advance socially and economically, as other ethnic groups have
done in this country? First, the question overlooks the fact that
African Americans have made significant socioeconomic and political gains since World War II. Second, the African American community has a strong tradition of self-help and self-reliance which
has made it possible to survive the degradation to which we have
been subjected and to withstand the varied (and sometimes vicious) attempts to divide us. Third, the question appears to ignore
the peculiar history of African Americans in this country, and the
fact that our progress has been artificially delayed by societal racism and official discrimination. Given the massive poverty and the
depth of the disadvantages that still beset the African American
community, self-reliance is not enough. To bring about the kinds of
economic and sociopolitical change that are needed is a public

responsibility. Thus, we must continue to demand of governmental bodies that they be active catalysts for change.

This essay is written to remind us of some of the difficulties African American communities face in using ethnicity as a tool for social and economic development. It is meant to serve as a corrective for those who would uncritically extol African American culture and African American heritage without first putting it within the larger socioeconomic context of U.S. society, as well as for those who would castigate the African American community for not doing enough to help itself. In this essay we are concerned with how the experience of exclusion has led African Americans to view themselves and others to view them.

ETHNICITY DEFINED

We address African Americans as an ethnic group, in which behavior becomes the most important distinguishing feature, and not as a racial group (that is, as a specific phenotype in which physical appearance is most important). An ethnic group may well include people of differing phenotype; and a recognized phenotype may create an identity that has marked behavioral consequences. Ethnic identity can be enduring, but because behavior has to be learned afresh in each generation, possibilities for rapid change exist.

According to most theorists, ethnicity has both a communal and personal dimension. For Enloe (1973, p. 15), ethnicity refers to a peculiar bond among persons that causes them to consider themselves a group distinguishable from others. The content of the bond is shared culture (beliefs, values, rules of interaction, and goals). "Cultural bonds grow out of the group's recognition of the distinctiveness of their own standards of behavior and prizing of those standards to the extent that the group members feel most secure when among persons sharing them" (Enloe, 1973, p. 16). On the personal level, ethnicity equips an individual with a sense of belonging; it anchors the individual in society.

Ethnicity depends on self-identification, not on objective categorization. However, the way individuals define themselves is partly a response to other people's perceptions of them. Enloe (1973, pp. 17–18) suggests that the following characteristics help define ethnic groups:

1. An ethnic group for the most part is biologically self-perpetuating.

2. An ethnic group shares *clusters* of beliefs and values. One value held in common by a number of persons is insufficient to sustain an ethnic community. These value clusters must find expression through associational forms. Ethnic groups possess communal institutions that parallel those of the larger society.

3. Finally, ethnic groups have internal differentiations. The width of the gap between intracommunal groups affects the community's political capacity to deal with outside pressure. For instance, class tensions within an ethnic group can frustrate its own politico-economic development. To be successful, an ethnic group has to be a network of regular communication and interaction.

Therefore, we may conclude that ethnic solidarity is *conscious* togetherness. This consciousness is generated and perpetuated through will, artifacts, and myths. It depends (in part) on the existence of other groups, and is often viewed in terms of "we" versus "them." Racial ethnicity, which is one of three main types (the other two being tribal and national), is characterized by values and bonds stemming from physical and biological distinctions. More than any other, racial ethnic groups are the result of someone else's prejudice (Enloe, 1973, pp. 24–25). Racial ethnicity has a physical base and is perpetuated largely by visual memory.

Bell (1975) and others suggest that ethnicity is best understood *not* as a primordial phenomenon[1] in which deeply held identities have to reemerge, but as a *strategic choice* by individuals who, in other circumstances, would choose other group membership as a means of gaining some power and privilege (Bell, 1975, p. 171: emphasis added). In other words, there is the joining of status issues to political demands through the ethnic group. For African Americans the heightened ethnic consciousness of the 1960s (commonly called the Black Power Movement, which succinctly juxtaposed the glorification of color and ethnic identity with the quest for greater power) led to significant political and social change. Ethnicity was consciously used to assert claims against the government.

However, African American ethnicity has proven almost useless in fighting economic marginality. Other ethnic groups have been able to use their ethnic identity to advance themselves not only politically and socially but also economically. There are countless stories of the economic success in this country of Koreans, Vietnamese, Chinese, Germans, and Italians. Patterson's (1977, pp. 54–65) discussion of the various kinds of ethnicity may help us to understand the reasons for differential success among ethnic groups. Three kinds of ethnicity are important to our discussion. First, there is *adaptive* ethnicity, in which the ethnic group becomes strongly conscious of itself as a distinct entity only when placed in an alien setting: the ethnic experience is temporary and prepares the group for entry into the wider society. Adaptive ethnicity is possible, however, only where the host society is essentially tolerant and inclusive of displaced minorities in its midst. In the United States, displaced persons who are not too ethnically different from the majority, such as the Germans during and after World War II, have been welcomed. Others have found their entry into U.S. society marred with obstacles.

Another kind of ethnicity discussed by Patterson is what he calls *symbiotic ethnic groups,* those with a highly developed sense of ethnic cohesiveness which predates their becoming aliens in the host country. Misfortune in war or economic necessity force them to migrate to the new land. They proceed to perform crucial middlemen roles in the new setting, such as shopkeeping or various skilled crafts. The economic roles these groups play for the host society are critical for the survival of the symbiotic ethnic group. The group uses its ethnic distinctiveness to advantage in playing its economic role. Jews have historically been included among this group. Today Vietnamese and other Asians in the United States may also be included.

A third kind of ethnicity, what Patterson terms *revivalist ethnic groups,* perhaps explains best the state of ethnicity among African Americans. Revivalist movements usually come about during the last stages of complete absorption by the dominant society when all that remains are fragmentary and largely sentimental cultural patterns which have little vitality or relevance to the absorbed group. *The group uses cultural symbols to express grievances.* The reinvesting of empty symbols with cultural potency becomes the means of expressing discontent, whether of a social, economic, or political nature. Whether African Americans can be said to be in the last stages of absorption by the dominant group and culture is a disputable point, but clearly during the height of the Black Power Movement cultural symbols were used to express discontent and articulate specific grievances.

"Black Power" can be seen as an attempt to define blacks ethnically by and for ourselves—to recapture blacks from self-negation. Therefore, it is a statement of cultural viability.[2] Yet for some, blacks and whites alike, black ethnicity has lacked the quality of authenticity. Kilson (1975, p. 243) suggests that black ethnicity has a "curiously dependent cultural cluster. It borrows from white society much, though not all, of its culture-justifying ingredients." Kilson goes on to suggest that in order to gain greater viability, black ethnicity has become wedded to politics. Yet participation in the political arena, which is dominated by the majority culture, is fraught with danger, especially for movements whose indigenous culture is ideologically diffuse or poorly differentiated from the dominant culture. Kilson (1975, p. 251) argues that this is true of black culture:[3] "so much of what it means to be black in America is intricately linked to white society, and the formation of black ideas, values and institutions occurs in complex dialectical interaction with this society." This dialectical interaction is historical and complex. Thus Kilson and others argue that the Black Power Movement served to consolidate power among blacks, but it did not broaden the power base significantly, nor did it eliminate the growing underclass.

THE FRAGILITY OF AFRICAN AMERICAN ETHNICITY

What appears as the fragility of African American ethnicity stems from several sources. First are the *cleavages within the African American community,* which have evolved in large part from the "white bias" that is prevalent throughout American life. The first cleavage, in the leadership itself, is between the established African American bourgeoisie and the bourgeois newcomers. Relatively well socialized into American politics and acculturated to middle-class lifestyles for two generations, the established African American bourgeoisie was at first marginal if not opposed to the black ethnic movement. Only through the effective politicization of black ethnicity by the bourgeois newcomers (the black middle class of the 1950s and 1960s) did a section of the established bourgeoisie discover (and participate in) the black movement. Yet the tension within the movement between the moderates and the "militants" remains to this day.

Physical differences among African Americans have also made it difficult to foster and maintain a viable African American identity. African-Americans are distinguishable by skin color and hair type. Color and hair have carried real symbolic potency and have served to divide us. Lighter color and straighter hair have always provided greater access to white patrons, which in turn has generally meant entrance to the middle class as a result of better educational opportunities, jobs, and housing. Besides color, other cross-cutting cleavages among African Americans include nationality (for example, blacks who are more recent immigrants from the Caribbean and Africa), class (the elite, the recent middle class, the working poor, and the ever-increasing underclass), and religion (fundamentalists, old-line Protestant groups, and Catholics).

For years the dominant society has tried to use the apparent differences among us to divide us and play one group off against another. The latest version is to blame the African American middle class for moving from the inner city and leaving behind a "disastrously isolated under class" (Lemann, 1986). As Billingsley (1987, pp. 105–106) points out, a number of fallacies exist with this argument: (1) It exaggerates the number of African American middle class who have left the inner city; (2) it assumes and asserts that moral values account for the ascendancy of the African American middle class and that the absence of those values on the part of the poor accounts for their lack of progress, even though we know that the poor have the same basic values that other Americans have—they simply lack the resources to actualize these values; and (3) it exaggerates the resources which the African American middle class took with them from the inner city and ignores the more powerful resources that took flight from the inner city even earlier—the white middle class and industry.

Cross-cutting cleavages would not be so problematic were it not for the second major source of the fragility of African American ethnicity, what Patterson (1982, p. 5) terms "natal alienation." *Natal alienation* is a loss of ties of birth in both ascending and descending generations, resulting in a "shallowness of genealogical and historical memory." African American ethnicity has been uniquely and indelibly impacted by the long and savage experience of slavery. Patterson argues that natal alienation is achieved in a unique way in slavery, for society's definition of a slave, however recruited, is as a socially dead person. Alienated from all "rights" or claims of birth, slaves ceased to belong in their own right to any legitimate order. Thus they experienced a secular excommunication. Patterson continues:

> Not only was the slave denied all claims on, and obligations to, his parents and living blood relations but, by extension, all claims and obligations on his more remote ancestors and his descendants. He was truly a genealogical isolate. Formally isolated in his social relations with those who lived, he also was culturally isolated from the social heritage of his ancestors. . . . Slaves differed from other human beings in that they were not allowed freely to integrate the experience of their ancestors into their lives, to inform their understanding of social reality with the inherited meanings of their natural forbears, or to anchor the living present in any conscious community of memory. (1982, p. 5)

To reach out for the past and for the related living, which records show the slave attempted, meant struggling against the master, his laws, and his security mechanisms.[4] Within their own communities slaves created a sense of legitimacy, based on values which they held dear. These values—among them, primacy of family, the necessity for individual enterprise and hard work, and an appreciation of the rights and responsibilities of freedom—have continued to be fundamental to African Americans. But the slave communities were not self-contained entities; they were constantly being permeated. In their interaction with whites, which was ever present, a new set of rules was forced upon them, rules which went against their very sense of humanity.

Thus there was the constant walking of a tightrope between what was viewed as legitimate behavior in their own communities and what was mandated as legitimate by the dominant, white community. For instance, slaves succeeded in establishing strong social ties among themselves. Yet these relationships were never recognized as legitimate or binding. American slaves had regular sexual unions, but such unions were never recognized as marriages. Both sets of parents were deeply attached to their children, but the parental bond had no social support. The master could and did forcibly separate slave couples and children from parents.

The sense of not belonging, of loss of ties in both ascending and descending generations, of loss of honor in having to recognize the slavemaster's authority, were the distinguishing marks of slavery and what gave slavery its peculiar value to the master. The slave was "the ultimate human tool, as imprintable and as disposable as the master wished" (Patterson, 1982, p. 7).

Institutionalized marginality (or social) death was the ultimate cultural outcome of the loss of natality, as well as honor and power. Patterson argues that it was in this that the master's authority rested. For without him, the slave does not exist. "The slave came to obey [the master] not only out of fear, but out of the basic need to exist as a quasi-person, however marginal and vicarious that existence might be" (Patterson, 1982, p. 46). One final point from Patterson is instructive for our discussion. Although slaves were socially nonpersons and existed in a marginal state, they were not outcasts. Slavery was primarily a relation of personal domination.

> There was an almost perverse intimacy in the bond resulting from the power the master claimed over his slaves. The slave's only life was through and for his master. Clearly, any notion of ritual avoidance and spatial segregation would entail a lessing of this bond. Second, the assimilation of the slave to the status of an occupational specialized caste would undermine one of his major advantages—the fact that he was a natally alienated person who could be employed in any capacity precisely because he had no claims of birth. . . . The essence of caste relations and notions of ritual pollution is that they demarcate impassable boundaries. The essence of slavery is that the slave, in his social death, lives on the margin between community and chaos, life and death, the sacred and the secular. (Patterson, 1982, pp. 50–51)

The experience of enslavement has been hard to overcome, not only because of the psychological damage that has been wrought upon us, but also because many see our color as a continuing visible mark of servitude. The color cannot be denied (although some have found ingenious ways of trying to overcome it), but the dilemma remains whether to enhance it or hide from it. The problem is made all the more acute because the cultural heritage that would make our ethnicity authentic was brutally stripped from us, and often we find only a mimicry of the dominant culture in our search for survival and acceptance.

Not only did our early history in this country force us to become culturally marginal, but it also forced us to become economically marginal. This *economic marginality* is the third and most important reason for the fragility of black ethnicity. The forces of law, tradition, and public regulation have perpetuated our inability to generate sufficient economic resources to ensure ethnic viability. Unlike some other groups, African Americans historically were not allowed to develop any economically or occupationally specialized roles. Slaves, of course, could be physically forced to perform whatever roles the master required. Shortly after emancipation, African Americans found their economic choices limited by the laws, customs, and regulations of Jim Crowism. The effects of racial discrimination, which, until relatively recent times, could be practiced with impunity, led us into economic positions that were precarious at best. Historically, African Americans have owned, managed, or controlled few businesses and have accumulated little wealth. We have depended largely on our ability to attain opportunities or resources from within the dominant community.

More recently, several major changes have served to keep African Americans in ever-increasing numbers at or below the poverty level. These include the structural changes in the economy, in which the United States has moved from a manufacturing-based economy, where wages were higher and upward mobility greater, to a service-based economy within a matter of decades; the "credentializing" of the society, where more and more years of schooling and degrees are needed to obtain even basic jobs; and the welfare system, where rules encourage the degradation of the family unit, and the provision of food and shelter is seen as a privilege instead of a right. Except perhaps for the established bourgeoisie, even those in the middle class fear that their economic roles are being diminished. African Americans have historically been, and continue to be, *economically surplussed.*[5] That is, the plethora of customs, laws, and government regulations have resulted in an African American work force that is generally underpaid and underemployed, if not outright unemployed. For instance, Swinton (1987, p. 69) has estimated that the net impact of the total labor market disadvantages experienced by African Americans in 1984 was about $60.2 billion, or 49.5 percent of the existing earnings of whites.

The economic situation in the United States, specifically the scarcity of jobs and the resulting increased competition among workers for jobs, has meant that some workers lose under these circumstances. African Americans have been disproportionate losers in this increased competition, primarily because of racial discrimination and the legacy of historic disadvantages. Consider the following national statistics:

- Blacks receive only 59 cents for each $1.00 attained by whites.
- The median income for black families is about 58 percent of white family income.
- Fourteen percent of black families receive less than $5,000 in annual income.
- About 33 percent of black families have incomes below the poverty line.
- The unemployment rate for blacks is still twice that of whites.
- The unemployment rate for black teenagers is approximately 44 percent.
- The majority of black children live in poverty. (Brown, 1988, p. 109)

The empirical data presented provide indisputable evidence that, for more than ten years, little progress has been made in attaining the national goal of ending the extensive inequality and poverty that have historically characterized the situation of blacks in this country. The empirical evidence shows that some black families have made impressive economic gains—in fact, there has been an increase in the proportion of blacks who can be classified as upper middle class. However, this limited upward mobility for a few cannot offset the stagnation and decline experienced by the larger numbers of black families whose economic status has deteriorated.

In a recent study comparing the wage levels of black and white workers between 1979 and 1987, Bennett Harrison and Lucy Gorhan found that the 1980s were especially bad for African American workers (see Harrison, 1990). For example, between 1979 and 1987, the number of "full-time-equivalent" white workers with wages below the poverty level for a family of four grew by 31 percent. For African Americans, the increase was 44 percent. By 1987, an African American was three times as likely to earn an income below the poverty line as a white worker. Even more disturbing was their finding that during the past decade the number of African American men aged twenty-five to thirty-four who have found jobs but who still earn a poverty wage increased by 161 percent.

Harrison suggests that the most disturbing finding was that higher education does not necessarily solve the problem. In 1987, the wages of one out of six white male college graduates were below the poverty line. For African Americans it was one out of three. Among female college graduates, three out of eight whites earned poverty-level wages in 1987, versus nearly half the African Americans. Even among African-American professionals, the findings are not good. in 1987, 300,000 *fewer* college-educated African American men earned $36,000 or more than earned the equivalent in 1979. The number of African American women with the same amount of income grew by a meager 7 percent during the decade.

STRATEGIES FOR ETHNIC SUCCESS

The African American community has been alarmed by these kinds of statistics for years and has sought ways to keep young people in school, families intact, and individuals at work. But to wonder why such statistics as Harrison reports exist or why African Americans have not been as successful as some other groups in using their ethnicity to achieve economic and social self-sufficiency is to deny the historical experience of blacks in this country. The brutality that forced us here and kept us as slaves, the marginal economic and social roles we have been forced to play, and the systematic discriminations to which we have been exposed limit our ability to generate resources. This is not to suggest that African Americans have not banded together to maximize the resources that we do have.

The idea of self-help is no stranger to the African-American community. The "self-help" tradition of building institutions and initiating efforts both to defend ourselves and to advance within a hostile society has long been a hallmark of African American life. The historic link to the tradition of self-initiated efforts to improve the lives of African Americans has never been broken. But greater leadership is needed to mobilize and enhance those efforts and the values they represent. These efforts must reach more broadly and find ways of sustaining coalitions that include the poorest among us and those who have been more fortunate. We must continue to draw upon our own resources, the most basic of which is the special value structure that has sustained us. Those values include the primacy of the family, the importance of education, and the necessity for individual enterprise and hard work. We need to renew our commitment to those historic values as a basis for action today.

Yet self-help alone is not enough. We must remember that ethnicity is learned behavior, based not only on how we interact with each other but also on how others react to us. The legacy of racism and covert and overt discrimination has resulted in problems in the African American community that are well beyond our capacity to resolve (see Committee on Policy for Racial Justice, 1987, p. 11). Job creation on the scale needed, restoration of the physical infrastructure in our neighborhoods, and the development of human resources (in terms of education, training, and health) require a concentrated effort by the government. However, during the Reagan presidency, the government retracted on all fronts. Estimates of the cumulative effects of federal social spending cuts between 1981 and 1987, as determined by the National Urban League, are approximately $114 billion (Jacobs, 1988, p. 7). The most severe budget cuts were in programs that invested in providing individuals with skills and opportunities, such as job training, which were a third smaller in 1987 than they were in 1981. Welfare and food stamp programs were also cut heavily. In the 1980s federal money for subsidized housing was slashed by 78 percent. The Reagan administration was also involved in a systematic attempt to undermine effective enforcement of civil rights. A new commitment by the government to work toward the eradication of all vestiges of poverty and discrimination must be pursued.

Thus the National Urban League's recent call for a "Domestic Marshall Plan" funded by the federal government speaks to the need for a coordinated national program against poverty and inequality (Jacobs, 1990). Inadequate housing, education, and jobs lessen the ability of African Americans to function as purposeful individuals within American society. By addressing some of our basic needs, the proposed $50 billion plan would begin to enable more African Americans to enter the social and economic mainstream of the United States. Enhancing the human potential of African Americans will allow us to begin to participate more competitively in the opportunities provided by American society. Only then will African Americans be able to create a stronger sense of community and cultural identity. That greater sense of self will help us to struggle against the injustices to which all African Americans are exposed.

A proper education would help to nurture our cultural heritage and pass the heritage along to succeeding generations. A proper education would also remind us of our peculiar history in this country and of the fact that the inexcusable disparities between African Americans and whites are the result of official and societal discrimination that denied us earlier access to equality and opportunity. Thus to compare ourselves uncritically to other ethnic groups is unfair and unproductive. But to be aware of our history is to embolden us, particularly our young people, to demand that adequate resources flow to African American communities. Such demand making will help give a sense of purpose to the lives of our young people. Their lives will take on greater meaning as they understand that the civil rights struggle continues and they have a significant role to play in that struggle. As Ronald Walters of Howard University has said so well, "There can be no civil rights without civil resources. . . . Gaining access to those resources must become the new civil rights agenda." Education can help us take up the struggle and advance the civil rights agenda. In the process African American ethnicity can become a greater force for social and economic change.

NOTES

1. Much of the literature is devoted to ethnicity as being nonrational, emphasizing primordiality and intensity of involvement and putting ethnic allegiance above all else. Thus the view was held that with "modernization" (that is, political and economic development) ethnicity would cease to be important. Clearly that has not been our experience in this country or elsewhere around the world. Often, in fact, economic and social progress has led to heightened ethnicity.

2. I would like to thank Dennis H. Young for suggesting this point.

3. There is little consensus on the characterization of the black culture. The debate begins with Melville J. Herskovitz, *The Myth of the Negro Past* (New York: Harper, 1941) and progresses through E. Franklin Frazier, *The Negro in the United States* (New York: Macmillan, 1948), Ralph Ellison, *Shadow and Act* (New York: Random House, 1964), and chapters by Nathan I. Huggins and Houston Baker in Nathan Huggins,

Martin Kilson and Daniel Fox, eds., *Key Issues in the Afro-American Experience* (New York: Harcourt Brace Jovanovich, 1971).

4. For a discussion of the current lively debate about the history of slavery, see Michael P. Johnson, "Upward in Slavery," *The New York Review of Books,* December 21, 1989, pp. 51–55.

5. This term comes from Janet Abu-Lughod, in a lecture at the University of New Orleans entitled "New Orleans as a Third World City," October 2, 1986.

REFERENCES

Bell, Daniel. (1975). Ethnicity and social change. In Nathan Glazer and Daniel P. Moynihan (Eds.), *Ethnicity: Theory and practice* (141–174). Cambridge: Harvard University Press.

Billingsley, Andrew. (1987). Black families in a changing society. In *The state of black America 1987* (94–111). New York: National Urban League.

Brown, Lee P. (1988). Crime in the black community. In *The state of black America 1988* (95–113). New York: National Urban League.

Committee on Policy for Racial Justice. (1987). *Black initiative and government responsibility.* Washington, DC: Joint Center for Political Studies.

Enloe, Cynthia H. (1973). *Ethnic conflict and political development.* Boston: Little, Brown.

Harrison, Bennett. (1990). The wrong signals. *Technology Review,* January, p. 65.

Jacobs, John. (1988). Introduction, In *The state of black America 1988* (8). New York: National Urban League.

Jacobs, John. (1990). Discussion on the *McNeil-Lehrer News Hour,* January 9.

Kilson, Martin. (1975). Blacks and neo-ethnicity in American political life. In Nathan Glazer and David P. Moynihan (Eds.), *Ethnicity: Theory and practice* (236–266). Cambridge: Harvard University Press.

Lemann, Nicholas. (1986). The origins of the underclass. *Atlantic Monthly,* June and July.

Patterson, Orlando. (1977). *Ethnic chauvinism: The reactionary impulse.* New York: Stein and Day.

Patterson, Orlando. (1982). *Slavery and social death: A comparative study.* Cambridge: Harvard University Press.

Swinton, David. (1987). Economic status of blacks 1986. *The state of black America 1987* (49–73). New York: National Urban League.

Multiculturalism

CHAPTER 12

Multicultural Approaches to Racial Inequality in the United States

Cameron McCarthy

Multicultural education emerged in the United States, in part, as a minority response to the failure of compensatory education programs launched by the Kennedy and Johnson administrations in the 1960s. Multicultural education is therefore a product of a particular historical conjuncture of relations among the state, contending racial minority and majority groups, and policy intellectuals in the United States, in which the discourse over schools became increasingly racialized. Black and other minority groups, for example, began to insist that curriculum and educational policy address issues of racial inequality, minority cultural identities, and the distribution of power within institutions such as schools themselves (Banks, 1988; Berlowitz, 1984). Proponents of multiculturalism were very much influenced by these radical possibilitarian themes. But, as we shall see, proponents of multicultural policies in education often "claw back" (Fiske and Hartley, 1978) from the radical themes associated with black challenges to the white-dominated school curriculum and school system.

In what follows, I will explore the theory and practice of multiculturalism as a contradictory and problematic "solution" to racial inequality in schooling. First, I will outline the historical developments in American schooling and state policy toward racial minorities that led up to the events of the 1960s and the emergence of multiculturalism in education. Second, I will closely examine the general perspectives, core ideological assumptions, and desired outcomes of three different types of multicultural policy discourses on racial inequality as embodied in various school curriculum and preservice teacher education program guides as well as in the articulated theories of proponents of multicultural education. As we shall see, there are subtle differences among these policy discourses. These differences, I will argue, have important ideological and political implications. The essay will conclude with a summary and some general observations.

HISTORICAL BACKGROUND

For over one hundred years and up until two decades ago, a basic assimilationist model formed the centerpiece of education and state policies toward ethnic differences in the United States. Schooling was looked upon as the institution par excellence through which American educational policymakers and ruling elites consciously attempted to cultivate norms of citizenship, to fashion a conformist American identity, and to bind together a population of diverse national origins (Kaestle, 1983; Olneck and Lazerson, 1980). This assimilationist ideology was rooted in the nativistic response of dominant Anglo-Americans to the waves of immigrants from southern Europe who came to work in urban factories at the turn of the century. These southern European immigrants were seen as a threat to a social order that was based on the values of earlier settled European American citizenry. The latter traced their ancestry to England, the Netherlands, and other northern European countries.

In 1909, Ellwood P. Cubberley, a proponent of "social efficiency" (Kliebard, 1986, p. 223), clearly stated the case for using civil institutions such as schools as vehicles for cultivating dominant Anglo-Saxon values among the new immigrants and their offspring:

> Everywhere these people [immigrants] tend to settle in groups or settlements, and to set up here their national manners, customs, and observances. Our task is to break up these groups or settlements, to assimilate and amalgamate these people as part of our American race, and to implant in their children, as far as can be done, the Anglo-Saxon conception of righteousness, law and order, and popular government, and to awaken in them a reverence for our democratic institutions and for those things in our na-

tional life which we as a people hold to be of abiding truth. (Cubberley, 1909, pp. 15–16)

In addition to promoting highly conformist practices and values in schools, policymakers turned to the coercive apparatuses of the state to control the flow of non-Anglo immigrants into the United States. Highly exclusionary clauses were written into the United States Immigrant Acts of 1917 and 1924 which drastically limited the number of immigrants that came from southern and eastern Europe, Asia, and Latin America (Banks, 1981).

For American minority groups, institutional assimilationist practices were even more stringent and definitively conformist. Efforts were made in educational institutions serving Hispanic, Native American, and black youth to rid these groups of "ethnic traits" (Banks, 1981, p. 4) that were considered inimical to the dominant American culture. Consequently, early twentieth-century institutions such as the Hampton Institute were designed to equip black and Native American youth with "the skills that would bring them to the level of the white middle class" (Kliebard, 1986, p. 126). The course in economics at Hampton, for example, "attempted to get blacks and American Indians to abandon certain undesirable practices in specific areas of practical concern such as the purchase of clothing and the consumption of food" (Kliebard, 1986, p. 126).

For most of the first half of the century, this assimilationist model of education was not seriously challenged, even though black protest groups such as the United Negro Improvement Association, led by Marcus Garvey, championed separatism and pluralism. Indeed, many prominent black as well as white middle-class intellectuals regarded the assimilation and cultural incorporation of American ethnic groups as a highly desirable social goal. In the 1920s and 1930s, the so-called Chicago School of sociologists, led by Robert E. Park (a former secretary to Booker T. Washington), outlined the basic assimilation model that was so influential in shaping research and social policy on race relations during the period. Park postulated that all immigrant and ethnic minority-group members went through a "race relations cycle" or trajectory on their way to eventual incorporation into the mainstream of American life. This cycle consisted of four stages: *contact, conflict, accommodation, and assimilation* (Omi and Winant, 1986, p. 15).

But for minorities such as blacks and Native Americans, assimilation meant a special kind of cultural incorporation into a racial order in which they were accorded a secondary status. The ideology of assimilation clearly benefited white Americans. White "ethnics," over time, were able to share in the rewards of the society from which black Americans were systematically excluded (Banks, 1981). Blacks, Native Americans, and Hispanics continued to experience severe discrimination and racial exclusion in housing, employment, and education during the first half of this century. During this same period, European immigrants—Irish, Italian, and Greek—came, settled, and consolidated their status in American society.

By the 1950s and 1960s, policies of assimilation lost credibility among many groups of racial minorities and were subjected to unprecedented challenges by oppositional black groups and the civil rights movement. These challenges were particularly strong in the area of education. Black and other minority groups contended that schools as they were organized in America were fundamentally racist and did not address the needs and aspirations of minority peoples. Minority groups demanded more control of institutions in their communities. They demanded greater representation in the administration and staffing of schools. Even more significantly, black youth and their political leaders demanded a radical redefinition of the school curriculum to include black studies. The latter demand constituted a strategic challenge to the taken-for-granted Eurocentric foundations of the American school curriculum (McCarthy and Apple, 1988).

Essentially then, the assimilationist approach to race relations and to the education of minorities had become unstuck. Blacks and other oppositional racial minorities had begun to champion a radical pluralism (Berlowitz, 1984). It is in this context of radical black discontent with American schooling that educational policymakers and liberal intellectuals began to forge a "new" discourse of multiculturalism. Educators and social researchers such as Baker (1973), Banks (1973), and Glazer and Moynihan (1963) attempted to replace the assimilationist model that undergirded the American school curriculum with a pluralist model that embraced the notion of cultural diversity. Multicultural education as a "new" curricular form disarticulated elements of black radical demands for the restructuring of school knowledge and rearticulated these elements into more reformist professional discourses around issues of minority failure, cultural characteristics, and language proficiency.

MULTICULTURAL POLICY DISCOURSES

Over the years, policy discourses on multicultural education have consistently identified the variable of culture as the vehicle for the resolution of racial inequality and racial antagonism in schooling (Troyna and Williams, 1986). This central motif does represent a certain continuity with an earlier emphasis on minority culture identifiable in the proposals of liberal scholars for compensatory education. However, unlike the earlier liberal preoccupation with cultural deprivation, multiculturalism tends to emphasize the positive qualities of a minority cultural heritage. Proponents of multicultural education have therefore promoted curriculum models that emphasize the following: (a) *cultural understanding*—the idea, central to many ethnic studies and human relations programs, that students and teachers should be more sensitive to ethnic differences in the classroom; (b) *cultural competence*—the insistence in bilingual and bicultural education programs that students and teachers should be able to demonstrate competence in the language and culture of groups outside their own cultural heritage; and (c) *cultural emancipation*—the somewhat more possibilitarian and social reconstructionist thesis that the incorporation or inclusion of minority culture in the school curriculum has the potential to positively influence minority academic achievement and consequently life chances beyond the school (Grant & Sleeter, 1989; Rushton, 1981).

In this section of my essay I will discuss in some detail the contradictions and nuances that are embodied in these three multicultural approaches to racial inequality in education. First, I examine the policy discourse of cultural understanding.

MODELS OF CULTURAL UNDERSTANDING

Models of cultural understanding in multicultural education exist in the form of various state- and university-supported ethnic studies and human relations programs which place a premium on "improving communication" among different ethnic groups (Montalto, 1981). The fundamental stance of this approach to ethnic differences in schooling is that of cultural relativism. Within this framework, all social and ethnic groups are presumed to have a formal parity with each other. The matter of ethnic identity is understood in terms of individual choice and preference—the language of the shopping mall.

This stance of cultural relativism is translated in curriculum guides for ethnic studies in terms of a discourse of reciprocity and consensus: "We are different but we are all the same." The idea that racial differences are only "human" and "natural" is, for example, promoted in the teaching kit, "The Wonderful World of Difference: A Human Relations Program for Grades K–8," in which the authors "explore the diversity and richness of the human family" (Anti-Defamation League of B'nai B'rith, 1986). In their *Multicultural Teaching: A Handbook of Activities, Information, and Resources* (1986), Tiedt and Tiedt tell teachers and students that there are many different ways of grouping individuals in "our society." Income, religious beliefs, and so on are some of the criteria "we use" in the United States. One of the handbook's many activities requires students to make up a list of cultural traits that would be characteristic of "Sue Wong" (p. 144). Students are also asked to supply the appropriate cultural information that would help to complete the sentence "Sue Wong is . . . " (p. 144). This tendency to focus on the acceptance and recognition of cultural differences has led in recent years to a movement for the recognition of the cultural "uniqueness" of "white ethnic" groups (for example, Poles, Italians, Norwegians, and Swedes) to counterbalance demands for the study of black, Hispanic, and Native American cultures (Gibson, 1984).

But the emphasis on cultural understanding goes beyond the development of communication skills and respect for ethnic differences. Various preservice teacher education programs and state human relations guides emphasize the elimination of racial and sexual stereotypes and the development of positive attitudes toward minority and disadvantaged groups (Wisconsin Department of Public Instruction, 1986). This emphasis on attitudinal change is, for example, reflected in the Ann Arbor, Michigan, Board of Education's regulations of the 1970s:

Beginning in the 1972–73 school year, no student-teacher shall be accepted by the Ann Arbor schools unless he (she) can demonstrate attitudes necessary to support and create the multiethnic curriculum. Each student-teacher must provide a document or transcript which reflects training in or evidence of substantive understanding of multicultural or minority experience. (Baker, 1977, p. 80)

In a similar manner, the University of Wisconsin's Steering Committee on Minority Affairs, in its 1987 report, strongly emphasizes the need for course work that would promote racial tolerance:

The University must implement a mandatory six credit course requirement; and create and develop various Ethnic Studies Programs. These measures will recognize the contributions of ethnic minorities to American society and promote cross-cultural understanding and respect among the entire student body. (p. 4)

Cultural understanding models of multicultural education, such as the one promoted in the University of Wisconsin's Steering Committee on Minority Affairs report, generally take a "benign" stance (Troyna and Williams, 1986) toward racial inequality in schooling and consequently place an enormous emphasis on promoting racial harmony among students and teachers from different cultural backgrounds. The following are some of the ideological assumptions that centrally inform this approach to racial differences in education.

Core Ideological Assumptions   (a) The United States is a culturally and ethnically diverse nation. (b) This cultural diversity has had a positive effect on the overall growth and development of America as a powerful country (King, 1980; Tiedt and Tiedt, 1986). (c) All of America's ethnic groups have in their different ways contributed to the growth and development of America (Wisconsin Department of Instruction, 1986). (d) The educational system in the past has not sufficiently fostered this multicultural view of American society, and this has contributed to prejudice and discrimination against certain ethnic groups. (e) Schools and teachers must therefore positively endorse cultural diversity and foster an appreciation and respect for "human differences" in order to reduce racial tension and estrangement of minority groups in the school and in society (Tiedt and Tiedt, 1986).

Desired Outcomes   The principal expectation of those who promote the cultural understanding model of multicultural education is that American schools will be oriented toward the "cultural enrichment of all students" (Gibson, 1984, p. 99). It is assumed that teachers will provide such enrichment in their classrooms. By fostering understanding and acceptance of cultural differences in the classroom and in the school curriculum, it is expected that educational programs based on the cultural understanding approach will contribute toward the elimination of prejudice (Baker, 1977).

Commentary   Proponents of cultural understanding models of multicultural education attach enormous significance to the role of attitudes in the reproduction of racism. Human relations and ethnic studies programs based on this approach pursue what Banks (1981) calls the "prejudiceless goal." The strong version of these programs directly targets white students and teachers, who are portrayed as the flawed protagonists in their racial relations with blacks and Native Americans. It is expected that negative white attitudes toward minorities will change if these prejudiced individuals are exposed to sensitivity training in human relations programs. The weak version of the cultural understanding approach emphasizes the promotion of racial harmony and tolerance of social and ethnic differences.

Various pretest and posttest evaluations of multicultural education and human relations programs that emphasize attitudinal change and cultural understanding suggest that these programs have not been very successful in achieving their espoused goal of eliminating majority and minority prejudice. For instance, though in her evaluation of the University of Michigan's human relations program Baker (1973) claims modest changes in white "pro-irrational attitudes" (p. 307), these changes are not reported in the critical area of black-white relations. Thus, according to Baker, the Michigan students' perceptions of blacks remained at the "pretest level" and were not significantly changed by their participation in the university's human relations program: "No statistically significant differences obtained on the black anti-irrational or pro-irrational subscales. Therefore it can be concluded that the change in the perception of blacks held by the [white] students remained fairly constant" (p. 307).

Like Baker, Fish (1981) reports findings of "no significant effects" in his study of the impact of the field experience component of Wisconsin's human relations program on white students' perceptions of blacks and other disadvantaged groups. According to Fish, "Students who completed a fieldwork experience did not over a semester's time show significantly greater positive attitudes towards the population worked with than students who did not complete a fieldwork experience" (p. xi). Indeed, Fish indicates a worsening of attitudes toward blacks during the course of the Wisconsin program: "One semester after completion of a fieldwork experience, subjects' attitudes towards the mentally retarded and the physically disabled persisted at the pretest level, whereas subjects' attitudes towards blacks significantly worsened from the pretest level" (p. xii). Fish is not alone in his findings of unanticipated negative effects of attitudinal change programs. Buckingham (1984) draws similar conclusions in his case study of responses to "The Whites of Their Eyes"—a Thames Television educational program on "Racism in the British media." In his study of the responses of "a number of groups in London school pupils to the program," Buckingham drew the following conclusions:

> In general, for instance, pupils failed to perceive that the programme was concerned with racism in the media, and this led many to assume that the programme was suggesting that all white people are racist. Likewise few pupils picked up on the programme's arguments about the causes of racism, and fewer still seem to have noticed its implicit suggestions about how racism might be eradicated. While the programme provides a fairly clear historical context for the discussion of racism, pupils generally failed to make connections between this and the examples of racism in the media today. (Buckingham, 1984, p. 139)

American school critics have raised other concerns about attitudinal change and cultural understanding programs. Writers such as Pettigrew (1974) and Garcia (1974) have argued that the content and methods of these programs are significantly flawed. Pettigrew (1974), Garcia (1974), and Kleinfeld (1974) point to the tendency of proponents of cultural understanding models to overemphasize the difference among ethnic groups, neglecting the differences within any one group. They also draw attention to the unintended effect of stereotyping which results from multicultural approaches that treat ethnic groups as "monolithic entities possessing uniform, discernible traits" (Gibson, 1984, p. 100). For instance, Garcia contends that advocates of cultural understanding models tend to discuss "Chicano cultures as if it were a set of values and customs possessed by all who are categorized as Chicanos or Mexican Americans. . . . This fallacy serves to create the new stereotype which is found in the completion of the statement, Mexican American children are . . . " (quoted in Gibson, 1984, p. 100).

The rather disturbing and contradictory findings of Baker (1973), Fish (1981), and Buckingham (1984) and the complaints about methods and content raised by minority educators such as Garcia (1974) have cast doubt on the educational and practical value of cultural understanding approaches to racial differences in schooling. Some proponents of multicultural education have therefore suggested different curriculum and instructional approaches to race relations in school. These curriculum theorists, led by educators such as Banks (1981, 1988), assert that all students should be able to demonstrate cultural competence in the language and cultural practices of ethnic groups other than their own.

Models of Cultural Competence

Underpinning the cultural competence approach to multicultural education is a fundamental assumption that values of cultural pluralism should have a central place in the school curriculum. This concept of social institutions as representing a plurality of ethnic interests was first formulated by liberal social scientists such as Riesman, Glazer, and Denney (1969) and Glazer and Moynihan (1963). Some educators, such as Banks (1973, 1981), Cortes (1973), Pettigrew (1974), and Gollnick (1980), contend that there is a general lack of cross-cultural competencies, especially in the area of language, among minority and majority groups in the American populace. These educators argue for various forms of bilingual, bicultural, and ethnic studies programs based on pluralist values. These programs aim at preserving cultural diversity in the United States, particularly the language and identity of minority groups such as blacks, Hispanics, and Native Americans. Banks summarizes this pluralist approach to ethnic differences in the following terms:

The pluralist argues that ethnicity and ethnic identities are very important in American society. The United States, according to the pluralist, is made up of competing ethnic groups, each of which champions its economic and political interests. It is extremely important, argues the pluralist, for the individual to develop a commitment to his or her ethnic group, especially if that ethnic group is "oppressed" by more powerful ethnic groups within American society. (p. 62)

The American Association of Colleges for Teacher Education (AACTE), in their often-cited "No One American Model," also make a particularly strong case for cultural pluralism in education. AACTE maintains that

multicultural education is education which values cultural pluralism. Multicultural education rejects the view that schools should merely tolerate cultural pluralism. Instead, multicultural education affirms that schools should be oriented toward the cultural enrichment of all children and youth through programs rooted to the preservation and extension of cultural alternatives. Multicultural education recognizes cultural diversity as a fact of life in American society, and it affirms that this cultural diversity is a valuable resource that should be preserved and extended. It affirms that major education institutions should strive to preserve and enhance cultural pluralism. (AACTE 1974, p. 264)

Proponents of multicultural education as cultural competence, such as the AACTE's Commission on Multicultural Education (1973), argue that multiculturalism in education should mean more than the fostering of cultural understanding and awareness about America's ethnic groups. They argue that "teachers [should] help students develop ethnic identities, knowledge about different cultural groups . . . and competence in more than one cultural system" (Grant and Sleeter, 1985, p. 101). By integrating the language and culture of a plurality of ethnic groups into the curriculum, proponents argue that teachers can help to "build bridges" between America's different ethnic groups (Sleeter and Grant, 1986, p. 4). The target population of this cultural competence approach to multicultural education is mainly minority students. It is expected that minority students will develop competence in the "public culture" and the skills and the attitudes of the dominant white society (Lewis, 1976, p. 35). This familiarity with mainstream culture must not take place at the expense of the minority student's own ethnic heritage—a difficult balancing act indeed.

Core Ideological Assumptions   The cultural competence approach to multicultural education is underpinned by some basic assumptions about race relations in education and society in the United States. The following are some of the principal ideological assumptions and values of the cultural competence approach: (a) Previous assimilationist approaches to education, which characterized the United States as a melting pot of ethnic groups, actually helped to foster the hegemony of Anglo values. This has led to the virtual subordination or exclusion of minority culture from the American mainstream (Banks, 1981). (b) Cross-cultural interaction through bilingual and bicultural education programs will help to guarantee the survival of minority language and minority culture (Banks, 1981; Cortes, 1973; Ramirez and Castenada, 1974). (c) Cross-cultural interaction between America's ethnic groups is regarded as a powerful antidote to the racial prejudice that continues to limit the presence of blacks, Hispanics, and Native Americans in America's mainstream (Grant and Sleeter, 1989).

Desired Outcomes   Proponents of the cultural competence approach to multicultural education champion a pluralism which has as its principal objective the preservation of minority language and culture. Bicultural and bilingual programs associated with this cultural competence approach aim to prepare minority students for their social and cultural negotiation with dominant white mainstream society. At the same time, it is expected that white students will also acquire knowledge and familiarity with the language and culture of minority groups. It is felt that such cross-cultural interaction will contribute to reduced antagonism between majority and minority ethnic groups.

Commentary   Proponents of the cultural competence approach to multicultural education have attempted to developed programs that go beyond cultural awareness and attitudinal change. This approach to multiculturalism is particularly critical of earlier compensatory education programs, such as Headstart, which worked centrally on the assumption that minority students were "culturally deficient." Instead, proponents of models of cross-cultural competence valorize minority cultural heritage and language and argue for the meaningful inclusion in the curriculum of "aspects of minority culture that a teacher could build on" (Sleeter and Grant, 1986, p. 4).

But the emphasis on cultural competence as a set of curricular strategies for enhancing minority negotiation with mainstream society precipitates a central contradiction. On the one hand, the affirmation of minority culture in various bilingual, bicultural, and ethnic studies programs represents a direct challenge to the centrality of Anglo values in the school curriculum and the notion that minority culture and language are "naturally" deficient (McCarthy, 1988; Banks, 1988). On the other, the closely related objective of "building bridges" (Sleeter and Grant, 1986, p. 4) from minority groups to mainstream society privileges individual mobility over a collective identity politics oriented toward change in the current structure of race relations in schools and society. As such, the cultural competence approach to multiculturalism has a significant unintended consequence. Attempts to have minority students learn how to cross over to the language and culture of the Anglo mainstream also commit these students to a trajectory that leads toward incorporation and assimilation—an educational and social result that is antithetical to one of the principal concerns of biculturalism, the valorization and preservation of minority cultural identity.

In sum, then, despite the emphasis on diversity within the cultural competence model, the minority child is just like anybody else, free to make his or her choices in the marketplace of culture, ethnicity, and heritage. As Banks (1987) argues, minority and majority students "need to learn that there are cultural and ethnic alternatives within our society that they can freely embrace" (p. 12). Presumably, the responsibility that the enterprising minority youth undertakes in exchange for his or her participation in the cultural market is that of respecting the society's institutions and the rules that make them "work" for those in the American mainstream.

Within recent years, challenges to the cultural understanding and cultural competence approaches to multiculturalism have led to the reformulation and reconceptualization of multicultural perspectives on racial inequality in education. Proponents of multicultural education such as Suzuki (1984) and Swartz (1988) link the current demands for multiculturalism to a more reformist policy discourse of cultural emancipation and social reconstruction. It is this policy discourse that I would now like to discuss.

Models of Cultural Emancipation and Social Reconstruction

Like proponents of curriculum and educational policies of cultural understanding and cultural competence, educators who promote the idea of cultural emancipation within the framework of multiculturalism attach a positive value to minority culture (Grant and Sleeter, 1989; Suzuki, 1984; Swartz, 1988). These educators argue that multiculturalism in education can promote the cultural emancipation and social amelioration of minority youth in two vital ways. First, proponents of emancipatory multiculturalism argue that the fostering of universal respect for the individual ethnic history, culture, and language of the plurality of students to be found in American schools will have a positive effect on individual minority self-concepts. Positive self-concepts should in turn help to boost achievement among minority youth (Bullivant, 1981). This first set of claims therefore retraces some of the ground of the cultural deprivation theorists in that it is suggested that minority students do poorly in school because of their lack of self-esteem, among other things. But proponents of emancipatory multiculturalism add a new twist. They link the issue of minority underachievement in the classroom to the attitudinal prejudice of teachers and the suppression of minority culture in the school curriculum. These reformist educators then argue that a reversal in teacher attitudes and curriculum and instructional policies that suppress minority cultural identities will have a positive effect on minority school achievement. Individual minority school performance will improve since such students will be motivated by a multicultural curriculum and classroom environment in which teachers and students treat minority culture and experiences with respect (Olneck, 1989). For example, Swartz (1988) insists that students who come from family backgrounds in which ethnic pride and identity is emphasized are likely to do well in school, or at least better than those who do not:

> A curriculum which values diverse cultures in an equitable way is self-affirming. . . . It makes a statement to students about the importance of their present and future roles as participants and contributors to society. Research findings by Cummins (1984) and Ogbu (1978) point out that significant school failure does not occur in cultural groups that are positively oriented toward

both their own and others' cultures. These students demonstrate a higher educational success rate. (p. 6)

The second conceptual strand of this emancipatory agenda is related to the first, but more directly links race relations in the classroom to the economy. Proponents of multicultural education as an emancipatory program suggest that improved academic achievement will help minority youth break the cycle of missed opportunity created by a previous biography of cultural deprivation. The labor market is expected to verify emancipatory multicultural programs by absorbing large numbers of qualified minority youth. This thesis of a "tightening bond" between multicultural education and the economy is summarized in the following claim by James Rushton (1981):

> The curriculum in the multicultural school should encourage each pupil to succeed wherever he or she can and strive for competence in what he or she tries. Cultural taboos should be lessened by mutual experience and understandings. The curriculum in the multicultural school should allow these things to happen. If it does, it need have no fear about the future career of its pupils. (p. 169)

This emancipatory or "benevolent" type of approach to multicultural education (Gibson, 1984; Troyna and Williams, 1986) rests, in part, on an earlier curriculum philosophy of "social reconstructionism." Like earlier curriculum theorists such as Rugg (1932) and Counts (1932), proponents of the emancipatory approach to multiculturalism offer the powerful ideology of the "quiet revolution." They suggest that cultural and social changes in minority fortunes are possible if the school curriculum is redefined in response to the needs of minority youth (Grant and Sleeter, 1989; Troyna and Williams, 1986).

Ideological Core Assumptions Proponents of emancipatory multiculturalism operate on some basic assumptions about the role of education in the reproduction and transformation of race relations. These assumptions can be summarized as follows: (a) There is a fundamental mismatch between the school curriculum and the life experiences and cultural backgrounds of American minority youth (Swartz, 1988). (b) This mismatch exists because schools privilege white middle-class values while simultaneously suppressing the culture of minority youth (Williams, 1982). (c) Thus, schools play a critical role in the production of differential educational opportunities and life chances for minority and majority youth. (d) Educators should help to redress this pattern of inequality by embarking upon multicultural curricular reform that will provide equality of opportunity for academic success for minority students.

Desired Outcomes   A genuine multicultural curriculum which includes knowledge about minority history and cultural achievements would reduce the dissonance and alienation from academic success that centrally characterizes minority experiences in schooling in the United States. Such a reformed school curriculum is expected to enhance minority opportunities for academic success and better futures in the labor market. And, in keeping with this thesis, employers are expected to allocate jobs on the basis of market-rational criteria, namely, the credentials and academic qualifications of prospective employees (Bullivant, 1981; Rushton, 1981).

Commentary   Proponents of an emancipatory approach to multicultural education offer a "language of possibility" (Giroux, 1985) with respect to the school curriculum—a language that is not present within earlier assimilationist frameworks. In an ideological sense, such a multicultural program allows for the possibility that the scope of current school knowledge will be "enlarged" to include the radical diversity of knowledge, histories, and experiences of marginalized ethnic groups. It is possible, for example, that radical ideas associated with minority quests for social change would also find their way into the discourse of the classroom (Olneck, 1983).

In addition, the powerfully attractive "social reconstructionist" theme running throughout the thesis of emancipatory multiculturalism raises the issue of inequality in the job market itself. Models of cultural understanding or cultural competence tend not to venture so far beyond the textbook, the classroom, and the school.

However, radical school theorists have, with good reason, criticized the tendency of these multicultural proponents to lean toward an unwarranted optimism about the impact of the multicultural curriculum on the social and economic futures of minority students (McLaren and Dantley, 1990; Mullard, 1985; Troyna and

Williams, 1986). Indeed, the linear connection asserted by multicultural education proponents between educational credentials and the economy is problematic. The assumption that higher educational attainment and achievement through a more sensitive curriculum will lead to a necessary conversion into jobs for black and minority youth is frustrated by the existence of racial practices in the job market itself. Troyna (1984) and Blackburn and Mann (1979), in their incisive analyses of the British job market, explode the myth that there is a necessary "tightening bond" between education and the economy. In his investigation of the fortunes of "educated" black and white youth in the job market, Troyna (1984) concludes that racial and social connections, rather than educational qualifications per se, "determined" the phenomenon of better job chances for white youth even when black youth had higher qualifications than their white counterparts. The tendency of employers to rely on informal channels or "word of mouth" networks, and the greater likelihood that white youth would be in a position to exploit such networks, constitutes one of the principal ways in which the potential for success of qualified black youth in the labor market is systematically undermined. Of course, Carmichael and Hamilton (1967) and Marable (1983) have made similar arguments about the racial disqualification of black youth in the job market in the United States. Expanding this argument, Crichlow (1985) makes the claim that subtle forms of discrimination, job relocation, and increasing competition among workers for smaller numbers of attractive jobs, rising entry-level job requirements underline those employment difficulties experienced by young black workers. Having graduated from high school or not, blacks continue to suffer high rates of unemployment, despite possessing sound educational backgrounds and potential to perform productively as workers.

Besides the issues of naivete about the racial character of the job market, further criticism can be made of the multicultural thesis. Proponents of multicultural education as an emancipatory formula tend to ignore the complex social and political relations that are constituted in the internal order of the schools. Issues of policy formation, decision making, trade-offs, and the building of alliances for specific reformist initiatives have not really been addressed within multicultural frameworks. For these reformist educators, educational change hinges almost exclusively upon the reorganization of the content of the school curriculum. But, as Troyna and Williams (1986) have pointed out, attempts at the reorganization of the school curriculum to include more historically and culturally sensitive materials on minorities have not significantly affected the unequal relations that exist between blacks and whites in schools.

It is criticisms such as those advanced by Troyna and Williams that have seriously called into question the validity of liberal reformist claims about the emancipatory potential of multicultural education and its ability to positively influence minority futures in schools and society in the United States.

CONCLUSION

Spurred forward by minority-group pressure for equality of opportunity in education and society and by the efforts of liberal scholars to provide practical solutions to racial inequality, multicultural education became one of the most powerful educational slogans in the 1970s and 1980s. Federal legislation for ethnic studies and bilingual programs reinforced the state's ideological commitment to multicultural approaches to racial differences in schooling (Grant and Sleeter, 1989). A growing number of school districts and university-based teacher education preservice programs have also espoused various forms of multicultural education (Baker, 1977). In this essay, I explored the conceptual and practical claims of three approaches or discourses of multicultural education. I described these approaches as "models" of cultural understanding, cultural competence, and cultural emancipation. As we saw, each of these approaches represents a subtly different inflection on the issue of what is to be done about racial inequality in schooling. Thus proponents of cultural understanding advocate sensitivity and appreciation of cultural differences—a model for racial harmony. Cultural competence proponents insist on the preservation of minority ethnic identity and language and "the building of bridges" between minority and mainstream cultures. Finally, models of cultural emancipation go somewhat further than the previous two approaches in suggesting that a reformist multicultural curriculum can boost the school success and economic futures of minority youth.

But, as I have tried to show, these multicultural approaches to curriculum reform really do not offer viable explanations or "solutions" to the problem of racial inequality in schooling. School reform and reform in race relations within these frameworks depend almost exclusively on the reversal of values, attitudes, and the human nature of social actors understood as "individuals." Schools, for example, are not conceptualized as sites of power or contestation in which differential interests, resources, and capacities determine the maneuverability of competing racial groups and the possibility and pace of change. In significant ways, too, proponents of multiculturalism fail to take into account the differential structure of opportunities that help to define minority relations to dominant white groups and social institutions in the United States. In abandoning the crucial issues of structural inequality and differential power relations, multicultural proponents end up placing an enormous responsibility on the shoulders of the classroom teacher in the struggle to transform race relations in American schools and society.

REFERENCES

American Association of Colleges for Teacher Education. (1974). No one model American. *Journal of Teacher Education, 24,* 264–265.

Anti-Defamation League of B'nai B'rith. (1986). *The wonderful world of difference. A human relations program for grades K–8.* New York: Anti-Defamation League of B'nai B'rith.

Baker, G. (1973, Winter). Multicultural training for student teachers. *The Journal of Teacher Education, 24,* 306–307.

Baker, G. (1977). Development of the multicultural program: School of Education, University of Michigan. In F. Klassen and D. Gollnick (Eds.), *Pluralism and the American teacher: Issues and case studies* (163–169). Washington, DC: Ethnic Heritage Center for Teacher Education.

Banks, J. (1981). *Multiethnic education: Theory and practice.* Boston: Allyn & Bacon.

Banks, J. (1987). *Teaching strategies for ethnic studies.* Boston: Allyn & Bacon.

Banks, J. (1988). *Multiethnic education: Theory and practice.* Boston: Allyn & Bacon, 1988.

Berlowitz, M. (1984). Multicultural education: Fallacies and alternatives. In M. Berlowitz and R. Edari (Eds.), *Racism and the denial of human rights: Beyond Ethnicity* (129–136). Minneapolis: Marxism Educational Press.

Blackburn, R., and Mann, M. (1979). *The working class in the labor market*. London: Macmillan.

Buckingham, D. (1984). The whites of their eyes: A case study of responses to educational television. In M. Straker-Welds (Ed.), *Education for a multicultural society* (137–143). London: Bell & Hyman, 1984.

Bullivant, B. (1981). *The pluralist dilemma in education: Six case studies*. Sydney: Allen & Unwin.

Carmichael, S., and Hamilton, C. (1967). *Black power*. New York: Vintage Books.

Cortes, C. (1973). Teaching the Chicago experience. In J. Banks (Ed.), *Teaching ethnic studies: Concepts and strategies*. Washington,, DC: National Council for Social Studies.

Counts, G. (1932). *Dare the school build a new social order?* New York: John Day.

Crichlow, Warren. (1985). *Urban crisis, schooling, and black unemployment: A case study*. University of Rochester, Graduate School of Education and Human Development.

Cubberley, E. P. (1909). *Changing conceptions of education*. Boston: Houghton Mifflin.

Fish, J. (1981). *The psychological impact of field work experiences and cognitive dissonance upon attitude change in a human relations program*. Ph.D. Dissertation, University of Wisconsin-Madison.

Fiske, J., and Hartley, J. (1978). *Reading television*. London: Methuen.

Garcia, E. (1974). Chicano cultural diversity: Implications for competency-based teacher education. In W. Hunter (Ed.), *Multicultural education through competency-based teacher education*. Washington, DC: American Association of Colleges for Teacher Education.

Gibson, M. (1984). Approaches to multicultural education in the United States: Some concepts and assumptions. *Anthropology and Education Quarterly, 15*, 94–119.

Giroux, H. (1985). Introduction to P. Freire's *The politics of education*. South Hadley, MA: Harvard University Press.

Glazer, N., and Moynihan, D. P. (1963). *Ethnicity: Theory and experience*. Cambridge, MA: Harvard University Press.

Gollnick, D. (1980). Multicultural education. *Viewpoints in Teaching and Learning, 56*.

Grant, C., and Sleeter, C. (1985). The literature on multicultural education: Review and analysis. *Educational Review, 37*(2), 97–118.

Grant, C., and Sleeter, C. (1989). *Turning on learning: Five approaches for multicultural teaching plans for race, class, gender, and disability*. Columbus: Merrill.

Kaestle, C. (1983). *Pillars of the republic: Common schools and American society, 1780–1860.* New York: Hill & Wang.

King, E. (1980). *Teaching ethnic awareness.* Santa Monica: Good Year.

Kleinfeld, J. (1975). Positive stereotyping: The cultural relativist in the classroom. *Human Organization, 34,* 269–274.

Kliebard, H. (1986). *The struggle for the American curriculum 1893–1958.* Boston: Routledge and Kegan Paul.

Lewis, D. (1976). The multicultural education model and minorities: Some reservations. *Anthropology and Education Quarterly, 7.* pp N.A.

McCarthy, C. (1988). Reconsidering liberal and radical perspectives on racial inequality in schooling: Making the case for nonsynchrony. *Harvard Educational Review, 58*(2), 265–279.

McLaren, P., and Dantley, M. (1990). Leadership and a critical pedagogy of race: Cornel West, Stuart Hall, and the prophetic tradition. *Journal of Negro Education, 59*(1), 29–44.

Marable, M. (1983). *How capitalism underdeveloped Black America: Problems in race, political economy, and society.* Boston: South End Press.

Montalto, N. (1981). Multicultural education in the New York City public schools, 1919–1941. In D. Ravitch and R. Goodenow (Eds.), *Educating an urban people: The New York City experience.* New York: Teachers College Press.

Mullard, C. (1985). Racism in society and school: History, policy and practice. In F. Rizvi (Ed.), *Multiculturalism and educational policy* (64–81). Geelong, Victoria; Deakin University Press.

Olneck, M. (1983). *Ethnicity, pluralism, and American schooling.* Unpublished paper.

Olneck, M. (1989, March). *The recurring dream: Symbolism and ideology in intercultural and multicultural education.* Unpublished paper.

Olneck, M., and Lazerson, M. (1980). Education. In S. Thernstrom, A. Orlov, and O. Hanlin (Eds.), *Harvard encyclopedia of American ethnic groups* (303–319). Cambridge, MA: Harvard University Press.

Omi, M., and Winant, H. (1986). *Racial formation in the United States.* New York: Routledge & Kegan Paul.

Pettigrew, L. (1974). Competency-based teacher education: Teacher training for multicultural education. In W. Hunter (Ed.), *Multicultural education through competency-based teacher education.* Washington, DC: AACTE.

Ramirez, M., and Castenada, A. (1974). *Cultural democracy, bicognitive development, and education.* New York: Academic Press.

Riesman, D., Glazer, N., and Denney, R. (1969). *The lonely crowd.* New Haven: Yale University Press.

Rugg, H. (1932). Social reconstruction through education. *Progressive Education* 9, 11–18.

Rushton, J. (1981). Careers and the multicultural curriculum. In J. Lynch (Ed.), *Teaching in the multicultural school* (163–170). London: Ward Lock.

Sleeter, C., and Grant, C. (1986, April). *The literature on multicultural education in the U.S.A.* Paper presented at the American Educational Research Association Conference, San Francisco.

Suzuki, B. (1984). Curriculum transformation for multicultural education. *Education and Urban Society,* 16, 294–322.

Swartz, E. (1988). *Multicultural curriculum development.* Rochester, NY: Rochester City School District.

Tiedt, I., and Tiedt, P. (1986). *Multicultural teaching: A handbook of activities, information, and resources.* Boston: Allyn & Bacon.

Troyna, B. (1984). Multicultural education: Emancipation or containment? In L. Barton and S. Walker (Eds.), *Social crisis and educational research* (75–97). London: Croom Helm.

Troyna, B., and Williams, J. (1986). *Racism, education and the state.* London: Croomhelm.

University of Wisconsin–Madison Steering Committee on Minority Affairs Report, 1987.

Williams, M. (1982). Multicultural/pluralistic education: Public education in America "The way's it's 'spoze to be," *Clearing House,* 3, 131–135.

Wisconsin Department of Public Instruction. (1986). *A guide to curriculum planning in social studies.* Madison, WI: Wisconsin Department of Public Instruction.

A Curriculum of Difference

CHAPTER 13

The Politics of Race, History, and Curriculum

Joe L. Kincheloe

The kind of history William Bennett and his successors have advocated for the public school curriculum refuses to recognize culture as a terrain of struggle. The relationship between knowledge and power is ignored while concern with domination is buried alongside other skeletons of the past. The attempt to win the consent of the governed is used in the effort to diffuse the social conflict which inevitably emerges from domination. Of course, the creation of a one-dimensional national interest is the strategy employed to win the consent of the people—a national interest, it must be added, which excludes the black community. For example, the dominant definition of the classics in music, art, and literature which forms the cultural basis of the nation consistently excludes the contributions of black men and women. The underlying message of such a definition implies that black people are not a part of the American cultural heritage; they are outside the national interest. Framed in egalitarian rhetoric while excluding the history and culture of the black community, the struggle for consent masks the reality of a country stratified along racial, gender, and class lines (Carby, 1982, p. 184; Staples, 1984, p. 2). The surface harmony heralded by the media, the government, and education is merely an image in the minds of those individuals who are shielded by privilege from the injustice experienced by dominated peoples. Such a pseudo-harmony idealizes the future as it covers up the historical forces which have structured the present disharmony which it denies (Giroux, 1988, p. 125). The governed will not deliver their consent if the presence of the conflict becomes too obvious, too overbearing. In a nation where the economic disparity between black and white is great and continues to grow, the appeal to national unity is heard more frequently. Concerns with the pledge of allegiance in schools and flag burning legislation overshadow attempts to rectify injustice.

At least, right-wing critics do not attempt to hide their position that black history, especially the history of racial conflict, should not be emphasized in the curriculum. Conservative spokesperson Russell Kirk, for example, has argued unabashedly that the purpose of education is to lift a minority student out of his or her subculture rather than immerse him or her in the "trivialities" of ethnic history. What is to be gained by black studies? Kirk asks. Answering his own question, he argues that the only advantage derived from black studies is that a student might possibly find a job as a professor black of studies somewhere (Ford, 1973, pp. 6–7). Thus, the fact that the conquered and oppressed are not remembered is justified—their memory is not marketable in industrial capitalism. "Official history" grows even more amnesiac in regard to black people, and the past and present come to be seen as the inevitable triumph of the deserving. The European experience is assured to be universally applicable, the only valid historical experience—an idea which tacitly permeates E. D. Hirsch's *Cultural Literacy*. No account is taken of the historiographical idea that history cannot be relayed by a single method, that the differences in experience between black and European culture necessitate methodological alterations, not to mention different purposes for pursuing history in the first place (Harrison, 1985, p. 250; Dussel, 1981, p. 17). The result of such perspectives serves to exclude black history from the mainstream public school curriculum. This does not mean that black history is not mentioned—one finds more coverage in the texts of the 1990s than in the 1950s. Nevertheless, the nature of the coverage is so superficial, so acontextual, so devoid of conflict that the essence of the American black experience is concealed even as uncritical curricularists boast of "progress" in the area.

When black history is taught without a critical edge, students gain little insight into the problems facing black people in American history and how these problems affected American history in general. Black history has often been represented in the curriculum as a set of isolated events—slaves as bit players in the larger portrayal of the Civil War, brief "personality profiles" of Sojourner Truth, Booker T. Washington as "a credit to his race," George Washington Carver and the peanut, Martin Luther King, Jr., as the one-dimensional leader of a decontextualized civil rights movement now relegated to the past, c. 1955–c. 1970. The black history taught in the public schools has not really induced students to ask the question: What does it mean to be a black American? Indeed, the perfunctory manner in which black history has been included in the curriculum has served as a means of defusing the rising tide of black student consciousness in school settings (Brittan and Maynard, 1984, p. 160). This uncritical cooption of black history has allowed school leaders to point with pride to the "multicultural" nature of their curriculum, while at the same time maintaining a static view of the purpose of the curriculum in general. Pasted onto the curriculum in a marginal manner, black history is separated from the larger conversation about the curriculum and thus exerts no effect upon it. The "knowledge" transmitted in schools is untouched by a consciousness of black history.

Black history must be integrated into the curriculum on two fronts: (1) to transcend its supplementary role, black historical perspectives must be brought to existing courses in social studies, government, history, literature, science, art, and music; and (2) black perspectives should be studied as an area in its own right. Black history as simply an integrated aspect of the general curriculum would undermine the attempt to devise black-oriented conceptual frameworks and epistemologies (Sleeter and Grant, 1988, p. 120). Sulayman Nyang and Abdulai Vandi provide an excellent example of how an understanding of black history would affect the way mainstream educators teach the European Age of Exploration in the fifteenth and sixteenth centuries. Traditionally, the era has been taught uncritically as an age of heroes whose names were to be memorized along with their "discoveries." Nyang and Vandi place the "discoveries" in broader historical context, examining the assumptions of the Europeans about themselves and other peoples and the effects of European "heroics" on Africans and Asians. Not only do the authors examine the specifics of the Age of Exploration, but they trace the effects of the era on the lives of Europeans, Africans, Asians, and Native Americans (Nyang and Vandi, 1980, pp. 243–244). Bringing a black perspective to bear on the Age of Discovery changes the entire tenor of the pedagogical act. The rote-based memorization of the "discoveries" of Columbus, Cortes, Balboa, DeGama, et al. would give way to a thematic conceptualization of the reasons for European expansionism and the effect of such actions on African, Asian, and Native American peoples. The traditional curricular preoccupation with Europe would expand into a study of non-European cultures. The view of the Age of Exploration as an isolated historical event would be replaced by an understanding of the connections between the past and the present—especially the European past and the Afro-American present. The study of the Age of Exploration would lead naturally into an examination of colonialism and its effects on the daily events of the late twentieth century. Thus, questions generated by black history would fundamentally change what mainstream educators and standardized test makers have labeled "basic knowledge" about Western civilization.

Black history will not only uncover new dimensions of the black experience but will also reveal new ways of seeing dominant culture and dominant education. Having been situated in a state of oppression for so long, black experience may point the way to more sophisticated definitions of social theory and ethical authority. Oppressed groups often gain unique insights into the forces which move history. They comprehend the culture of their oppressors better than do the oppressors themselves. Such insights may dramatically alter that which we refer to as knowledge.

Yet schools continue to teach the black experience uncritically; units of study are added on to existing curricula which are otherwise unaltered. The uncritical presentation of slavery or stories from the "homeland" often estrange black students from their history more than they connect them. Such material is taught in lieu of thematic connections between past and present or the development of a sense of the problems which have faced black Americans. Writing of her own public school experience, Bell Hooks describes this detachment: "We are taught to love the system that oppressed us" (Hooks, 1981, p. 120).

Mainstream education has confused traditionalism with authentic tradition. Distinguishing between the two concepts, Enrique Dussel argues that traditionalism ends with superficial comprehension. Superficial traditionalism does indeed transmit something, but what it tells conceals more than it reveals. It dwells on the surface, thus hiding essence, inner nature, life. Authentic tradition is by nature critical. To be critical in a historical context means to "de-present" the present, that is, to take the mundane, hold it up to the light, and look at it from another angle. Critically grounded, authentic tradition never lets history slip by unquestioned; it requires that we really test and interrogate what tradition transmits, to uncover what has been concealed in the obvious (Dussel, 1976, p. 13). For example, black Americans know they are Afro-Americans, but the important point is to know what that means. It is one thing to know that black people gained educational opportunities in the last portion of the nineteenth and the first part of the twentieth century; it is another idea entirely to understand what the dominant culture perceived the purpose of that education to be.

Textbooks inform students that America from the beginning was a melting pot, a land without great conflict. No history books, Bell Hooks writes, mentioned racial imperialism. Our minds were filled with romantic notions of the new world, the American dream, America as the land where all the races lived together as one (Hooks, 1981, p. 119). Fearful of authentic tradition and the reality of oppression and conflict, many textbook publishers and curriculum developers do not believe that students need to understand the role of racism in America over the last four centuries. With their emphasis on national unity, spokespeople such as William Bennett contend that emphasis on matters such as race and culture are inappropriate. We should concentrate less on racial concerns in the modern curriculum, Bennett maintains, and focus our attention on the *great facts* of American history, that is, a sanitized, whitewashed view of America, the greatest nation in history (Kincheloe, 1989, pp. 71–72).

Bennett's perspective is not unlike the position taken by mainstream curriculum developers since the origins of the common schools. A survey of modern public school social studies texts reveals that the word *racism* does not appear in their indexes. When this central theme of the Afro-American experience is not raised, serious political consequences result. Indeed, any measured treatment of racism in American history would need to focus on the variety of forms it takes at different historical moments. Racism is not a fixed principle but a contradictory phenomenon which is constantly changing its form in relation to the alterations of wider political and economic structures (Hale-Benson, 1986, p. 156; So-lomos, Findlay, Jones, and Gilroy, 1982, pp. 10–11). No public school textbook, for example, examines the history of the northern urban Afro-American experience. As a result no textbook studies the evolution of institutional racism and its dramatic impact on northern black communities. If the question of racism is raised, it is viewed in a southern slavery or Jim Crow context where it was mandated by law and quite overt. Such was not the case in the North. Left without historical explanations of the nature of racism which developed in the urban, industrialized North, students have no conceptual experience which might help them understand why blacks in Chicago could not gain the same employment and educa-tional opportunities as immigrants from Poland. An understanding of the black experience in the labor markets of the North is critical in modern America, where children of immigrants from Europe ask (as did one of my undergraduate students of Greek heritage while I was writing this essay), "We worked hard and succeeded in America, why didn't Blacks?" Thus, as James Anderson concludes, it is easy for such students to buy into popular theories of black social pathology and blame the black victim of racism for the difference in status between Afro-Americans and white immigrants in the urban North (Anderson, 1986, pp. 266–272).

Liberal multicultural programs have often framed racism as simply a struggle over representation, an imagistic battle which effectively serves to hide the social relations of domination in which racism is situated. A central function of black history as a component of the school curriculum must involve its ability to expose naive notions about the nature of racism, such as the belief that it is simply an attitude which needs to be changed. Such treatment of racism perpetuates a cultural blindness which sub-merges the recognition of the social relations of the lived world. Historical myths of "progress," the success of racial integration, and the conquest of racial prejudice eclipse the power relationships which sustain institutional racism and which are reproduced in the very classrooms which point out the decline of prejudice (Carby, 1982, p. 197; Harrison, 1985, p. 247; Carby, 1980, p. 67). Al-though curricular reformation has often concerned itself with the removal of racist stereotyping from textbooks or with the artifacts produced at specific cultural sites, such as art, religion, music, dance, and food, a decline in racial discrimination has not followed a decline in overt prejudice.

Here is where black history intervenes; here is where it plays a particularly critical role in the effort to develop a critical consciousness. The history of racism reveals a tendency for viruslike mutation. In the last fifty years the dominant form of expression has moved from individual racism involving overt acts by individual whites toward individual blacks to institutional racism which takes the form of public policies and socioeconomic arrangements which deny blacks access to legal, medical, or educational facilities. Institutional racism, of course, is particularly insidious because it perpetuates policies which are promoted as racially neutral but which exert a discriminatory impact.

During my tenure at a community college in Louisiana, for example, I submitted a proposal for a History of Black Education course to be offered in the college of education. Located in a city where the percentage of black and white residents was roughly 50-50, the college's student enrollment was 93 percent white and 7 percent black and, as a result, was under a federal court order to desegregate. Nevertheless, my proposal was rejected by the university courses and curricula committee with the justification that such a course would be racially divisive. "We want to maintain a policy of racial neutrality," committee members argued, "we do not want to offer classes which promote racial hatred." The result of this and other such actions was the promotion of a hidden form of institutional racism which in the name of justice denied the validity of black experience as a topic of academic analysis. Thus the black community remained outside the purview of the college's mission, many black students refused to attend the "white college," and the few black students and faculty who did study and teach at the school felt marginalized and soon left. College administrators publicly expressed dismay over the failure of their many attempts to desegregate the college, but privately they confided that their vision of a high-quality, selective college was incompatible with the attempt to raise black enrollment. A critically grounded black history reveals these mutations of racism, their genesis and their contextual development. Such revelations set the stage for the deconstruction of the racial meanings embedded in words such as *merit, quality education, reverse discrimination, tuition tax credits,* and *law and order.* Proceeding from these understandings, we come to realize that people are not just black and white in terms of racial stereotypes but also in relationship to their power and status (Bowser, 1985, p. 307; Piliawsky, 1984, pp. 141–

142; Brittan and Maynard, 1984, pp. 99–100). Thus racism is not simply a matter of prejudice, a cultural phenomenon—it is also grounded in the way certain groups are economically and politically located in society.

Understanding this political-economic location of black Americans, this evolution of racism, this authentic tradition, permits those who are historically conscious to move closer to an awareness of Afrocentric visions, philosophy, and curriculum. Subjugated peoples have to establish their own visions—visions which stand in stark contrast to the worldviews assumed by those established in the current centers of power. The ultimate power of black history is in its truth telling. As it removes history from the afternoon shadows cast by the dominant culture, its truth telling reshapes the present as it creates new visions of the future. The historiographical assumption embedded in this concept is that the future is somehow imprinted in the past (Holt, 1986, p. 10). It is not just black consciousness which stands to be remolded but dominant consciousness as well. The possibility offered by black history confronts teachers with the question of what constitutes official knowledge (Inglis, 1985, p. 18). If successful, black history will force teachers, curriculum developers, and hopefully the public to ask where knowledge does come from, who certifies it, and what its political impact is.

Michel Foucault's notion of subjugated knowledges helps us theorize the possible curricular roles of black history. Foucault would resurrect these subjugated knowledges: (1) history which has been buried or disguised, typically a history of subjugation, conflict, and oppression lost in a dominant theoretical framework or wiped out by a triumphant history of ideas; and (2) knowledges that have been disqualified as inferior to the dominant definitions of scientificity, knowledges regarded as primitive by mainstream intellectuals (Foucault, 1980, pp. 82–83). The knowledges of the culturally different fall into this latter meaning, since Western intellectuals have traditionally viewed non-Western epistemologies as illogical, not worthy of serious philosophical analysis. One theme runs through both meanings: the historical consciousness of struggles, of conflicts. Foucault admonishes the dominant culture to end its suppression of the role of conflict in history, in discourse—a role that is suppressed in a variety of contexts, the mainstream curriculum included. Foucault used the term *genealogy* to describe the process of remembering and incorporating these memories of subjugated knowledges, conflict, and the dimensions of power they reveal into active contemporary struggles (Welch, 1985, pp. 19–20, 25).

Foucault's genealogy is reminiscent of Herbert Marcuse's concept of "dereification', which implied a certain type of remembering. Something extraordinarily important had been forgotten in the modern world, Marcuse argued. What had to be retrieved were the human origins of a socially constructed world which had been buried by industrialization and the power of Enlightenment rationality (Jay, 1982, pp. 2–5). Foucault's genealogy picks up where Marcuse left off. Specifying the nature of excluded contents and meanings, Foucault prepares us for the strategic struggle between the subjugated and the dominant knowledges. He begins with the realization that the insurrection of subjugated knowledges exists among the oppressed, as in his study of prisons and prisoners. The insurrection is not something that dominant intellectuals can theorize into existence—historians simply acknowledge its reality. Obviously, Afrocentric knowledge is a prime example of Foucault's notion of subjugated knowledges; no intellectual systematically theorized it—it was already there. W. E. B. Du Bois recognized its existence decades prior to Foucault. To understand ourselves as black people, he wrote in 1946, we must understand African history and social development—one of the most sophisticated worldviews, he added, the planet has witnessed (Du Bois, 1973, p. 143).

How might a teacher build his or her practice on the foundation provided by such understandings and theoretical insights? A practice grounded on an understanding of a history of subjugated black knowledge would be aware of the way schools are structured around specific silences and omissions (Giroux, 1988, pp. 100, 109). Teachers would thus seek to incorporate subjugated black knowledge by forging links with the black community—not just the dominant culture's definition of the "successful" elements of that community but a variety of groups and subgroups in the black community. The *diverse* resources to be found in the community open the school to a variety of community traditions, histories, and cultures discredited within the culture of the school. The stories, the worldviews, the music, the politics, the humor, the art of the black community become a central part of everyday school life, never viewed in isolation or as supplements to the "real work" of the school but always viewed in the context of the general curriculum. How do these knowledges, teachers would ask, fit with the dominant knowledge? What dynamics are at work in their interrelationship? The attempt to answer such questions lays the foundation for an authentic curriculum, an education which takes the black experience seriously. The dominant curriculum, with its unproblematic, standardized definitions of knowledge and its standardized tests, has no room for such activities—it is too busy being accountable. The isolation from community which results eventually sets up adversarial relationships between teachers and black parents, black citizens, and black political leaders.

Teachers informed by Foucault's nation of subjugated knowledges thus rewrite history in their classrooms—not in the sense of a totalitarian regime (China's official account of the Tiananmen massacre, as an example) which manufactures a pseudo-history to control its people. This authentic rewriting of history involves the inclusion of subjugated knowledges and the new perspectives such countermemories provide. E. P. Thompson in *The Making of the English Working Class* alludes to this process of historical rewriting as he describes the task of the labor leaders in nineteenth-century who were industrializing Britain. They had to write a new past, Thompson tells his readers, create forms of unprecedented political organization, and draw upon this new history to invent class traditions from a largely invisible past. There is something pedagogically important here—something which provides a peek at the subtle and complex ways history influences curriculum theory and political practice. Nineteenth-century labor leaders took the subjugated historical experience of the working class and theorized it into knowledge—a knowledge which affected the consciousness and pedagogical and political practice of those who grasped it. A solidarity between those who understood the new knowledge was forged, and thereby a community of learning was established (Inglis, 1985, p. 61). The subjugated history, the countermemory of the English working class, like the historical experience of Afro-Americans, was not just "dead old history"; within it were found the origins of the problems, the debates, the oppression of the present. This is what happens when the oppressed draw upon their subjugated knowledges and speak for themselves. Insurrections of subjugated knowledges elicit critical interpretations of educational and school codes, symbols, and texts, institutional structures of public education, and the possibility of an educational praxis built on the wisdom gleaned from these recognitions (Welch, 1985, pp. 44–45).

Critical black history in its essence is concerned with repressed memory, subjugated knowledge and the influence of such repression on the life of the present. The power of the memory of repression is nowhere better represented than in the Afro-American experience—among those who have been denied a useful past. Memory finds itself intimately connected to the present as its cultivation helps liberate the knowledges of peoples long separated from their pasts. With oppressed groups memory engenders consciousness, which leads to a panoply of possible futures. Black historians must draw upon its power in the attempt to secure a place in the public discourse about education.

Thus, once the often-eclipsed relationship between past and present is recognized, the ties between history and politics can be exposed. History is a discourse that exists in a dialectical relationship with political thought (Kaye, 1987, p. 336). If such a relationship seems paradoxical or dangerous, it is because we often hold such a narrow view of politics. In the popular sense of the term, *politics* typically refers to public office seeking at the least and the great public issues at the most (Popular Memory Group, 1982, p. 244). If the definition is expanded to include the larger moral and ethical dimensions of power sharing in a society, the relationship of history and politics is rendered less threatening. In the dialectical interplay between history and politics (and education), the way one makes sense of the past is essential in the determination of what political (or educational) perspective one will view as realistic or socially responsible (White, 1987, p. 73). Indeed, some would argue that all political and educational reasoning is basically a form of historical argument (Popular Memory Group, 1982, p. 213). Thus, like other forms of history, black history is never disinterested. Disinterested history is a luxury only dominant groups can afford. When W. E. B. Du Bois viewed the past, he saw a useful chronicle of methods employed by his black ancestors to fight slavery and oppression—methods, he believed, which could be put to use in present struggles against racial tyranny. The blueprints for the black future, he theorized, must be built on a base of our problems, dreams, and frustrations; they will not appear out of thin air or based exclusively on the experience of others (Du Bois,

1973, p. 144). Echoing this theme, Maulana Karenga argued almost forty years later that Afro-American history is not only a reflection of what black people have done but of what they can do (Karenga, 1982, p. 49). The black past holds out possibility because it served the political function of destabilizing the existing order by revealing its social construction and thus its bogus suprahistorical character.

The possibility that black history holds does not involve the presentation of past heroics, resistances, and dreams for simple imitation. The past cannot unproblematically be repeated; present circumstances are unique and will not allow such a tack. The mere repetition of a past formula is bogus—the possibility of black history rests in its fresh restatement for each new age and new generation. Authentic black history is no panacea; it simply immerses students in the vital flow, the whitewater of tradition—in the process they come to see the possibilities for liberation in the everyday stream of events. Because history does not lead automatically to our finding the *right strategy* for the present, several other steps of emancipatory socioethical analysis must be pursued if individuals are to come to a reflective sense of what they are to do. These steps, Beverly Harrison writes, includes the delineation of our solidarities and loyalties. Every political and curricular stance is influenced by the solidarities and loyalties to groups it aims to serve (Harrison, 1985, p. 251). As Rebecca Chopp agrees, since there are no *purely* individual categories for meaning, freedom, or reason, solidarity forms the basis for ideological critique and historiographical theory. Solidarity with marginated and oppressed groups forms the cornerstone of black history—the black curriculum holds little meaning outside the bounds of such solidarity (Chopp, 1986, p. 43).

Drawing upon the insights of Chopp and Harrison, oppositional educators have come to realize that insight into black history alone does not provide a pedagogy sufficient for the emancipatory task. A truly emancipatory black pedagogy must begin with authentic black tradition, confirm it as a subjugated knowledge, *and* interrogate it critically in order to understand its relationship to present realities and mutated forms of racism and oppression. Black history becomes a starting point for curriculum theorizing about what students and others need to learn in addition to their own cultural, racial experience, that is, the relationship between dominant and subjugated knowledges. William Pinar clarifies the issue when he writes, "After self-revelation, the question becomes, what do I make of what is revealed?" All people are more than just their history, their experiences, what they have been conditioned to be (Pinar, 1988, p. 272). In other words, once black history is laid bare, what are we to make of it: how are we to connect it to our own lives and the lives of others?

REFERENCES

Anderson, James D. (1986). Secondary school history textbooks and the treatment of Black history. In Darlene Clark Hine (Ed.), *The state of Afro-American history: Past, present, and future.* Baton Rouge, LA: Louisiana State University Press.

Bowser, Benjamin P. (1985). Race relations in the 1980's: The case of the United States. *Journal of Black Studies,* 15(4), 307–324.

Brittan, Arthur, and Maynard, Mary. (1984). *Sexism, racism, and oppression.* New York: Basil Blackwell.

Carby, Hazel. (1980). Multi-culture. *Screen Education,* 34, 62–70.

Carby, Hazel V. (1982). Schooling in Babylon. In Centre for Contemporary Cultural Studies, *The empire strikes back: Race and racism in 70s Britain.* London: Hutchinson.

Chopp, Rebecca S. (1986). *The praxis of suffering.* Maryknoll, NY: Orbis Books.

Du Bois, W. E. B. (1973). The future and function of the private Negro college (1946). In W. E. B. Du Bois, *The education of Black people,* ed. Herbert Aptheker. Amherst: University of Massachusetts Press.

Dussel, Enrique. (1976). *History and the theology of liberation,* trans. John Drury. Maryknoll, NY: Orbis.

Dussel, Enrique. (1981). *A history of the church in Latin America,* trans. Alan Neely. Grand Rapids, MI: William B. Eerdmans.

Ford, Nick Claron. (1973). *Black studies: Threat or challenge?* Port Washington, NY: Kennikat Press.

Foucault, Michel. (1980). Two lectures. In *Power/knowledge: Selected interviews and other writings.* New York: Pantheon.

Giroux, Henry. (1988). *Schooling and the struggle for public life.* Minneapolis: University of Minnesota Press.

Hale-Benson, Janice E. (1986). *Black children: Their roots, culture, and learning styles.* Baltimore: Johns Hopkins University Press.

Harrison, Beverly Wildung. (1985). *Making the connections: Essays in feminist social ethics.* Boston: Beacon Press.

Holt, Thomas C. (1986). Whither now and why? In Darlene Clark Hine (Ed.), *The state of Afro-American history: Past, present and future.* Baton Rouge: Louisiana State University Press.

Hooks, Bell. (1981). *Ain't I a woman: Black women and feminism.* Boston: South End Press.

Inglis, Fred. (1985). *The management of ignorance: A political theory of the curriculum.* New York: Basil Blackwell.

Jay, Martin. (1982). Anamnestic totalization. *Theory and Society,* 7, 1–16.

Karenga, Maulana. (1982). *Introduction to Black studies.* Los Angeles: Kawaida Publications.

Kaye, Harvey J. (1987). "The use and abuse of the past: The new right and the crisis of history." *Socialist Register,* 332–365.

Kincheloe, Joe L. (1989). *Getting beyond the facts: Teaching social studies in the late twentieth century.* New York: Peter Lang.

Nyang, Sulayman S., and Vandi, Abdulai S. (1980). Pan-Africanism in world history. In Molefi Kete Asante and Abdulai S. Vandi (Eds.), *Contemporary Black thought: Alternative analyses in social and behavioral science.* Beverly Hills, CA: Sage.

Piliawsky, Monte. (1984). Racial equality in the United States: From institutionalized racism to 'respectable' racism. *Phylon,* 45(2), 135–143.

Pinar, William F. (1988). Time, place, and voice: Curriculum theory and the history moment. In William F. Pinar (Ed.), *Contemporary curriculum discourses.* Scottsdale, AZ: Gorsuch Scarisbrick.

Popular Memory Group. (1982). Popular memory: Theory, politics, and method." In Centre for Contemporary Cultural Studies, *Making histories: Studies in history-writing and politics.* Minneapolis: University of Minnesota Press.

Sleeter, Christine E., and Carl A. Grant. (1988). *Making choices for multicultural education.* Columbus, OH: Merrill.

Solomos, John, Findlay, Bob, Jones, Simon, and Gilroy, Paul. (1982). The organic crisis of British capitalism and race: The experience of the seventies. In Centre for Contemporary Cultural studies, *The empire strikes back: Race and racism in 70s Britain.* London: Hutchinson.

Staples, Robert. (1984). Racial ideology and intellectual racism: Blacks in academia, *The Black Scholar,* 15(2), 2–17.

Thompson, E. P. (1963). *The making of the English working class.* London: Gollanz.

Welch, Sharon D. (1985). *Communities of resistance and solidarity.* Maryknoll, NY: Orbis Books.

White, Hayden. (1987). *The content of the form.* Baltimore: Johns Hopkins University Press.

CHAPTER 14

Toward Emancipation in Citizenship Education: The Case of African American Cultural Knowledge

Beverly M. Gordon

INTRODUCTION

One of the issues that has been a special concern is how a particular society is able to reproduce the functional relations of power and dominance that characterize its existing social and political arrangements. This social reproduction involves not simply the reproduction of capital and labor, but also the reproduction of models of social control, including specific social relationships and specific forms of social consciousness. Antonio Gramsci (1971) and Raymond Williams (1976), among others, refer to this aspect of social control as ideological hegemony; and they argue that society reproduces itself partly through the transmission of a system of values, attitudes, beliefs, social practices and norms which function at once to convey and legitimate the ideology and social practices which serve the interests of the dominant class in the established order. The dominant world view of the society is thus perpetuated, in part, by schools as well as by families and other agencies of socialization. While the dominant world view in American society is far from monolithic, it nonetheless exercises a powerful influence in shaping and legitimating social structure and the normative social relationships of our society as a whole.

Ideological hegemony, thus broadly construed, represents a crucial starting point for examining the basic notion of citizenship education, and the nature of the relationship between schools and the larger society. The role that schools play as social and economic institutions—i.e., as agents of social, cultural, and economic reproduction—becomes critically problematic when the schools are designed to legitimate and reproduce a society that is marked by enormous inequities in wealth and power, and when the underlying world view is conveyed as citizenship education. The question is whether we, as educators, intend education for citizenship simply to function as a mode of ideological domination, conforming students to the demands of dominant society; or whether citizenship education should be designed to foster social reconstruction, by helping students (and others) to become creative, critical thinkers and active social participants, and to become capable of redefining the nature of their own lives in the society in which they live. The author's bias must be evident there. Our task, then, is to determine how it is that citizenship education functions either to reproduce the social condition of labor and the mechanisms of social control that reinforce a class-stratified society; or, alternatively, how citizenship education can be designed to equip students to challenge and reconstitute society according to the principles of social justice and equitable economic opportunity. I recommend that teachers, especially at the preservice level, start with some very readable descriptions of emancipatory pedagogy, e.g., Warner's work with Maori children in New Zealand (1964); Searle's work with poor working class children in England (1975); Freire's work with Brazilian peasants (1973); and Brown's work with minority and poor children in Oakland, California (1978). All of these master teachers incorporated the authentic language, the generative words, or the organic vocabulary and original writings of their students. The pedagogy employed also seems to be historically situated in the real life-world conditions of the students and to use these conditions as guides to classroom praxis.

What I believe to be critical to effective emancipatory citizenship education is the linkage of practical experiences generated from the "life-world" of a community culture—those experiences that its scholars have identified as part of the cultural knowledge base of a particular community—to classroom experience. Such cultural knowledge, which pervades the history and present-day reality of a community, is what scholars distill and formulate as the philosophy and social theory of their constituency.

THE CASE OF AFRICAN-AMERICAN CULTURAL KNOWLEDGE

Philosopher Lucius Outlaw (1983) argues that in order for leaders (e.g., teachers, as Fontaine will tell us) to assist African-Americans in their efforts to emancipate themselves from their subordinate position in American society, and in order to be a guiding influence in their struggle against cultural imperialism, domination, and ideological hegemony, they must make sure that praxis is grounded "in the concrete needs and aspirations of African-Americans (Outlaw, 1983:66). Outlaw also believes that the cultural modes of rationality which hold the most promise for emancipation will be found in the "life-world" of African-Americans, and along with Harold Cruse (1967) he explicitly rejects the notions of the American melting pot and assimilation through the ideal of integration. Instead, he contends that truly emancipatory life-world orientations for African-Americans can be found by looking inward:

> . . . in the mediated folk tales; in religious practices; in political language and practices prevalent during various times, under various conditions; in forms of music, poetry, language of common currency, etc. As these forms of expression, in their concreteness as life-praxis, are constitutive elements of the life-world of African-American people, then the meanings they hold, in symbolic and/or explicit form, contain fundamental orientations. Reclaiming them through acts of reflection will provide understandings of the historically conditioned concerns of black people (Outlaw, 1983:66).

African-American cultural knowledge itself can be uniquely emancipatory for African-Americans—because it is born out of the African-American community's historic common struggle and resistance against the various oppressive effects of capitalism and racism which have kept them in a subordinate position in American society. In fact, a number of specific, indigenous emancipatory currents of thought have pervaded African-American philosophical, sociological and educational scholarship over the past century and more; self-help, service, nationalism, economic autonomy, and political power (Gordon, 1983). These indigenous themes or currents of thought have generative meaning for the African-American community from which they came. After a brief examination of the genesis of these currents of thought, I will explain their potential emancipatory power in classroom pedagogy. In this effort, I believe I am working toward what Giroux (1980) envisions as emancipatory citizenship education.

Educational Science and Ethnocentrism in American Education

The application of "educational science" to curriculum development in the early part of this century seems to have played an unfortunate role in the perpetuation of the cognitive inferiority theory and its consequential second-class subordinate status for African-Americans. Furthermore, at the same time that educational science was employed as a means of differentiating cognitive ability in children, the psychological and scientific principles of business management were introduced into the public schools as administrative conveniences for handling the influx of children of immigrants and former slaves into the cities. Edward L. Thorndike's educational psychological theories in particular, most notably his principles of intelligence testing, provided a rationale for Snedden the social engineer, and the curricularists Bobbit and Charters. Their paradigms of social efficiency and the "differentiated" curriculum legitimized the distribution of different kinds of knowledge among certain ascribed categories of children, to prepare them to assume different roles and functions in adult society (Gordon, 1982). Unfortunately for African-Americans, their position within this ethnocentric hierarchical framework was considered to be inferior to whites, and this belief was repeatedly "verified" by the empirical "scientific" research which became a legitimated part of the quoted literature (Gordon, 1980).

It is of signal importance that while there is a voluminous literature written about education for African-Americans in the first decades of this century, the extensive literature written *by* African-American scholars and educators on this subject is neither represented nor referenced in the dominant educational literature. We cannot any longer afford to overlook the important corpus of endogenous knowledge generated and implemented by African-American scholars that speaks to educational philosophy, theory, and pedagogy. Moreover, as pointed out by Berry and Blassingame (1982), Franklin and Anderson (1978) and Gordon (1983), a new body of literature that provides a new perspective on black educational history from 1896 to the present has also begun to emerge. This substantial body of knowledge generated by modern black scholars has also been largely overlooked by the dominant historical texts—a point that is painfully obvious when studying, for example, Fitzpatrick (1936), Woefel (1933), or Mulhern (1946).[1]

I do not believe there is a conspiracy to underdevelop African-Americans, or to deny them to advancing knowledge, or to negate or ignore their scholarship; the effects of ethnocentrism and racist attitudes that permeate American (and Western) society are much more fundamental than to withstand such simplification. As I have argued elsewhere, the subtle currents of the ethnocentrism and racism which inhere in the Anglo-Saxon world view pervade the dominant culture in American society at every level (Gordon, 1983).

African-American scholars have illuminated and analyzed from an African-American perspective the internal structure of the black community, the effects on African-Americans within their subordinate position in the larger society, and various forms of resistance which African-Americans have developed in order to survive—and advance—in the capitalist and racist society in which they find themselves. It is this kind of self-knowledge that emancipates people. African-Americans must learn their own seldom-explored history, because their own history makes the dominant society's "commonsense" interpretive knowledge problematic. Exploring their own history also provides the opportunity for African-Americans to critique the dominant culture's world view, and to formulate their own cultural and epistemological statements. Furthermore, we can trace in the evolution of black scholarship the evolution of a uniquely African-American cultural mode of rationality.[2]

The Legacy of African-American Cultural Knowledge and Black Educational Philosophy

During the period from 1890 to 1920, the United States experienced thoroughgoing change in all aspects of its economic, political, and industrial structure, as the country was transformed from a mercantile to an industrial society. The earliest African-American scholars, William E. B. DuBois, Kelly Miller and Booker Taliaferro Washington (among others) experienced this industrial and social change and generated historical perspectives on the place of African-Americans in the newly developing industrial era.

Much has been written elsewhere concerning the Washington/DuBois controversy. Although DuBois clashed with Washington over the most effective means of uplifting and developing the black race, they shared the same goals: economic autonomy for political power, self-reliance, and community service. Both Washington and DuBois also envisioned a cultural knowledge base, upon which subsequent political, economic, philosophical thought would be developed. While Washington argued for an agricultural scientific basis, to serve the masses of African-Americans still in the South in the 1890s and early 1900s, DuBois argued that emphasis had to be given to the best and the brightest, and that their education should be more classical, theoretical, and conceptual. The debate over these conflicting educational paradigms—the intellectual and the practical—within the African-American community may itself have served to further the development of a black intelligentsia.

Washington and DuBois each played a significant role in the production and dissemination of knowledge. As theorists, they developed paradigms and conceptual frameworks, and organized institutions into knowledge-producing systems to clarify and explain the condition of African-Americans in American society. Then, as pragmatists, they applied their knowledge to the challenges of building an industrial base and achieving economic autonomy.[3]

Kelly Miller of Howard University, writing in 1908, reflects a theme that is characteristic of much of the early twentieth-century black scholarship: the nationalist view. Miller was concerned about the progress and the development of African-Americans, and argued that they should strive primarily for economic independence and self-reliance. Along with DuBois, he rejected the social darwinist theories which dominated English and American sociological thought. While he squarely blamed white racism for attempting to thwart black progress, he also addressed the problems which he felt existed within the African-American community itself.

Miller reasoned, first, that the "Negro's Part in the Negro Problem" was the schism between the educated African-Americans and the African-American masses. Miller argued that when the black bourgeoisie accepted white intellectual and educational paradigms, they came to hate themselves and the masses as well. This theory foreshadows what Carter G. Woodson would say twenty-five years later. Miller (and later Woodson) also recognized the necessity of both a theoretical approach (DuBois) and a practical approach (Washington) to education in the struggle to advance the black race. Miller argued that African-Americans should receive training in both the intellectual, classical field (which he called "higher education"), and in manual skills and agricultural and industrial science, since each served an essential role in the overall effort for advancement and progress (Miller, 1908:267). Echoing DuBois, he wrote, "A most significant indication of progress is the emergence of a superior class. The talented tenth constitutes the controlling factor in the life of any people" (Miller, 1908:105). Yet he also realized the potentially symbiotic relationship between higher education and industrial activities (Miller, 1908:267).[4]

Early black thought, especially with regard to the role of education in uplifting and the development of African-American people as a group, was very nationalistic in its beliefs. Early black scholars believed that the need for African-Americans to take charge of every aspect of Afro-American life and culture was axiomatic. In these early writings (1890s to early 1920s, black scholars sought a collective self-knowledge and critical understanding which could form the basis for a cultural mode of rationality. The pervasive themes in these early writings were an ideology of emancipation (freedom from domination); self-help; self-reliance; economic autonomy (independence); and political power.

These early nationalist themes were soon seriously challenged, however, by an alternative exogenous influences on black scholarship. A new crop of young African-American scholars, from the mid 1920s to 1930s, was trained in social science paradigms that supported instead the dominant culture's interpretations of the African-American condition; and these paradigms haunted black scholarship and hindered black progress throughout most of the next sixty years.

In the ten years between 1926 and 1936, more black students graduated from college than in the entire previous century (Fontaine, 1940). Where these students were educated, and the paradigms they were grounded in, is critical in understanding the deviation of the new black social theory from the traditional (a more natural) nationalist perspective.

These young African-Americans were schooled in a new alien model grounded on ecological assimilationist/integrationist perspectives. Elsewhere I have examined the profound influence of the Chicago school of sociology on black scholarship (Gordon, 1983). The sociological theories of Robert Parks and Ernest Burgess, which are grounded in social Darwinist theory, shifted the second generation of young black scholars from the very independent endogenous black paradigms of nationalism, economic autonomy, political power, self-help, and self-reliance, and service to a dependency ideology grounded in a culturally 'alien' technocratic rationality paradigm.

The influence of the Chicago school has also recently been discussed by other black scholars (e.g., Ellison, 1973; Ibn Alkalimat, 1973; Jones, 1973; Bowser, 1981). The main conclusion of these scholars is that the Chicago school paradigms profoundly altered the ways in which the condition and the plight of African-Americans were perceived—by African-Americans as well as by whites. Black scholars trained in this school then proceeded to collect "accurate" socioeconomic data on the black urban community; but their theory-bound conclusions and non-emancipatory policy recommendations could go no further than the ethnocentric phenomenological constructs they employed and the particularly inappropriate investigative framework within which they worked (Bowser, 1981).

How African-Americans were to be educated and for what purpose continued to be a central concern of black scholarship during the late 1920s and the 1930s. However, Carter G. Woodson and William T. Fontaine examined this issue and formulated a methodology and an ideology which revitalized the traditional black concept of black nationalism and economic and political independence, which African-Americans trained in the influential Chicago school had rejected.

A Critique of the New Negro: Carter G. Woodson and William T. Fontaine on the Education and Mis-Education of African-Americans

The decade between 1926 and 1936 produced a record number of black college graduates. They attended colleges such as Yale and Harvard as well as Fisk, Howard, and many other schools across the country, both in the South and in the North. Somewhat ironically, at the height of this outstanding effort and achievement in higher education, Carter G. Woodson presented a thesis that criticized the education that African-Americans were receiving and set forth an alternative philosophical and ideological roadmap for the development of African-Americans.

In *The Mis-Education of the Negro* (1933), Woodson argued that the education African-Americans were receiving was having a debilitating, crippling effect on African-American youth, and that it was inhibiting their social development and hindering their economic advancement. Woodson's thesis was that African-Americans were, in effect, being miseducated, since the 'knowledge' they were taught also systematically taught them self-hatred and a self-image of inferiority. In this important critique of the status of black education in America, Woodson explained how the predominant ecological paradigms in which African-Americans were being educated and the assumptions underlying these paradigms, by their very nature, served to legitimate white racism and to rationalize the colonial or subordinate status of African-Americans in American society. Woodson saw how difficult it was for African-Americans to break away from these theories, which had taken on the aura of the conventional wisdom and were presented as commonsense knowledge, because few students were ever encouraged to question or challenge the assumptions that shaped these theories of social reality. After all, "[w]hen you control a man's thinking, you do not have to worry about his actions. . . . He will find his proper place and will stay in it" (Woodson, 1933:xiii).

Woodson's primary criticism was that what African-American students were being taught as unquestioned objective reality were only unfounded and ethnocentric theories which supported the notion of black inferiority. He argued that the academic training African-American students received at the university level was discouraging them from attempting to play an active, constructive role in the development of the race (Woodson, 1933).

Woodson believed that the ethnocentric paradigms they studied caused these young "educated" African-Americans to acquiesce in the notion that African-Americans were inferior, and made them contemptuous both of themselves and of the masses. Woodson theorized that when educated African-Americans then tried to rationalize this self-hatred, their self-limiting paradigms produced only self-defeating rationalizations of why the masses of African-American people in America were not capable of building an independent economic power base. The ironic consequence of this miseducation, then, was that instead of empowering the African-American intelligentsia to join with the masses in a collective effort to advance the race, the "education" of the young African-American intelligentsia, the theorists, and the scientists, had instead served only to alienate them from the masses. Woodson consequently believed that it was African-American businessman, not the miseducated African-American intelligentsia, who could be most helpful and influential in the advancement and development of African-Americans.

For Woodson, as for many earlier writers, the most important obligation incumbent upon any individual African-American was to serve the race in its development. He insisted that African-Americans had to gain control over their own institutions and he urged African-Americans to follow the example—if not the teachings—of Booker T. Washington, who was the only African-American man who had ever actually built and controlled an institution of higher learning (Woodson, 1933:57).

Woodson also believed that in white schools African-Americans did not receive adequate preparation in either industrial or classical education. In the former, African-Americans did not receive sufficient practice or opportunity, and upon graduation were barred from trade unions. In classical education, African-Americans did not fare much better, he reasoned, because it was evident that such training had failed to produce any sizeable cadre of outstanding thinkers and philosophers: "They have not risen to heights of black men farther removed from influences of slavery and segregation" (Woodson, 1933:15).

In the matter of curriculum, the kinds of study that should be done, Woodson advocated that it be both practical and applicable to the real world situation. Woodson thus transcends the Booker T. Washington/W. E. B. DuBois controversy by calling for a collaborative dialectic between theorists and pragmatists.

Woodson believed in African-American "self reliance" to uplift the race. He argued that African-Americans must serve each other and must pull together as a community, forgoing individual strife and conflict. He thought community and interpersonal cooperation were essential if the condition of African-Americans were to be improved; and he even advocated several forms of collective enterprises (Woodson, 1933).

The Legacy of an African-American Cultural Rationality

Collectively, Woodson's efforts and those of his predecessors form component parts of a broader endogenous African-American cultural mode of rationality, wrought out of the reality and history of the African-American experience in America. Woodson spoke about African-American history and about the necessity of viewing oneself from an historical perspective, situated within the racist and capitalist structure of American society. Woodson's thinking reawakens our sensibilities to our own social experience, and to our own history and aesthetics and values. Here, especially, the oral tradition in African-American culture comes to mind, as well as the emphasis on physical prowess. The philosophy Woodson promoted was also centered around the tradition of service and the development of the Afro-American community.[5] He tried to awaken African-Americans to the realization that imitating whites was an admission of self-hatred and rejection.

From this theoretical perspective on the nature and importance of culture, Woodson also provides us with an understanding of how studying their own culture can help a people to determine, at any given point in time, the kind of knowledge they need to pursue. Furthermore, Woodson, by effectively politicizing culture, adds further cogency to Giroux's argument that cultural history is essential for an emancipatory pedagogy. Studying the African-American cultural heritage thus not only teaches the truth about those who oppress, and demystifies domination and colonial rule; cultural self-knowledge is also self-instructive in that it can point out weaknesses and illuminate ways in which the community as a whole can improve and advance.[6]

In his "new program," Woodson's reconceptualization of higher education as a mechanism of service is nationalistic and seems to carry overtones of "Booker T-ism." His call for "radical reconstruction" of the analytical framework and paradigms used to view the black experience in America, however, is as current as Giroux's call for an emancipatory rationality. It should be noted here that Woodson was anti-Marxist. Not that he was against Marxism, but he viewed the Marxist influence as an alien force attempting to invade the African-American community—another Euro-American ethnocentric tradition—and believed it was not germane to the situation of African-Americans in America. Woodson believed that an endogenous radicalism would have to emerge from within the African-American community if it were to succeed. On the other hand, Woodson also believed that African-Americans should not depend on or wait for general white support; Woodson believed fervently that African-Americans should do for themselves.

Woodson's notion of developing a new pedagogy to teach people about themselves and their neighbors and heroes, and his ideal of the "real teacher," precede Freire's notions of education for critical consciousness by thirty years; and so does the research methodology he suggests as preliminary step in establishing a curriculum for African-Americans (Woodson, 1933:151). Woodson recognized the critical necessity of formulating our indigenous philosophy, and of generating endogenously our own social theory and ideology, so that African-American people would be able truly to think for themselves and act in their community's own true interest. But perhaps the most important of Woodson's contributions was his realization of how social science paradigms and their underlying assumptions both shape our perceptions of reality and influence social policy, and his insistence that African-Americans must critique these taken-for-granted paradigms, challenge their validity, and generate their own.

Seven years after Woodson's critique of black education William Fontaine challenged the naive and uncritical way in which African-Americans envisioned democracy as the heavenly antithesis to their servile state, and expected that democracy alone would somehow automatically bring them equity and freedom (Fontaine, 1940). Fontaine believed that democracy was slow and ineffective from the standpoint of the aspirations and ambitions of African-Americans. He questioned how a democracy which was "powerless to prevent simultaneous existence of poverty and wealth, intelligence and ignorance, dead-end kids and prep school Buster Brown" could possibly bring equity and equality to descendants of slaves, who were confined to a low-caste status in American society. Fontaine argued that African-American scholars must reject the "democratic liberal science Weltanschauung" and adopt a "defensive psychology" posture, generated from the black perspective on the African-American experience. The "knowledge" generated within this defense psychology was "socially determined," as a response to the ascribed low-caste status of African-Americans; i.e., "there is a correlation between the knowledge propounded by Negro scholars and the social situation confronting the Negro group" (Fontaine, 1944 in Harris, ed., 1983:105).

For example, African-American scholars such as Carter G. Woodson unmasked the "sins of omission and commission in writers like Hegel, Dunning, J. W. Burgess, J. F. Rhodes, A. D. White, etc." (Fontaine, 1940). These scholars (and also Charles Wesley) made invaluable methodological contributions in historiography by demonstrating the importance of subjectivity and point of view: "Dr. Wesley not only contends that 'history is an expanding concept embracing the ways in which ALL people have lived throughout the ages,' but in addition to the inclusion of facts about the Negro he believes that the Negro's perspective should be used in the interpretation of these facts" (Fontaine, 1940:8–9).

Reminiscent of Woodson's call for a "new" educational program to counter the mis-education of African-American people, Fontaine believed that the philosophy of African-American teachers would have to embrace would be one of *counter-indocrination*. Fontaine described this as a "toughminded" approach, a kind of provocative revolutionary thought involving black opposition to the "democratic-liberal scientific Weltanschauung" in all three areas of African-American scholarship, from history and sociology to literature. In essence then, Fontaine saw counter-indoctrination as a psychologically healthy, nationalistic stance.

Emancipatory Trends in Present-Day African-American Scholarship

Research and writings in black educational history and thought continued to provide much material on the topics of integration, desegregation, boycotts, and liberalism, and responses to these issues from both the African-American and white communities, etc. (Cox, 1948; Herbst, 1973). However a major shortcoming of the African-American intelligentsia which has persisted up until the present time has been their failure to take the work put forth by such scholars as Booker T. Washington, W. E. B. DuBois, Kelly Miller, Carter G. Woodson, and William T. Fontaine to synthesize it into a body of knowledge and to make it the basis of a common intellectual heritage that would give leadership and direction to the African-American community. The failure of African-American intellectuals to gain control over educational and other institutions, mass media, publishing houses, dominant societal national organizations, etc., also means that they have been excluded from influential participation in the political, theoretical, and ideological debates in the mainstream society. But even more critical for the advancement of African-American people, is that the failure of the African-American intelligentsia to formulate its own knowledge base has meant that African-Americans are still being schooled in the same (old) ideological hegemonic paradigms that still served to legitimate and reproduce the dominant culture.

The problem of the hegemonic impact of Euro-American theory, be it conservative or even radical theory, on black cultural and political thought has also long been recognized. It was raised as early as 1913 by Arthur Schomburg, and has recently been examined by such African-American scholars as Manning Marable (1981), John Brown Childs (1981) and James M. Jones (1979). Other theorists are also beginning to articulate the differences between the American and European social, cultural, and political contexts, and the reflections of these differences in the respective schools of neo-Marxist thought (Aronowitz, 1981).

Contemporary African-American scholars realize, for example, that socialism alone will not insure the abolition of racism. According to Marable (1981), "there is not . . . a body of knowledge which could be described as a Marxian theory of racism which can be directly applied to our understanding of American society."

There is thus a growing consensus among African-American scholars that what they must now do is return to their own traditions, history, and cultural thought, and begin to articulate their own cultural mode of rationality, independent of Western European domination. There has also been a significant resurgence of interest in the African-American concept of culture. Raymond Williams, for example, views culture as "a record of a number of important and continuing reactions to changes in our social, economic and political life" (Childs, 1981:43). Also along this line, John Brown Childs, in his study of DuBois conception of culture within the African-American community, has defined culture as "a historically grounded way of existence" (Childs, 1981). We can thus observe, within contemporary African-American literature, an emerging awareness of the existence of a distinct cultural mode of rationality, although at the present time there is little formal writing on the topic in the educational literature. Awareness of such a mode of rationality has increased as a result of the persistent efforts of African-American scholars to conceptualize alternative scientific and philosophical paradigms for the purpose of systematically analyzing African-American culture (Berry and Blassingame, 1982; Boykin, 1979; Childs, 1981; Franklin and Anderson, 1978; Gordon, 1982; Jones, 1979; Ladner (ed.), 1973; Marable, 1981).

While all of these scholars, and many others, are grappling with issues and concerns within their respective disciplines, there is still a need for a synthesis of this body of knowledge into what I believe will form an African-American epistemology. One way of getting a handle on this massive amount of knowledge would be to continue to look for emancipatory categories or currents of thought (such as those referred to in this paper: self-help; service; nationalism; political power, economic autonomy) generated from the daily experiences of the African-American people, and use these in systematic study. With continued research, the categories may, under scientific scrutiny, collapse, be subsumed into another category, or be refined or expanded. One would suspect that the categories will change shape and form during the dynamic process of generating theory hued from black consciousness. But this process is the first step toward true cultural emancipation and self-realization for African-Americans.

IMPLEMENTING EMANCIPATORY PEDAGOGY FOR CHILDREN (AND TEACHERS): CHALLENGES AND IMPLICATIONS

Emancipatory pedagogy requires the reconceptualization of knowledge into new forms of ideology, paradigms, and assumptions that can help illuminate and clarify African-American reality. Emancipatory pedagogy also requires counter-indoctrination against the blind acceptance of the dominant culture's concepts and paradigms. Emancipatory pedagogy is the freeing of one's mind to explore the essence and influence of the African-American race throughout the world, and the ability to pass on that information to the next generation as a foundation upon which to build. This information can generate emancipatory perspectives: for example, black Egyptian civilization lasted a thousand years, while the United States is little more than two hundred years old. When a child ponders this historical fact s/he develops a different perspective on Africa and her rulers. In essence; it triggers a "gestalt switch" that enables one "to see" something s/he had not seen before, but which was there all along.

In teacher education courses, this type of critical awareness can also be taught. For example, in teaching social studies, student teachers (and the children they teach) can be taught to critically examine the descriptive language and the knowledge in elementary school history books that is presented as objective fact, true and unbiased (see Cynthia Brown [1973], for example). Student teachers might critically examine how history is disseminated in various way: take, for example, a pamphlet *Highlights Of Ohio History,* published by The Bell Telephone Company for Ohio elementary school children:

> LaSalle Discovers the Ohio River. In 1669, the famous French explorer LaSalle wrote his name in Ohio History by his discovery of the Ohio River. . . . Told about the river by the missionaries, he was warned of the fierce Iroquois who guarded it . . . (Ohio Bell Telephone Co., 1953:5).

Words such as *discover, fierce,* and *missionaries* become problematic and under examination take on very interesting, self-serving properties.

In the next example, from the same booklet, we can analyze the knowledge disseminated about Ohio's Native American population:

> *The Indians in Ohio.* Ohio pioneers not only had to conquer a vast wilderness; they had to come to terms with the many Indian tribes that inhabited the territory. Many of these Indian chiefs and their tribes have left their mark on the pages of Ohio's history. Among them are . . . Chief Tecumseh . . . Many others, such as the Delawares . . . gave up their struggles against the settlers in the Greenville treaty. In 1842, the Wyandott tribe was the last tribe to leave the Ohio Country and open the entire territory for peaceful settlement (Ohio Bell Telephone Co., 1953:6).

By studying the meaning and contextual usage of words such as *conquer, hostile, struggles, treaty,* and *peaceful settlement* in this section, and the assumption behind them, student-teachers and children (in both intermediate and upper elementary grades, as demonstrated in Brown [1973]), begin to discern what is and is not being taught. They also realize that "facts" and values are interrelated, and that if the paradigms and assumptions are already determined, the intended interpretations will have also been decided. This kind of critical analysis through the reconceptualization of knowledge enables teachers and students to fairly consider the righteous indignation on the part of the Native American nations, and to detect and unpack colonialism and racism in such reading materials. Moreover, this kind of critical analysis allows both students and teachers to study in a more open and broad fashion such issues of genocide and the history of the displacement of indigenous peoples, as well as war and refugees in the world today.

PARADIGM TO PRAXIS

Pedagogy, of course, must be susceptible of understanding and implementation. In the spirit of Woodson, I propose some interpretations and suggestions for applying theory to praxis in promoting an emancipatory rationality.

Returning to the African-American categories of self-help, economic autonomy, political power, nationalism, and service, I postulate that citizenship education for African-American children, in fact for all children, must shift away from models based on rationalizations of colonialism, and emphasize instead the emancipation of the mind and spirit. Instead of teaching children with negative imagery, we must allow students to speak with their own authentic voices (cf. Warner), and then engage them in formal classroom work which uses their own cultural capital as a bridge between their own life-world and classroom experience. In such an effort to teach "from the bottom up," using the cultural capital of the children, it may be appropriate to use reading material like DuBois' *Dusk of Dawn* (1940) and *The Dark Princess: A Romance* (1928), or the autobiographies of Woodson, Malcolm X, and one of the 1984 presidential candidates, the Reverend Jessie Jackson. While such material would be a challenge (and perhaps even a struggle), it is through conflict and struggle that students grow and learn. Moreover, this would introduce them to a body of classical literature heretofore generally omitted from the public school curriculum.

Many African-American people, however, have not fully enjoyed reading because the acquisition of those skills has been mystified, and made, I believe, unnecessarily difficult and at times painful for minority and poor folk. My second practical suggestion would therefore be to ask each member of the Afro-American intellectual community to promote the reading of (and buy or somehow supply copies of) the works mentioned in this article to public, school and/or church libraries so that the community has access to them to be read and discussed. The beauty of these books, especially Woodson's book, is that it is very readable, would promote discussion and would hopefully encourage further reading. To actualize such an idea within our communities would, no doubt, be a challenge, but the longest journey begins with one step. This suggestion also follows our traditional categories of self-help and service, so that the means is as culturally valid as its intended end.

My final suggestion centers around the concept of nationalism. It behooves African-American scholars to generate a list of basic readings for the academicians as well as the lay population. We can start the list with the pivotal works of Woodson, W. E. B. DuBois, and Booker T. Washington. Woodson described the best teacher as one who taught people using their own heroes and telling them about themselves; and if we let these key figures "speak for themselves," their works will come to serve as common intellectual touchstones for all African-Americans, and as reference points in our new emancipatory paradigms.

CONCLUSION

This discussion is not merely another effort to rationalize the teaching of African-American history in schools. My first thesis is that we as teacher-educators and teachers can learn how better to educate African-Americans by studying black scholarship; my second thesis is that exploring the African-American experience in classroom learning situations, coupled with an emancipatory paradigm, can be a liberating experience for all our children. I am not just advocating some African-American equivalent of (or alternative to) the indoctrination of dominant American patriotism (what the dominant culture calls teaching American history). My goal was to share my understanding of the emancipatory process, and how teachers can implement a methodology to educate minority children to become creatively thinking and effectively active citizens in this society (even though it is not at all clear to me that the dominant culture in this society wants a critically thinking and active citizenry).

It is my contention that one methodology which recommends itself is to begin by understanding the tradition of resistance among African-Americans, and to use the emancipatory modes of rationality that were born from their struggle as a basis for pedagogy. Citizenship education then ideally becomes education for informed political awareness, and in the practice of critically analyzing reality, and not simply a process of rote indoctrination. By attempting to illuminate the genesis of some of the indigenous African-American currents of thought, I have tried to provide a better understanding of the nature of emancipatory rationality and its appropriateness as a basis for preparing citizens to participate in building a socially just and economically humane society.

This discussion has come full circle: I began by talking about how a society reproduces itself, and have ended by proposing one means by which we can—I hope—challenge ideological hegemony through critical reflection and responsible, active communal participation, and regenerate our society along lines more in keeping with its own professed ideals.

NOTES

1. Merle Curti (1935) is an exception in this case, because he did, in fact, cite the work of Booker T. Washington in his research.

2. Elsewhere I have discussed in detail the interpretive history of African-American knowledge paradigms and influences in the education of Black people (Gordon, 1983). As I heard myself writing these words "African-Americans must learn their own history," first a great pain welled up within me and then the dawning awareness of the reason for that pain. I thought such questions had already been raised in the 1960s, and did not realize that this great awareness period waned, that the African-American children today seem to possess less cultural and historical knowledge of their people than I had as an adolescent and throughout my teens. (It should also be noted that during my high school years, I

listened to John Coltrane, Bobby Timmons and Thelonious Monk while my contemporary counterparts are listening to Michael Jackson and Prince.) I thought such battles had been won, and never really thought about them again, which is probably the most elegant statement as to why we are still fighting the same battles.

3.   One interesting aside is that in African philosophical thought, Cesaire (1972) and Mbiti (1970) both talk about the relationship between theory and practice: African philosophy and culture are a continued merging of theory and praxis.

4.   It should also be pointed out that Miller stated that what was needed to help the race was "not mere theorizers" but practical application. The relationship between atheory and practice (praxis) is another characteristic/current of thought that reappears through black scholarship and will be discussed later. Suffice it to say that Miller's belief that dynamic knowledge "which clarifies the vision, refines the feelings, broadens the conception of truth and duty . . . is of the highest and most valuable form of practicability," could be traced to African philosophy, where philosophy is in concert with action (Miller, 1908:272; Mbiti, 1969).

5.   One interesting side of Woodson in the book is his style. It is simple and straightforward. In a way, it is a demonstration of practicing his own philosophy. Although he was apparently criticized for this practical, simplified style, this style makes the information more accessible to the larger, less scholarly audience.

6.   Within this teaching of culture, Woodson even takes religion to task: "If Negroes got their conception of religion from slaveholders, libertines, and murderers, there may be something wrong about it, and it would not hurt to investigate it. It has been said that the Negroes do not connect morals with religion. The historian would like to know what race or nation does such a thing. Certainly the whites with whom the Negroes have come into contact have not done so" (Woodson, 1933:73).

REFERENCES

Abd el-Hakimu Ibn Alkalimat. The Ideology Of Black Social Science. In Ladner, Joyce, ed., *The Death of White Sociology.* New York: Vantage Books, 1973: 173–189.

Aronowitz, Stanley. *The Crisis In Historical Materialism.* New York: J. F. Bergin Pub., 1981.

Berry, Mary & John Blassingame. *Long Memory: The Black Experience In America.* New York: Oxford Press, 1982.

Bowser, Benjamin P. The Contribution of Blacks to Sociological Knowledge: A Problem of Theory and Role to 1950. *Phylon*, 42: 180–193, 1981.

Boykin, A. Wade. Psychological/Behavioral Verve: Some Theoretical Explorations and Empirical Manifestations. In Boykin, A. Wade, A. J. Franklin, & A. F. Yates, eds., *Research Directions of Black Psychologists.* New York: Russell Sage Foundation, 1979.

Brown, Cynthia. *Literacy in Thirty Hours.* Chicago: Alternative Schools Network, 1973.

Cesaire, Aime. *Discourse on Colonialism.* New York: Monthly Review Press, 1972.

Childs, John Brown. Concepts of Culture in Afro-American Political Thought, 1890–1920. *Social Text: Theory/Culture/Ideology,* II, no. 1 (1981): 28–43.

Cox, Oliver, C. *Caste, Class, and Race (1948).* New York: Modern Reader Paperbacks, 1970. 1948 (Gardon City: Doubleday).

Cruse, Harold. *The Crisis of the Negro Intellectual.* New York: William Morrow & Co., Inc., 1967.

Curti, M. E. *The social ideas of American educators.* New York: Charles Scribner's Sons, 1935.

DuBois, W. E. B. *Dark Princess, a Romance.* Millwood, NY: Kraus-Thomsen Organization, 1928.

DuBois, William Edward Burghurd. *Dusk of Dawn* (1940). New York: Modern Reader Paperbacks, 1970.

Ellison, Ralph. An American Dilemma: A Review. In Ladner, Joyce, ed., *The Death of White Sociology.* New York: Vantage Books, 1973: 81–95.

Fitzpatrick, Edward, ed. *Readings in the Philosophy of Education.* New York: Appleton-Century Co., 1936.

Fontaine, William Thomas. An Interpretation of Contemporary Negro Thought from the Standpoint of the Sociology of Knowledge. *Journal of Negro History.* 25, no. 1 (January, 1940): 89–102.

Franklin, Vincent, & James Anderson, eds. *New Perspectives on Black Educational History.* Boston: G. K. Hall & Co., 1978.

Freire, Paulo. *Education for Critical Consciousness.* New York: The Seabury Press, 1973.

Giroux, Henry. Critical Theory and Rationality in Citizenship Education. *Curriculum Inquiry,* 10, no. 4 (1980): 329–366.

———. *Ideology, Culture, and the Process of Schooling.* Philadelphia: Temple Press, 1981.

Gordon, Beverly M. Towards a Theory of Knowledge Acquisition for Black Children. *Journal of Education,* 164, no. 1 (Winter, 1982): 90–108.

———. *An Investigation into the Nature and Dimensions of Afro-American Episteomology and Its Implications for Educational Theory And Practice: A Proposal.* Columbus: The Ohio State University. January, 1983.

Gramsci, Antonia. *Selections from the Prison Notebooks.* Edited and translated by Quinten Moore and Geoffrey Smith. New York: International Pub., 1971.

Harris, Leonard, ed. *Philosophy Born of Struggle: Anthology of Afro-American Philosophy from 1917.* Dubuque, Iowa: Kendal Hunt Pub. Co., 1983.

Herbst, Jurgen. *The History of American Education.* Northbrook: AHM Publishing Corp., 1973.

Jones, James M. Conceptual and Strategic Issues in the Relationships of Black Psychology to American Social Science. In Boykin, A. W. et al., eds., *Research Directions of Black Psychologists.* New York: Russell Sage Foundation, 1979.

Ladner, Joyce, ed. *The Death of White Sociology.* New York: Random House, 1973.

Marable, Manning. The Third Reconstruction: Black Nationalism and Race in a Revolutionary America. *Social Text: Theory/Culture/Ideology,* 2, no. 1 (1981): 3–27.

Mbiti, John S. *African Religion and Philosophy.* New York: Praeger.

Mbiti, John S. (1970). *Concepts of God in Africa.* New York: Praeger, 1969.

Miller, Kelly. *Race Adjustment: Essays on the Negro in America* (1908). Miami: Mnemosyne Pub. Co., 1969.

Mulhern, James. *A History of Education.* New York: The Ronald Press Co., 1946.

Outlaw, Lucius. Philosophy, Hermeneutics, Social-Political Theory: Critical Thought in the Interest of African-Americans. In Harris, Leonard, ed., *Philosophy Born of Struggle: Anthology of Afro-American Philosophy from 1917.* Dubuque: Iowa: Kendall Hunt Pub. Co., 1983.

Searle, Chris. *Classrooms of Resistance.* London: Writers & Readers Pub. Coop., 1975.

Warner, Sylvia Ashton. *Teacher.* New York: Basic Books, 1964.

Woelfel, Norman. *Molders of the American Mind.* New York: Columbia University Press, 1933.

Wood, George. Beyond Radical Educational Cynicism. *Educational Theory,* 32, no. 2 (Spring, 1982): 55–71.

Woodson, Carter, G. *The Mis-Education of the Negro* (1933., 2nd rev.ed.). New York: AMS Press, Inc., 1977.

Conclusion:
Toward a Nonsynchronous Identity

CHAPTER 15

Separate Identities, Separate Lives: Diversity in the Curriculum

Peter M. Taubman

> Nothing is more to be feared than saying something that might be true. For if it were, it would become entirely so, and God knows what happens when something, by the very fact of its being true, can no longer be doubted.
>
> Jacques Lacan

> And as late as 1814, *mask* could be used to mean "to infuse." Surely these meanings lurk in our consciousness; certainly these resonances inform our usage. To net meanings not obvious; to enmesh a meaning somehow obscured; to remember, in this very act of decoding these subtle inferences now buried in artifice; to infuse with the newly translated or interpreted meaning—we imply all of these when we speak of the "mask-in-motion."
>
> Henry Louis Gates, Jr.

> The questions which one asks oneself, begin at last to illuminate the world, and become one's keys to the experience of others. One can only face in others what one can face in oneself. On this confrontation depends the measure of our wisdom and compassion.
>
> James Baldwin

If it is true that identity is central to understanding who we are and what we know, but not synonymous with either, then current approaches to multicultural and antibias education are simplistic and flawed. Not only have they failed to address how identity is formed, what it might mean, and how it functions, but they have also left unexplored the way the approaches themselves consciously or unconsciously are used to create identities.

I want to examine various approaches to multicultural and antibias education in terms of their treatment of identity. To do this I have defined three separate but interactive registers in which the construction, meaning, and function of identity are addressed. From these registers we can look at the approaches not only in terms of what they have to say about multicultural and antibias education, but also in terms of the way they create identity for themselves.

But I am nagged by a question, and that is: What identity am I assuming in this paper, and how does that identity function for me? Perhaps in examining the various approaches from the three registers, I will be able to answer that question. Perhaps I shall find the face I need to lose in order to create an identity.

THE REGISTERS

I call the first register *fictional* because identity emerges here primarily as a construct of language and certain preverbal relationships and as an artifice imposed on the plenitude of the individual. Within this register identity is seen as objectifying and alienating the individual or as a violence done to the ineffable. The register is characterized by poststructuralism, particularly the work of Lacan, Foucault, and Derrida. It is here that occur the attempts to endlessly evoke and utter the unutterable, to map the uttered and to expose the absence under the fading presence of the word.

The second register I call the *communal* for it is in this register that identity is activated and given meaning by and through the group, and in turn can illuminate experience. In this register movements mobilize around identity, and identity serves as the ground for action and reflection.

In the third register, which I call the *autobiographical*, identity emerges as a personally meaningful and continually developing aspect of one's Self, as a private center of being or as an autonomous subject capable of excavating his or her own history in the service of transcending it.

Although these registers are not *commensurable*, there are points at which they touch. However, they may be most helpful in looking at multicultural and antibias education if they are used stereoscopically and seen as being in dialectical tension with one another. Let me sketch each of these registers in a little more detail.

For Lacan the subject is at bottom split and alienated. This split occurs, according to Lacan, in the "mirror stage" during which the fragmented, uncoordinated human is squeezed or sucked into a unity formed in the gaze of the Other, a unity called an ego and misrecognized as synonymous with the subject, and a unity which is "orthopedic" and provides a certain sense of power. This necessary but alienating ego-identity precipitates out what, when language is introduced, will become the unconscious and the elusive "I" of consciousness. The ego-identity is not, according to Lacan, synonymous with the "I." The ego "is something else—a particular object within the experience of the subject. Literally the ego is an object . . . which fills . . . the Imaginary function" (1977, p. 44). The residual "I" speaks, as Lacan said, from nowhere, from where it is not. "I think where I am not," he wrote; "therefore I am where I do not think" (Lacan, 1977, p. 166).

The gaze of the Other in which the fragmented subject congeals both freezes the subject as object and becomes itself an object of desire. The gaze is not, however, synonymous with the look or with literal vision. The gaze is to the look what the ego is to an impossibly unified subject. It narrows the field of vision and freezes the object. Because it sees only partially or incorrectly, Lacan referred to it as a "blind gaze."

Thus the gaze objectifies, but it can also be an object of desire. The narcissistic pleasure gained from its apparent fascination is a lure which seduces and traps, for as the subject becomes entranced with the fascinated gaze of the Other which carries back the subject's ego-identity, the subject wants to be seen more fully, to be seen in its plenitude. The impossibility of fulfilling this need is profoundly unsatisfying and results in the desire to become that which the Other is seemingly fascinated with, to become that which the Other desires. Lacan wrote, "You never look at me from the place from which I see you" (Lacan, 1981, p. 103). The gaze, then, is a weapon, an evil eye that is also mistakenly desired and fundamental for the constitution of identity.

The ego that is formed during the "mirror stage" is, according to Lacan, shot through with aggressivity and paranoia. The very circularity of dependence that is established between the subject and the Other leads to aggression, for, as Lacan stated, "Whatever it is that the first is oriented toward will always depend on what the Other is oriented toward. . . . [A]n ego which hangs completely on the unity of another ego is strictly incompatible with it on the plane of desire. An apprehended desired object, it's either he or I who will get it, it has to be one or the other. And when the Other gets it, it's because it belongs to me" (Miller, 1988b, p. 51).

Paranoia haunts the ego because a subject solely and only identified with an alienated ego needs the Other to affirm that identity and thus is continually fearful of the Other acting unpredictably or of losing the Other's gaze.

When the Hegelian dialectic of the "mirror stage" emerges in the symbolic, the ego fortress is cemented and the unconscious seeps out, which, as Lacan taught us, is structured like a language and is the discourse of the Other, is a discourse addressed to the Other.

Only the recuperation of what Lacan called "full speech" can alleviate the bleakness of such an alienated and mistaken subject. To achieve "full speech" the alienated identity must be shattered. The subject must follow back the threads of discourse until in the alienated speech that is spoken can be heard the shadow speech emanating from the unconscious and going to the original Other.

The problem of the subject is not of particular concern for Foucault since, unlike Lacan, he sees identities as being primarily surface phenomena. The hinted Platonism of Lacan's formless ideal—the unconscious—is rejected by Foucault's stringent attention to the horizontal plane. There is no depth to Foucault's subject. Whereas Lacan tries to evoke the "real hollowed out by speech," Foucault maps the discursive terrain on which emerged identities or, as he called them, "figures."

Identity for Foucault does not exist in some space anterior to discourse, in an Imaginary; nor does it preexist itself, held back by some obstacle. Rather, identities such as "man," "woman," "homosexual" or "heterosexual," and "the black" and "the white" appear only within discourses which may be inserted into certain nondiscursive practices. Genet's quote which introduces his play *The Blacks* (1960) captures the discursive formation of identity: "One evening an actor asked me to write a play for an all black cast. But what exactly is a black? First of all, what is his color?"

In such a discursive analysis of identity the subject is replaced by various subject positions or positions of enunciation. There is no antecedent for the subject or an ego or an "I" except where that antecedent is found on a horizontal plane in other discursive formations which, like masks, provide shape for, even as they constitute, the unsayable.

Although Foucault's work argues against and deconstructs totalizations, although his work reveals and resists the oppression of discursive practices, and although he rejects universalism and any notion of depth, any beach beneath the paving stones, his very attempt to map a surface, to present the paving stones, maintains the structure of surface and meaning. It is this structure and meaning that Derrida will subvert.

As Allan Megill suggests, Derrida is like Homer's Penelope who by day ravels her tapestry and by night unravels it. Raveling and unraveling discourse, Derrida entangles and disentangles the central threads running through the tapestry of logocentric thought. Essentialism, foundationalism, transcendence, and presence become so many dropped stitches.

Carried out in terms of literature, Derrida's enterprise extends beyond literary criticism. He critiques any movement toward meaning and searches out the speech that is always more than what is meant. Unlike Lacan, who found in the excess speech a shimmering of full speech which might return the subject to its senses, Derrida finds only non-sense in speech. There is only the continual deferral of meaning. As Derrida has suggested, he takes the risk of not meaning anything.

Lacan's and Foucault's positions are extended and subverted in Derrida's project just as all positions are subverted, including the position of identity. For Derrida, identity is unstable and only an ephemeral moment in the act of endless interpretation. Derrida insists that nothing is outside the text. Under the endless raveling and unraveling of thought in language there is only a violated ineffable.

What can we say about this register I am calling the "fictional"? First, identity emerges within the register as alien, alienating and oppressive. It imprisons the subject in an armored and illusionary ego or can be inserted into a variety of oppressive nondiscursive practices. The danger of founding a program or anchoring a discourse on such an identity becomes apparent. Furthermore, whenever an identity, an "I" and the plenitude of the subject are collapsed onto each other, paranoia and aggression are increased.

Second, within the register language serves to evoke rather than inform. As Lacan states, "The function of Language is not to inform but to evoke" (Lacan, 1977, p. 86); or, as Derrida writes, "The referent is lifted, but the reference remains; what is left is only . . . a fiction that is not imaginary" (Megill, 1985, p. 283); or, as Foucault said, "I am well aware that I have never written anything but fiction" (Megill, 1985, p. 234).

Third, within this register the relationship with the Other evokes danger and desire. The gaze, for example, is both destructive and desirable, and thus, within this register, certain questions can be asked. For example, what does it mean to say that the dominant gaze is "white" or "male" beyond what it means in terms of objectification? Of what consists the lure in this gaze? Who or what is fascinated by it? And how does it relate to the phrase "color blind" or the demand addressed by those in power to the powerless to "lower your eyes" when in fact the desire is for the gaze?

Fourth, within this register we can suspend a variety of unities that constitute identities and thus put them into question and deconstruct them. We can also ravel and unravel centric or centered thought. Thus within this register logocentric, gynocentric, or ethnocentric thought, for example, may be examined.

Finally, the register offers an opening onto or into the ineffable or the unconscious, which may be endlessly spoken, may offer the possibility of full speech, or may simply serve as a space of detachment or spiritual rest.

It is from within this register that the discussions about multicultural and antibias education may be analyzed in terms of how they perpetuate or maintain oppression and alienation, how they block understanding through a kind of massification, or how they produce paranoid knowledge and how they prevent subjects from achieving full speech.

The problem, of course, with this register is that taking a position becomes a bit like standing in quicksand, and it leaves unquestioned who or what puts the period at the end of its speech and thus reintroduces meaning. The problem ultimately with the register is its bloodlessness. Thus, to put it glibly, when a homosexual, who for Foucault is a figure constituted by discourse and who for Derrida is a borderless deferred identity, is beaten up, that identity doesn't disperse; it bleeds.

It is in the second register that identity takes on a certain weight, and it is this register that along with the third can hold the first in a dialectical tension and thus give it flesh.

If identity emerges in the first register as fiction, it emerges in the register I call the "communal" as an identity-in-motion. To understand this register, it will be helpful to explore what Henry Louis Gates has to say about Yoruba masks, in which he sees "contained as well as reflected, or coded, a secret hermetic world, a world discovered only by the initiate" (Gates, 1987, p. 167).

According to Gates, the Yoruba mask is only a piece of wood until, before an audience, it is worn or carried by the artist. Only as "mask-in-motion" and only as it exists among or in front of the chorus or audience can the mask signify. Thus only when the mask is in motion does it produce meaning. The mask-in-motion and in relation to others evokes a "complete hermetic universe . . . an autonomous world, marked by a demonstrably interior cohesion and by a complete neutrality to exterior mores or norms" (p. 168).

The mask becomes immobility fused with the essence of mobility. In a collective as well as a functional sense, the mask-in-motion "effects the 'spiritual consolidation' of the race. . . . [It] transubstantiates the motley, disarrayed audience into the unified, homogeneous, choral community. The mask evokes a view of reality, of human experience, in the truest sense of a theatrical presence" (Gates, 1987, p. 168).

The mask-in-motion both covers the wearer—the artist becomes the mask—and recovers by re-covering the group's sense of community.

I would suggest that this discussion of the Yoruba mask-in-motion captures the communal register, since it is in this register that identity and Self merge in the mask, which activates and gives meaning to the group and group member as well as derives meaning from that group. It is within this register that a particular personality bearing a particular identity may coalesce with a group or may sing the memory song of a people, a song, Alice Walker writes, which "transformed by experiences of each generation . . . holds (the people) together" (p. 373 (201)).

Within the communal register identity is made the ground for action. The identity is not taken as a formation of language but as an identity-in-motion. Thus in this register a women's studies program or a black student union (BSU) may constitute "communities" unified by the acceptance of an identity which comes into being in motion and in relation to others. The group which coalesces around this identity-in-motion forms a hermetic world which operates according to certain codes, movements, and rhythms. In such a world only those who are members can explore the meaning of the identity.

By an identity-in-motion I mean an identity which produces meaning and is both inseparable from the person who participates in the identity and also exists as a sense which a group of people share about themselves. An identity-not-in-motion exists in the first register. Lacan's ego, Foucault's figures, and Derrida's dissolving subject are either fixed or ineluctable flux. Either way they signify only in discourse. In the communal register identity signifies only in action, that is, as a ground for action and/or reflection. As we shall see, though, what keeps the identity mobile is the relationship this register has with the other two registers.

Within this register, multicultural and antibias education assumes a particular shape. It is here one hears, for example, proposals for Afrocentric or gynocentric curricula. Each of these centrisms represents a community activated by an identity-in-motion. Each is intended to establish a community which will enlarge the individual's sense of self through participation in the community. We can hear this echoed in Alice Walker's comments about her story "Saving the Life That Is Your Own." "In that story I gathered up the historical and psychological threads of the life my ancestors lived, and in the writing of it felt joy and strength and my own continuity. I had that wonderful feeling . . . of being with a great many people, ancient spirits, all very happy to see me consulting and acknowledging them, and eager to let me know through the joy of their presence, that indeed, I am not alone" (quoted in Braxton and McLaughlin, 1990, p. 311).

It is this register that allows us to understand our collective experiences, that enables the individual to find speech which may already have been said but which dissolves mute isolation. It is also within this register that our "cultural literacy," to use a common phrase, or choral community can be denaturalized and analyzed in terms of the identity-in-motion which brings together the culture or community. Thus, for example, the report last year of the Central Park jogger's attack emerged differently within different communities, for example, as a racist attack, as an excuse for the persecution of blacks, as a class-based attack, and as an example of brutal misogyny. Each of these versions may be analyzed in terms of the identity-in-motion that animates them and thus be used to supplement or interrogate one another.

The danger with this register is that if it loses relationship to the other registers it can essentialize identity and reduce a complex human being to what Du Bois called a "rough work of propaganda." Franz Fanon's eloquence captures the problems with the communal register wrenched from the dialectical tension with the other registers and takes us to the third register, the autobiographical. He writes,

> No attempt must be made to encase man for it is his destiny to be free. The body of history does not determine a single one of my actions. I am my own foundation . . . I the man of color want only this: That the enslavement of man by man cease forever. . . . That it be possible for me to discover and love man, wherever he may be.
>
> The Negro is not. Anymore than the white man . . .
>
> Was my freedom not given to me then in order to build the world of the You? (1967, pp. 228–232)

In Fanon's words we hear the cry of Mounier's individual, who is always more than his identities or mask. We hear the murmur of a core self which constitutes a moral center in the brutal flux of reality. We hear a resistance to a power which inspires fear and adoration. We see a self which must free itself from the nightmare of history and assume responsibility for itself and the world. We hear the "autobiographical" register, in which in the beginning was not the word but, as Goethe said, the act. The construction of identity in this register is developed in the work of those writers who share what Jessica Benjamin calls the "intersubjective view," that is, writers such as Daniel Stern, Jurgen Habermas, and Benjamin herself.

Within this register, the infant, unlike Lacan's chaotic, fragmented, and nonindividuated infant, appears "primed from the beginning to be interested in and to distinguish itself from the world of others" (Benjamin, 1988, p. 18). This emergent self through a relationship to other subjects develops, according to Stern, a sense of a core self, then a subjective self, and finally a verbal self. Such a development requires that the Other, generally the mother, recognizes the infant's independent existence, but it also reveals the infant's need to "recognize the Other as a separate person who is like us yet distinct" (Stern, 1985 p. 23). Thus autonomy and relatedness are equally important for the development of identity and do not necessarily lead to the Hegelian master-slave dialectic we saw in Lacan's construction of identity.

Stern and Benjamin replace Lacan's house of mirrors with the existence and recognition of real separate subjectivities. "I" and "You" replace "ego" and "Other." The "I" emerges here not as alienated but as a mode of being-in-the-world which should be strengthened and thus made capable of not only acknowledging and sustaining relationship but also of self-knowledge. Such an "I" is neither doomed to alienation nor destined to embrace an objectified identity. Benjamin writes: "The spurious embrace of difference only defines the Other in minor opposition to the Self. It thus precludes the necessity of dealing with the contradictory tendencies within the self. This escape from the knowledge of self is what constitutes temptation in the struggle to deal with the complexity of life outside the garden" (p. 223).

The "I" or identity that develops in this register is not completely unified, however, for there can be different selves. For Stern these exist along a continuum which may be loosely divided into the "social self," the "private self," the "disavowed self," and the "not-me self." Although one hears in these categories echoes of Lacan's armored ego and split self, the self that emerges in this register is not by definition bent out of shape or constituted by language or the desires of others.

Within the autobiographical register, unlike the fictional register, the narrative which the subject constructs does not create the real experience of living but rather posits the possibility of external validation. One's recounted autobiography therefore does not create one's experience but captures it. Thus autobiography as a means to self-knowledge is possible since a dialectic exists between narrative and actual experience. This autobiography is the ground for both action and for what is to be transformed. Because within this register there is assumed a unified subject with agency, action at this level implies responsibility.

We can see, then, in this register the belief in a rational subject which makes possible Habermas's ideal speech situation and communicative rationality. It also makes possible the evaluation of various hermetic universes which emerge in the communal register.

Thus the white student unions or the fraternities and the black student unions or women's groups activated by an identity-in-motion in the communal register but immobilized by the denial of other registers may be evaluated according to ethical standards agreed on in the autobiographical register. Any individual in a group would also be held responsible for his or her actions. Thus the register evokes the existential subject, responsible, free, capable of surfacing submerged aspects of self and unfolding within relationships with other subjectivities.

When we view antibias and multicultural education from this register, several things become apparent.

- First, individuals are always more than and are always capable of transforming their social identities. They are not *only* intersections formed by grids of gender, class, race, ethnicity, religion, or physicality.

- Second, an ethical position can be articulated and assumed here which may put into question phenomena emerging in the first two registers.

- Third, an excavation of self can occur here which may reveal one's own embeddedness in or complicity with oppressive structures.

- Fourth, the register allows us to analyze the dynamics of oppression not in terms of victim and victimizer but in terms of the collusion in oppression.

- Fifth, within this register relatedness, intimacy, and intersubjectivity are privileged without valorizing an original world, pre-Oedipal or otherwise, of oneness. Thus a space is opened for an imaginative empathy, what, as Benjamin reminds us, Keats called "negative capability."

- Finally, in this register volition or agency is assumed, thus providing a basis for values such as commitment and responsibility. But it is exactly this belief in freedom and agency that points to the dangers in this register.

The assumption of agency frees us from a determinism but also denies the very real sense in which identity and knowledge are informed by race, gender, ethnicity, class, and the unconscious. Thus, when James Baldwin (1985) says that being white is a moral

choice, he is speaking from this register, but so is Shelby Steele
when he writes: "The only way we will see the advancement of
black people in this country is for us to focus on developing ourselves as individuals and embracing opportunity . . . that American society offered me and blacks in general. . . ." (pp. 20–21) We
see here a naive individualism that may be existential but is also
terribly incomplete.

We can also see how it is not a big step from Steele's comments
to a belief in a color-blind curriculum, for the implication is that in
the core self there is a universal truth. The question is, of course,
who articulates this truth and in what language. With this question
we arrive back in the register of fiction.

All of these registers, the fictional, the communal, and the
autobiographical, exist in a dialectical tension with each other.
They supplement and elaborate on one another and at the same
time problematize one another. If we are going to seriously consider and implement multicultural and antibias education, then it is
imperative that we design an approach which is informed by each
of these registers. If we do not, we will wind up with a curriculum
and pedagogy that promise an increased understanding of identity
and culture but that deliver alienated identities and arrested intellects.

Let us look, then, at some of the current approaches to antibias
and multicultural education.

THE CRITIQUE

Perhaps the most widely known approach suggests that groups
of a particular identity should be exposed to positive, fulsome, and
accurate representations of that identity. Recently that approach
was advocated by the New York State Task Force's "Curriculum of
Inclusion." The task force maintains that nonwhite students would
develop higher self-esteem and be more likely to learn if greater
recognition were given to the contributions of nonwhite cultures to
American society.

The approach finds a more extreme representation in the current establishment in Milwaukee of schools specifically set up for
black males and offering an Afrocentric curriculum, or in the Afrocentric programs being established in the Indianapolis school sys-

tem. The approach has historically been associated with parochial schools and same-sex private schools where the curricula and structures offered positive representations of and opportunities to develop specific identities.

The approach generally consists of courses or units which present the contributions of a particular group or curricula which represent the group in a generally positive light. It should be obvious that these approaches are carried out in the register of the communal and can be extremely important. Certainly a sense of community which elaborates and expands one's sense of self and generates a communal ethos is a great achievement.

However, we can also see certain dangers in this approach, for if the dialectical tension is not maintained with the fictional and autobiographical registers, the identity-in-motion of the communal register will become immobile.

Let me explain. The cohesiveness of the group activated by an identity-in-motion is premised on its members sharing a particular identity which, when set in motion, becomes meaningful as a way to illuminate and interpret experience. Thus, for example, 'woman' or 'Black' become identities-in-motion insofar as they help establish a dialectic between the mobile identity and the experiences seen through it. A community of women, for example, united by the identity-in-motion of 'woman' can examine and interpret a variety of themes in female experience through the identity-in-motion of 'woman'. Autobiographically, the identity-in-motion may also serve as a means of illuminating experience. But what keeps the identity in motion is the tension between it and the two other registers. Relinquish the tension and the identity freezes.

Thus, if the identity-in-motion becomes the *fixed* origin and horizon of experience, if, to continue our example, 'woman' is taken as a predetermined face found on the bottom layer of an archaeology of self, then the identity-in-motion has stopped and become the frozen identity emerging in the first register.

Unfortunately, much of the approach to antibias and multicultural education we are discussing falls into this trap. For example, blackness or Afro-Americanness, rather than an identity-in-motion which can be used to illuminate experience and serve as a ground for action and reflection, becomes a fixed and sedimented identity over which may be erected a *monumentalized* history and culture, one which in the process of memorializing history forgets it. For example, in the monumentalizing of Martin Luther King, Jr., his possibility-in-the-present is forgotten.

When the identity-in-motion becomes immobile, that is, when the tension is lost with the fictional and autobiographical registers, individuals, now frozen by an immobile identity, are thrown into the Lacanian dialectic of alienation. Let me give an example which, although transpiring outside of school, could as easily have occurred within school.

The example concerns a Korean grocery store owner, a Haitian customer, and New York City politics. The Haitian woman accused the Korean of beating her. He said he was only restraining a hysterical woman. The encounter set in motion two groups who unified around racial and ethnic identities. Various ethnic groups, for example, Haitians, West Indians, and Afro-Americans, coalesced around a particular black identity-in-motion. Koreans coalesced around a particular Korean identity-in-motion. Both groups were represented to the public by a group unified by a particular white identity which, unlike the first two, was blind to itself and thus particularly alienated.

The black communal group was represented as demanding from Korean merchants respect for their (black) women as daughters, wives, and mothers. The Korean communal group was represented as condemning the criminality and rudeness of the blacks. Both groups talked of losing face and wanting the other to look at them with respect. The trap in this dynamic was that the identities-in-motion lost dialectical tension with the other registers and became immobile. Since each group crystallized around an immobile identity which was necessarily alienating, neither group could possibly attain the gaze desired, nor could either group become more than what the gaze of the other returned to them. No member of either group could be seen as what the member wanted to be seen as, since each member embodied the group and thus would always remain less than what he or she was, while thinking he or she was more.

The Lacanian dialectic which is activated when the identity-in-motion is immobilized ensured that neither Koreans nor blacks could unite around another identity-in-motion, for example, class, nor could they analyze the economic situation which contributed to the tension, nor could they see gender as a factor, nor, finally, could they mobilize against the frozen images of each presented in the white media.

I want to turn now to the criticism of and implicit approaches to multicultural and antibias education as represented by the writings of more conservative educators such as Diane Ravitch and Chester Finn. Their criticism of multicultural education comes, in part, from the autobiographical register. In brief, the work of Ravitch, Finn, and their cohorts suggests that multicultural or antibias education is basically special interest politics and will lead to fragmentation. The arguments decry "particularism" and what is seen as ethnic chauvinism. Ravitch and Finn argue that whites are massified as oppressors and that history itself, written, they claim, by committee as opposed to disinterested scholars, is distorted into a false glorification of various ethnic groups. Finally, they argue that the insistence on racial or ethnic pride denies the individual and the transcendent humanity of the subject.

This critique becomes quite interesting if we analyze it from the register of the fictional. What we see from this register is an "I" which is completely collapsed onto the ego, resulting in aggressivity, paranoia, and the fear of loss of control. We also see the dynamic of the gaze played out in terms of knowledge and self.

To begin with, Finn and Ravitch cannot see that the curriculum has always been ethnocentric, particularist, and politicized, because, to use Lacan's terms, their "I" is completely conflated with their ego. Thus, they see the world through a kind of nictitating membrane constituted by whiteness and maleness but they are incapable of seeing the membrane. They are assimilated into an alienated ego, which is alienated because it comes into being in the gaze of the Other. Baldwin taught us that when he wrote,

> Part of the price of the black ticket is involved fatally with the dream of becoming white. This is not possible because white people are not white; part of the price of the white ticket is to delude themselves into believing that they are . . .
>
> The Irish middle passage, for but one example, was as foul as my own, and dishonorable on the part of those responsible for it. But the Irish became white when they got here and began rising in the world, whereas I became black and began sinking. (Baldwin, 1985)

The alienated ego of Ravitch's and Finn's text is thus dependent on maintaining the Other as massified other. Any particularization threatens to decenter such an ego, making it one among many. When they complain of an attack on the "common culture,"

they reveal their inability to see that culture as already partic-
ularized.

What becomes apparent in their writings is their desire for and
hatred of the gaze of the Other. Because they have conflated the "I"
and ego, and further, because they identify that ego with a corps of
study which again they mistake for a universal corps when it itself
is alienated and partial, they desire the gaze of the Other to remain
fascinated. They desire that the Other see that corps as universal,
as the subject in its plenitude. At the same time they hate that gaze
for they are dependent on it. That dependence turns quickly to
aggression and paranoia.

We can see the paranoia in the writing. Finn suggests if the
"curriculum of inclusion" is adopted in New York, America will
become Lebanon. Ravitch warns that it will lead to race war. The
knowledge these writers privilege is itself shot through with paranoid structures because it is seen as transparent to itself and con-
tainable. For these writers, knowledge, like consciousness, knows
itself in its plenitude. Thus any suggestion that it is not True or that
it is interested in Habermas's sense produces terror.

In these writers we hear the distortions of a subject totally
armored in an alienating ego. We hear an immobile identity of
"European whiteness" which posits itself as the origin and horizon
of consciousness itself. Finally, we hear the generic subject of an
autobiographical register which is no longer in dialectical tension
with the fictional and communal registers. Such a subject becomes
then the self-interested individual whose soul is a free-floating
empty transcendence.

The last approach to multicultural and antibias education I
want to look at is certainly a sophisticated one. It often concerns
issues of "empowerment" or presents stages in which various marginalized groups might be incorporated into the curriculum or
concerns the different ways "racist, classist, sexist, ablest and other
oppressive dynamics" which are nonsynchronous operate in the
school to produce knowledge and identity.

Certainly the approach is insightful and reveals a broader understanding of multicultural and antibias education than most other approaches do. I would suggest, though, that the approach is
finally incomplete. What this approach tries to do is establish
communities activated by various identities-in-motion (the physically challenged, Native Americans, Asians, Hispanics, African-

Americans, women). Unfortunately, the identities are not in motion. They are immobilized because the approach posits oppression as the origin and horizon of the identity. One is an oppressor, an oppressed, or both. One's identity is determined always along an axis of oppression. In such an approach, the communal register is severed from the autobiographical register.

What is missing is exactly what Jessica Benjamin calls for when she says, "Once we understand submission to be the desire of the dominated as well as their helpless fate, we may hope to answer the central question, How is domination anchored in the hearts of those who submit to it" (p. 52). What is missing is the dialectical tension with the first and third registers which would mobilize the identity of oppressed and/or oppressor and turn it into an identity-in-motion which could be used to illuminate the dynamics of oppression and investigate one's own being as well as the relationships one has with others.

I have attempted in this paper to outline an approach to multicultural and antibias education that takes the construction, meaning, and function of identity as starting points. The approach requires that we utilize three registers, *the fictional, the communal,* and *the autobiographical.* Although the registers cannot be collapsed onto one another, they can be held in a dialectical tension with each other. They are *only* useful if they are in tension with one another. If multicultural or antibias education is introduced from within only one register, the result is a distortion in thought and action.

We have seen that the autobiographical and communal registers provide the anchor for the fictional register. And we have seen how the fictional and communal registers prevent the autobiographical from collapsing into a transcendental individualism. Finally, we saw how the autobiographical and the fictional registers activated the identity-in-motion of the communal register and kept identity from becoming immobile and thus alienating and destructive.

These registers then *must* be kept always in a dialectical tension with one another so that identity itself can be investigated *and* used as a means for exploring and illuminating our experience. Any discussion and introduction of multicultural or antibias education must occur simultaneously on the three registers, must be viewed stereoscopically.

A question remains, though, the question I raised at the beginning of this paper, the question of identity as it is shaped by and gives meaning to this paper, to me and to others in the field.

On one level this paper is a critique of other approaches. Written in a detached, disembodied voice, the paper masked me with a particular identity—that of the one whose approach was *not* simple or flawed, that of the one-who-knows. Wanting to stake out a place in the discussion on multicultural and antibias education, I took an aggressive position; that is, I tried to reveal the flaws in other approaches. I defined myself against everyone rather than in relation to anyone and collapsed myself onto an observing eye/I, and thus my identity as the one-who-knows became fixed.

Frozen in its position of separateness, however, it could, therefore, be analyzed within the first register. And from there I can see how the discourse of this paper is the discourse of the Other—in this case the academic voice of the law of the field, of the phallic Other. And so perhaps a gender appears.

And now I can read back through the paper listening to the unconscious voice that speaks to the field identified now as phallic Other. And indeed, I hear the defensiveness, the fear of being cut, the paranoia and aggression. There is a kind of methodical point-by-point development in the paper. No vulnerability will show. No confusion. No doubts. And I can feel the desire to be recognized, to be seen from where I see the Other to whom I talk. And I talk to that Other over the objectified bodies of the approaches I have critiqued. And I anticipate my recognition in the gaze of that Other, a recognition that will of course never be enough.

The voice is also colorless. I can hear the resistance to embodying myself, because if I do, I run the risk of being collapsed into my color as social and political identity. And then the Other will see me as Other, so better to hide in a sexless and colorless paper.

But of course it was there at that fixed identity that I caught myself as a white man.

And now reading back through my whiteness and maleness, do I recover myself as Peter, the subject of some autobiographical search?

Shelter in the unique autobiographical narrative is tempting. Stories told in an isolated third register can be comforting and safe, as can the disappearing act of the first register, but I can neither disperse my identity nor turn it into the story of my life, for the pull of the communal register reminds me of my voice and body and how these do exist in the world.

So where am I? I don't know.

I know that somewhere in these words, in the effort behind them, in the hope that went before them, in the unspoken that speaks through them, there emerge different identities, and all I can do is try to understand the world and myself through them as I view each through the different registers.

And perhaps, finally, that is what all of us in this field must do. We who cling to our various identities and freeze ourselves and others in them, we who become the critical theorists or poststructuralists, the feminists or postmodernists, the autobiographers or the Marxists, we who look at multicultural and antibias education from these identities, we might ask how we have used and been used by those identities and how we have distorted ourselves and distorted others with them. In what way do we use these identities to save face, and in losing face, what identity will we save? What do these identities tell us about who we are, about our separate lives, our separate identities, our diversity? And finally, how can we look at and through these identities so that we can begin to see ourselves in one another and one another in ourselves, so that we can hold unity and differentiation in a tension that holds us all together?

BIBLIOGRAPHY

Baldwin, James (1985). *The price of the ticket: Collected non-fiction 1948–1985*. NY: St. Martin's Press.

Benjamin, J. *The bonds of love.* (1988). New York: Pantheon Books.

Braxton, J. M., and McLaughlin, A. N. (1990). *Wildwomen in the whirlwind*. New Jersey: Rutgers University Press.

Ellsworth, E. (1989). Why doesn't this feel empowering? Working through the repressive myths of critical pedagogy. *Harvard Educational Review*, 59(3), 297–324.

Fanon, F. (1967). *Black skin, white masks*. New York: Grave Press.

Finn, C. E., Jr. (1990). Narcissus goes to school. *Commentary*, 89(6), 40–45.

Garrow, D. J. (1988). *Bearing the cross*. New York: Vintage Books.

Gates, H. L., Jr. (1986). *"Race," writing and difference*. Chicago: University of Chicago Press.

Gates, H. L., Jr. (1987). *Figures in black*. New York: Oxford University Press.

Genet, J. (1960). *The blacks: A clown show.* New York: Grove Press.

Goldberg, D. T. (1990). *Anatomy of racism.* Minneapolis: University of Minnesota Press.

Lacan, J. (1977). *Ecrits: A selection.* New York: W. W. Norton.

Lacan, J. (1981). *The four fundamental concepts of psycho-analysis.* New York: Norton.

McCarthy, C. (1988). Rethinking liberal and radical perspectives on racial inequality in schooling: Making the case for nonsynchrony. *Harvard Educational Review,* 58(3), 265–279.

Megill, A. (1985). *Prophets of extremity.* Berkeley: University of California Press.

Miller, J. A. (1988a). *The seminar of Jacques Lacan, Book I.* New York: Norton.

Miller, J. A. (1988b) *The seminar of Jacques Lacan, Book II.* New York: Norton.

Pinar, W. F. (1991). Curriculum as social psychoanalysis: On the significance of place. In Joe Kincheloe and William F. Pinar (eds), *Curriculum as social psychoanalysis* (167–186). Albany, NY: State University of New York Press.

Rampersad, Arnold. (1990). The art and imagination of W. E. B. DuBois. New York: Stockten Books.

Ravitch, D. (1979). Multiculturalism E. Pluribus Plures. *The American Scholar.* (pp. 332–354).

Said, E. W. (1979). *Orientalism.* New York: Vintage Books.

Steele, Shelby (1990). Ghettorized black unity. Harper's Magazine (20–22).

Stern, D. N. (1985). *The interpersonal world of the infant.* New York: Basic Books.

Taubman, P. M. (1980). Gender and curriculum: Discourse and the politics of sexuality. *Journal of Curriculum Theorizing,* 4.

Taubman, P. M. (1987). Notes on James Baldwin, a Native Son. Kastendick Chair lecture, Poly Prep Country Day School, Spring.

Torgovnick, M. (1990). *Gone primitive: Savage intellects, modern lives.* Chicago: University of Chicago Press.

Verhouek, S. H. (1990). New York education chief seeks new stress on non-white cultures. *New York Times,* February 7.

CONTRIBUTORS

Louis A. Castenell, Jr., is dean of the College of Education at the University of Cincinnati.

Patricia Hill Collins teaches in the Department of African-American Studies at the University of Cincinnati.

Roger L. Collins teaches in the College of Education at the University of Cincinnati.

Susan Huddleston Edgerton teaches multiculturalism at the University of Illinois, Chicago.

Jewelle Gomez is a writer, poet, and critic.

Beverly M. Gordon teaches in the College of Education, Ohio State University.

Brenda G. Hatfield is director of the Center for Instructional Media and Technology for the New Orleans Public Schools.

Joe Kincheloe teaches in the College of Education at Florida International University in Miami.

Jonathan Livingstone was a postgraduate student at University College, Cardiff, at the time of his article's publication.

Wendy Luttrell teaches sociology at Duke University.

Cameron McCarthy teaches in the Department of Education at Colgate University.

Lindsay Murphy is a writer living in the United Kingdom.

William F. Pinar teaches curriculum theory at Louisiana State University.

Peter M. Taubman teaches English at Poly Prep Country Day School in Brooklyn, New York.

Mariamne H. Whatley teaches in the School of Education, University of Wisconsin.

Alma H. Young teaches in the College of Education, University of New Orleans.

NAME INDEX

SUBJECT INDEX